BITTER WOUNDS

Unidentified German soldier. (Photo: Militärverlag, German Democratic Republic)

BITTER WOUNDS

German Victims
of the Great War, 1914–1939

ROBERT WELDON WHALEN

CORNELL UNIVERSITY PRESS

ITHACA AND LONDON

First published 1984 by Cornell University Press.
Published in the United Kingdom by Cornell University Press Ltd., London.

International Standard Book Number 0-8014-1653-1
Library of Congress Catalog Card Number 83-45938
Printed in the United States of America
Librarians: Library of Congress cataloging information
appears on the last page of the book.

The paper in this book is acid-free and meets the guidelines
for permanence and durability of the Committee on Production
Guidelines for Book Longevity of the Council on Library Resources.

Listen, you leaders of Jacob, you rulers of Israel,
should you not know what is right?
You hate good and love evil;
you flay people alive and tear the very flesh from their bones;
you devour the flesh of my people,
strip off their skin,
splinter their bones;
you shred them like flesh into a pot,
like meat into a cauldron.

—Micah 3:1–3

. . . there were bitter wounds to be healed and no time to heal them.
—Peter Gay, *Weimar Culture*

Contents

Plates

Acknowledgments

You get attached to some things. When I discuss Germany's war victims nowadays, I find myself talking about "my" war victims. The possessive is revealing; it reflects the impact this book has had on me. The singular, however, is wrong. They are not "my" war victims, and it is not entirely "my" book.

Many people and institutions helped me with this work. R. Laurence Moore, Walter Pintner, John Weiss, and especially Isabel Hull, of Cornell University, read the manuscript at various stages in its evolution, and I thank them for their criticism and encouragement.

Research funds were provided by the Germanistic Society of America, the Fulbright-Hays Program, the Western Societies Program of Cornell University, and the Jacob and Louise Ihlder Fellowship of Cornell University.

As the notes and bibliography demonstrate, I am indebted to the staffs of many libraries and archives in the Federal Republic of Germany, the German Democratic Republic, and the United States.

Lawrence J. Malley, Kay Scheuer, and their colleagues at Cornell University Press saw the manuscript into print with professional skill. A generation of Cornell history graduate students waited patiently for this book to hatch, encouraged its first flights, and cheered it on its way. Janice Jannett and Francesca Verdier of Cornell's Computer Services helped me prepare the text; their assistance was invaluable.

Finally, two extraordinary people, Weldon and Genevieve Whalen, my parents, provided aid and comfort over a very long haul. This project, along with many others, would never have gotten off the ground without their unflagging support. To them I owe a debt of gratitude I can neither adequately express nor ever repay.

ROBERT WELDON WHALEN

Ithaca, New York

BITTER WOUNDS

Wounded soldiers returning home. They appear to be Austrians. (Photo: Ullstein, Berlin)

The Memory of Mass Violence

Es fielen in den Jahren 14 bis 18: einemillionachthundertachttausendfünf-
hundertundfünfundvierzig Deutsche, einemilliondreihundertvierund-
fünfzigtausend Franzosen, neunhundertachttausenddreihundertundein-
undvierzig Engländer, sechshunderttausend Italiener, einhundertund-
fünfzehntausend Belgier, einhundertneunundfünfzigtausend Rumänen,
sechshundertneunzigtausend Serben, fünfundsechzigtausend Bulgaren,
zweimillionenfünfhunderttausend Russen und Polen, fünfundfünfzig-
tausendsechshundertachtzehn Amerikaner. Zusammen: achtmillionen-
zweihundertfünfundfünfzigtausendfünfhundertvierunddreissig   Menschen.

—Edlef Köppen, *Heeresbericht*

There fell in the years '14 to '18: one million eight hundred and eight
thousand five hundred and forty-five Germans, one million three hundred fifty-four thousand Frenchmen, nine hundred and eight thousand
three hundred forty-one Englishmen, six hundred thousand Italians, one
hundred fifteen thousand Belgians, one hundred fifty-nine thousand
Rumanians, six hundred ninety thousand Serbs, sixty-five thousand Bul-
garians, two million five hundred thousand Russians and Poles, fifty-five
thousand six hundred eighteen Americans. Altogether: eight million two
hundred fifty-five thousand five hundred thirty-four men.

There were no casualties in the Great War. "Casualties" is an
abstraction, a cloak that conceals the fact that millions of human beings
died violently between 1914 and 1918. War hurts people and often kills
them in great numbers, and when wars are over, all the people whose lives
have been shattered do not simply return to normal. Everyone involved in
a war is in some way a war victim. But some can reconstruct their lives
more or less; others cannot.

Books about wars usually talk about kings and queens, generals and
admirals, geopolitics and grand strategy. Armies march here, fleets sail
there. War is more complicated than this, of course, and historians have

increasingly examined economic imperatives and domestic class tensions as well as battles. Oddly, though, the fundamental fact of war, the fact that it kills and widows and orphans people sometimes in appalling numbers, is often all but forgotten.

This neglect of human cost has long held true regarding writing about the First World War, but recently writers such as Antoine Prost, Paul Fussell, and Klaus Vondung have tried to recover the lives of common soldiers and ordinary citizens.[1] This book shares their concern with the experience, perceptions, and illusions of ordinary soldiers and their survivors. In particular, it examines the lives of the human wreckage that the war left in Germany: the disabled veterans, widows, and orphans.

What to do for, or with, the millions of victims of the Great War was the Weimar Republic's most intractable social problem. War victims were everywhere. Nearly 10 percent of the German nation, some six million people, were either disabled veterans and their families or dependent survivors of the dead. Thousands of civil servants tried to provide care for them at a cost of billions of marks. Of the funds available to the German government between 1920 and 1932, at least one-third was tied up in pension costs.

This social welfare problem was fundamentally a political problem, with profound implications for the Republic's stability. The instability of the Republic's government is often exaggerated. There were constant changes of cabinet, but the same people reappeared, and more important, the same social groups held power. More important still, the various institutions of power, such as the bureaucracy, the judiciary, and the army, were fairly stable during the period of the Republic. Decisions about pensions and social services, however, involved basic decisions about the division of national wealth and the setting of national priorities, and the failure of the Republic to meet the war victims' needs had an ominous effect on citizens' loyalty to the state. The story of the war victims and their movement is central both to the Weimar Republic's life and to its death.

Politics in the narrow sense of cabinet changes or elections was, to be sure, largely irrelevant to the politics of pensions. Care for war victims evoked a rhetorical consensus among politicians of every persuasion, and the matter was rarely debated publicly. War victims themselves insisted that care was "above" politics. Moreover, the pension system was so labyrinthine that few people outside it had any idea how it all functioned. Basic political decisions were made outside formal political channels, shaped by the often stormy relationship between the pension bureaucracy and the war victims.

Politics in the broader sense, however, the setting of public priorities, was crucial to the pension program. Without exception, the various

Weimar governments insisted that social policy was subordinate to economic policy, and subject to the restrictions the latter imposed. War victims countered that economic policy had to be made to achieve social goals, and this fundamental debate about priorities was at the heart of the politics of pensions.

Of course, the issue had social and psychological dimensions as well. Terrible things had happened to these people, and they responded sometimes with passivity and despair, sometimes with anger and violence. Swept up in the Republic's violent politics, though constantly proclaiming their neutrality, they did not even refrain from attacking one another. In the end, many of them jubilantly welcomed National Socialism. The illusions, myths, and symbols war victims used to order and interpret their experience are as important to a study of their lives as an examination of their attitudes toward public affairs. Therefore this book begins with an investigation of the apparently simple word "hero," then discusses bureaucracy and politics, and concludes with a reflection on melancholy.

One theme echoes throughout the work—the yearning for concord—with two variations: organized benevolence and epic politics. Prewar Germany was a badly shaking structure, in which the desire for social stability was directly proportional to increasing centrifugal tendencies. Civil war was always just over the horizon, yet both left and right wanted the same thing. When the right threatened to launch a coup or the left to spark a revolution, both promised that the resulting violence would be a first step toward a conflict-free society. Everyone longed for social peace, and everyone suffered from the inescapable sense of being torn.

Though the state in Wilhelmine Germany was certainly not a neutral regulator, its aim was as much coordination as repression. To this end, it constructed the welfare state, with the object not of redistributing wealth but of stabilizing German society. This organized benevolence, however, was never able to achieve social harmony, even before the war put incredible strains on the system.

That it made for such strain was ironic, for the Great War was itself, in a sense, an effort to achieve concord. In the decade or so before 1914, German foreign policy had less and less to do with foreign affairs and more and more to do with domestic troubles, and instead of being a matter of cautious bargaining and grudging compromise, it became a fantasy world of twilight struggles between good and evil. The aesthetics of politics uncoupled from ethics and logic, and politics became poetic, adventurous, epic. Style became the only substance. By 1914, epic politics, in which the idea of violent explosion took on a cathartic appeal, seemed to the German governing classes a promising way to direct attention away from domestic discord. This was not, however, simply calculated diversion. It was an

Red Cross nurse caring for a wounded soldier. (Photo: Bundesarchiv Koblenz, Federal Republic of Germany)

article of faith among the governing classes that internal disorder was caused by external enemies; they were sure that opponents at home were in league with enemies abroad. The destruction of foreign enemies was a necessary step in establishing domestic peace.

Creatures of the warfare state, the German war victims were denizens of the welfare state, and their career seems a type of our own. Their movement, like their lives, was fraught with paradox. It was led by veterans, but its largest organization was fiercely antimilitarist. Men dominated the movement, but women's concerns were basic to some of its most important demands. It was something totally new at the same time that it reincarnated chronic dilemmas of German society. The war victims' movement offers a unique perspective from which to view the political culture of the Weimar Republic and to attempt to understand what mass violence does to people.

The first five chapters of this book explain what happened to the war victims and how they struggled to comprehend what was happening to them. Chapters 6–12 discuss how the war victims and the state tried to overcome the consequences of mass violence, but at the end arrived at National Socialism. In conclusion, I will consider three constants of the war victims' symbolic universe: melancholia, suicide, and total mobilization.

Berliner Illustrirte Zeitung, front cover, August 16, 1914. The young officer is shouting "Charge!" (Photo: Ullstein, Berlin)

CHAPTER I

The Return of the Red Baron

Es braust ein Ruf wie Donnerhall,
Wie Schwertgeklirr und Wogenprall;
Zum Rhein, zum Rhein, zum deutschen Rhein!
Wer will des Stromes Hüter sein?
    Lieb Vaterland, magst ruhig sein,
    Fest steht und treu die Wacht,
    Die Wacht am Rhein.

Der Schwur erschallt, die Woge rinnt,
Die Fahnen flattern hoch im Wind:
Am Rhein, am Rhein, am deutschen Rhein,
Wir alle wollen Hüter sein!
    Lieb Vaterland, magst ruhig sein, u.s.w.
"The Watch on the Rhine"

And they still go on dying, wrote Heinrich Mann in a letter intended for his brother "Tommy." The brothers Mann, those most representative of modern Germans, had been estranged for years, but their disagreement about the Great War added passion and grief to their division. Thomas justified the war as a cruel but necessary defense of German culture. Heinrich condemned the war as a barbarity. In the winter of 1917, Thomas had severely criticized a new play by Heinrich and had, in effect, spurned Heinrich's efforts at reconciliation. In a letter written in January 1918, which bears the notation "never sent," Heinrich tried to explain to his brother his opposition to the war: "I do not know if anyone can actually help his fellow-men to live, but for God's sake don't ever allow our literature to help them to die! . . . And they still go on dying. . . . The time will come, I hope, in which you will see people, not shadows; and then perhaps me."[1]

Individual human beings, not abstractions, died in the Great War, and they died violently and in vast numbers. The realization that people, not shadows, were dying horrified Europeans and Germans, not suddenly but slowly, not everyone, but, as the war went on, more and more people. The pervasive experience of death, Sigmund Freud argued in 1915, was the most important consequence of the war. Europeans, Freud wrote, had denied that they were capable of such enormities; they had systematically obscured the reality of death itself. Events had overwhelmed illusions. Understanding death, finding a language with which to express the reality of death, had become the haunting task of Europeans. In his opinion, Freud wrote: "the bewilderment and the paralysis of capacity, from which we suffer, are essentially determined among other things, by the circumstance that we are unable to maintain our former attitude towards death, and have not yet found a new one."[2]

Finding language and ritual to comprehend death is a profoundly important task of any culture and, as Philippe Ariès has demonstrated, the symbolic comprehension of death can vary widely.[3] So long as death is located in some symbolic order it is tolerable, but if the symbols shatter, death becomes horrifying. The confrontation with death, the bewilderment and paralysis of which Freud spoke, made everyone who survived the Great War a kind of war victim. Gradually Thomas Mann's attitude toward war approached Heinrich's. Thomas, though he was not a soldier, suffered the wounds of war; in his *Betrachtungen eines Unpolitischen,* he wrote that he too was a war victim.[4]

War wounds were not, though, simply metaphorical. The war left in its wake millions of crippled soldiers, widows, and orphans in Germany. It was as if the awful WAR in Georg Heym's prewar poem, "Krieg,"[5] had branded all these people as witnesses to his devastating power. How did these people, whose lives had been shattered, react to their experience? How did they solve Freud's dilemma of developing a new attitude toward death and life? These questions must be postponed until a prior question is answered: What did the war mean to Germans in general? The war victims were ordinary citizens, too, who shared the illusions and hopes of other Germans.

The question is a gigantic one, and invites immediate objections. The war meant different things to different people: men and women, proletarians and capitalists, soldiers and civilians, children and adults. The poets and artists who tried to express their feelings about the war were not necessarily representative of anyone but themselves. Moreover, some attitudes toward the war changed over time, though others remained fixed.

Yet recurring themes, words, and ideas appeared in home-front propaganda and front-line diaries. Despite the diversity of German society, the ubiquity of some terms suggests a minimum common vocabulary. In the early stages, the central explanation of the war had as its keystone *Heldentum,* heroism. But as the war went on, this explanation became less and less believable. *Heldentum* lost its magical ability to order reality. Disillusion was not the result; something much more complicated occurred. The very failure of heroism made it all the more necessary, and some people clung to it frantically, even as others rejected it as useless. The resulting torn-ness, strife, and discord, or *Zerrissenheit,* was bitterly painful to everyone. *Heldentum* and *Zerrissenheit* are basic to an understanding of what the Great War and its aftermath meant to Germans.

I

An image from the first weeks of the Great War: a locomotive, that roaring, clanging symbol of the industrial world, rushing across Germany. Aboard the train, hundreds of young men in new field-grey uniforms, gaily singing. One song they always sang that summer was "Die Wacht am Rhein," full of waving banners, clashing swords, and heavenly heroes. Especially for troops moving west, the singing of this song was an important rite. As the train crossed the Rhine, soldiers, no matter what the time of day, sang "Die Wacht am Rhein," their voices carrying through the countryside:[6]

> There sounds a call like thunder's roar,
> Like the crash of swords, like the surge of waves.
> To the Rhine, the Rhine, the German Rhine!
> Who will the stream's defender be?
>   Dear Fatherland, rest quietly.
>   Sure stands and true the Watch,
>   The Watch on the Rhine.

> Through all the feeling surges,
> And all eyes glow brightly:
> The German youth, pious and strong,
> Protects the holy Mark.
>   Dear Fatherland, *etc.*

> To heaven he gazes.
> Spirits of heroes look down.
> He vows with proud battle-desire:
> O Rhine! You will stay as German as my breast!
>   Dear Fatherland, *etc.*

> Even if my heart breaks in death,
> You will never be French.

As you are rich in water
Germany is rich in hero's blood.
    Dear Fatherland, *etc.*

So long as a drop of blood still glows,
So long a hand the dagger can draw,
So long an arm the rifle can hold- -
Never will an enemy touch your shore.
    Dear Fatherland, *etc.*

The oath resounds the waters run,
The banners flutter high in the wind
On the Rhine, the Rhine, the German Rhine!
We all will the stream's defenders be!
    Dear Fatherland, *etc.*

Comical, one might say, for an officer wrote in August 1914 that many of the young men bellowing out the song had never seen the Rhine before in their lives.[7] Paradoxical, one might add, that young men would sing about banners, swords, and heavenly heroes as the creature of advanced technology carried them off to the first industrial war. It is from this paradox that an understanding of the heroic must begin.

Heldentum, heroism, in a myriad of guises, was the term constantly used in interpreting the war. Heroism was an enchanted word, charged with meaning. Every belligerent nation used the word; what did Germans mean by it?

They meant a great deal. The young men in field-grey were, first of all, not just soldiers, but young heroes, *Junge Helden.* They fought in the heroes' zone, *Heldenzone,* and performed heroic deeds, *Heldentaten.* Wounded, they shed hero's blood, *Heldenblut,* and if they died, they suffered a hero's death, *Heldentod,* and were buried in a hero's grave, *Heldengrab.* At home, a hero's grove, *Heldenhain,* might be planted in their memory. If the hero were wounded, he might enjoy, while recovering, heroes' books, *Heldenbücher,* borrowed from a heroes' library, *Heldenbibliothek.* Thus, it is not surprising that the political economist Werner Sombart argued, in 1915, that the war was really a clash of cultural values in which Germany represented the heroic ideal. "To be a German," Sombart wrote, "is to be a hero."[8]

The heroic is not, of course, a German invention. The hero is an archetype, a symbol which appears in every culture, under many forms. The heroic myth unites apparently antithetical ideas like death and life, and it implies a certain ontology, a certain way of seeing the world.[9]

The hero is, above all, a man of action (with few exceptions, the hero is male). He performs great deeds and undertakes harrowing adventures. The hero's most important task is the confrontation with the mysterious, the unknown, often represented by some monster which threatens his people. As the purest, bravest, noblest member of his tribe, the hero does battle with the monster and redeems the people. Even if he dies, he slays the dragon and rescues the nation. Though the hero does not always die in the story, his battle with the monster always transforms him, and he returns to his people to teach them all that he has learned. The hero sees things normal people never see; he does things ordinary people can never do; he leaves the world in order to come back to it; he dies and is reborn so that others might live. Joseph Campbell writes: "A hero ventures forth from the world of common day into a region of supernatural wonder; fabulous forces are there encountered and a decisive victory is won; the hero comes back from this mysterious adventure with the power to bestow boons on his fellow man.[10]

In late nineteenth-century Germany, the heroic enjoyed a tremendous revival, especially among the bourgeoisie.[11] Heroic metaphors were integral to Wilhelmine official culture. Wagner and Nietzsche, despite their profound differences, were merged with the posturing of Wilhelm II in a single extravagant complex. Psychologists like Rank and Jung were deeply interested in the idea of the heroic.[12] Rilke's sentimental knightly adventure, *Die Weise von Liebe und Tod des Cornets Christoph Rilke*, was an enormous popular success in 1912. The bourgeoisie, Engels sarcastically but accurately wrote, is the least heroic of classes—why, then, did the heroic achieve such popularity with the German bourgeoisie?

To this question there are several interrelated answers. The relationship between the bourgeoisie and the aristocracy was extremely complex. Part of the "feudalization" of the bourgeoisie involved the adoption and adaptation of aristocratic values. The incongruous image of bankers and industrialists absorbed in tales of high adventure and deadly struggle is not really so bizarre when one recalls that a goal of the bourgeoisie was to be accepted as equals by the old noble families. The bourgeoisie also adapted the feudal ideal of the heroic to their own needs. The heroic was separated from a distinct social class and transformed into a social ideal which, ostensibly, anyone could achieve. A primer on German Hero-Sagas, designed for Gymnasium students, stressed that no one class had a monopoly on heroic virtue.[13] The heroic ideal offered a way to transcend class boundaries. Anyone, even a worker, could escape from the modern world by becoming absorbed in stories of adventure and battle in far-away worlds, as in the tremendously popular stories of Karl May.[14] Anyone could act like a hero, abandoning his or her narrow interests, pledging loyalty to the people, and defending the nation. "Die Wacht am Rhein," written in 1840, became especially popular after the 1870–1871 war with France; it is striking that the song urges defense not of the monarchy, but of the Rhine and the nation.

War, then, became mysterious, rationally inexplicable; it was not the result of political calculation or miscalculation, but was a defense of the community from the dragon. Politics became poetry. Thus, Alfred Biese could write in 1916: "Never before had the God of War, the greatest poet of life, created such a mighty heroic-poem like the one we experience now with throbbing hearts."[15] The self-sacrifice required of the hero might involve the sacrifice of his own life. This, however, was nothing to be feared, for it was proof of heroism. Self-immolation was the highest form of self-affirmation.

The religious overtones of this ideal are important. In late-nineteenth-century Germany, nation, God, father, and monarch merged in the heroic metaphor. In Leipzig's Thomas Church, there is a crowned figure in one of the stained glass windows—a warrior holding a mighty sword with angels kneeling on either side of him. Since the window is in a church, one might assume that the image is that of the King of Kings. The face, however, is that of the King of Prussia, Wilhelm I. In "Die Wacht am Rhein," a "pious" youth gazes at heaven as spirits of heroes look down at him. To young men in 1914, ancient heroes/God/the nation/the monarch looked down at them and judged them. The way to placate the "heavenly heroes" was to become like them. In his 1931 novel, *Reinhold im Dienst*, Paul Alverdes writes that to the story's naive protagonist, God and nation seem to be one. The ultimate consequence of the pervasive heroic metaphor was that religious and idealistic motives were harnessed to the aims of the state. Rushing off to war was an act of love.

This was a defensive war; the Emperor himself had said so. In a decree naming August 5, 1914, a day of national prayer, Wilhelm explained the cause of the war: "In defense against a totally unjustified attack, I have been forced to draw the sword. . . . With a pure conscience concerning the cause of this war, I am certain of the justice of our cause before God. The defense of the Fatherland, forced on us by the enemy challenge, will demand hard sacrifices of blood and treasure. But I know that my people will stand by me with the same loyalty, unity, self-sacrifice and determination with which they stood by my Grandfather, now asleep in God, in earlier difficult days."[16] This was not cynical propaganda. It was a fully coherent explanation of the war within the context of the heroic metaphor.

Walter Flex, killed in action in 1918, was the most eloquent spokesman for the heroic, religious, nationalist metaphor. His *Wanderer zwischen beiden Welten* is the story of an ideal hero who, citing Jesus and Nietzsche, sets off to defend his people. The hero dies for his nation and, echoing "Die Wacht am Rhein," Flex writes,

> Er war ein Hüter getreu und rein
> Des Feuers auf Deutschlands Herde.
> Nun blüht seiner Jungen Heiligenschein
> Als Opferflamme im Heldenhain
> Über der blutigen Erde.
>
> .   .   .
>
> Dann leuchtet sein Leib aus der Toten Chor
> Ein Blitz aus wogender Wolke,
> Dann bricht er mit Fackel und Schwert hervor
> Und leuchtet durch der Ewigkeit Tor
> Voran seinem deutschem
> Volke.[17]

[He was a defender true and pure / Of the fire on Germany's hearth. / Now glows the halo of his youth / As a sacrificial flame in the hero's grove / Over the bloody earth. . . . Then his body glows from the choir of the dead / Lightning from the billowing cloud / Then he steps forth with torch and sword / And leads his German people / Through eternity's door.]

The war was a defensive war, and it was waged by "pious youth," not killers. Allied stories about German atrocities had to be contrived, as in fact many were, because from the German perspective they were impossible. Heroes did not commit atrocities. Heroes lived nobly; they died bravely. Langemarck, site of the "Slaughter of the Innocents," where scores of boys were killed in 1914 with patriotic songs on their lips, became a staple of wartime propaganda; it proved the nobility, the self-sacrifice, and the heroism of German youth.

The war was defensive, Germany's soldiers were pure, and (a third implication of "Die Wacht am Rhein") death was not in vain. The death of the hero was tied to the life of the nation, and because the nation was saved, the dead hero lived too. Death could be borne because it was not really death. "Reich wie an Wasser deine Flut, ist Deutschland reich an Heldenblut" (as you are rich in water, Germany is rich with heroes' blood), and heroes' blood would save the nation. The last line of Heinrich Lersch's popular poem, "Soldaten Abschied," a line that appeared on countless monuments after the war, stressed this voluntary self-immolation: "Deutschland muss leben, auch wenn wir sterben müssen"[18] (Germany must live, even if we must die). According to Leo Sternberg's "Heldenblut,"[19] rivers of heroes' blood would flow homeward and revitalize the nation. War ultimately meant peace, for the war would free Germany from the enemies who surrounded it and raise it to a higher moral plane. Thus Lersch in another wartime poem could write, "Ich hör das Friedenslied die Kugel singen"[20] (I hear the song of peace the bullets sing).

Images of sacrificial, redemptive death filled soldiers' letters, especially those written in the first years of the war. Christian soldiers could easily apply resurrection imagery to their experiences. Jewish soldiers described themselves as New Maccabees, ready to die so that Germany might live. Both called themselves a new type of sacrificial lamb ready to be offered on the altar of the Fatherland. A standard euphemism for battle death was "Opfertod," sacrificial death.[21] Otto Braun, a precocious young poet who was killed in action in 1916, wrote in his diary that for him, there were really only two kinds of life: "There are basically two ideals which conform to the two forms of human existence: to the 'vita activa' corresponds the hero; to the 'vita contemplativa' corresponds the priest, poet, and sage. Intermediate human ideals I do not consider, and so mine is certainly the hero."[22]

The heroic ideal reached its apogee in the most attractive German figure in the war, Manfred Baron von Richtofen. Richtofen was young, only twenty-two when the war broke out, twenty-four when he won the Pour le Mérite, Germany's highest decoration. He was handsome, modest, and brave. Like a knight, he defeated his enemies in single combat. The war department vigorously promoted him as a model for German youth. There were films and postcards of Richtofen setting off to battle; Richtofen, swathed in bandages, recovering from wounds. The Red Baron's war stories, *Der rote Kampfflieger,* were a schoolboys' favorite. When Richtofen was killed in April 1918, at the age of twenty-five, the nation was horrified. In his memory, *Vorwärts,* the journal of German Social Democracy, wrote:

Physical heroism will always have its brightness and magic, especially the more ideal and selfless the purpose for which it is practiced. There is and always will be something magnificent about the way a Richtofen dared hundreds of times to fight man to man for his Fatherland; it is a heroism always to be honored. Such action would be impossible without greatness and firmness of character. The working class, which too defends its Fatherland, also honors a man who has given such a high example of personal courage and fearless self-sacrifice.[23]

The Army's announcement of Richtofen's death had been terse:

24 April 1918: Squadron Leader Baron von Richtofen has not returned from

pursuing an enemy over the Somme battlefield. According to English accounts, he has fallen in battle.[24]

The announcement, brief though it was, seemed a frightful omen. The death of the hero should have contributed to the redemption of the nation, but certainly by the summer of 1918, disaster, not salvation, was impending.

The heroic metaphor did not lose its magic suddenly, and for some it never did. But, as letters from the front demonstrate, the value of the heroic for explaining the war, and especially violent death, rapidly deteriorated. Two letters, one from 1916, the other from 1918, bear witness to the appeal and the disintegration of the heroic ideal.

On November 5, 1916, Helmut Strassmann, a Berliner, was killed at the age of twenty-three. Eleven days later his brother Erwin wrote from France to their parents:

> Today I visited my brother's grave. . . . Dear parents, what you feared for two years has happened. But do not grieve too much. We should be thankful that we had him with us as long as we did, that he was full of joy and hope until the end, that he fought with his whole heart and soul, and that his soldier's death was painless. If everything seems as though it will collapse around you, just think what Helmut would say. With a few words, he would make you feel better, just as he always did. . . .
>
> Here in the field, on the Somme, death and mourning are very different. Everyone knows: comrades, the standard bearers, die every minute, but the ideal lives, the flag is held high. That's the important thing. Those who give their lives for us, give us and the whole nation life. They are the foundation of the future. That is why dying for the Fatherland is the highest fulfillment of life. . . .
>
> Today, at the cemetery, I had to smile despite the pain. Helmut lies first, in the first row. Even here, he is true to his motto: "always try to be first." I wish you could have seen the boys from the 5th Guards who visit the graves at night. They are such quiet, holy youth; in their eyes glows a peaceful, otherworldly infinitude. They visit once more their fallen comrades. It helps them, to stand next to the individual crosses, and to speak of those who lie below. The idea that they will join them soon gives them a quiet joy, for they yearn for sleep. But we must stay awake! Eyes open and to the front, lest we fall into temptation.[25]

Though the letter is a moving expression of the elements of the heroic ideal, the conclusion, with its allusion to Gethsemane, is disturbing. What is the "temptation" we might fall into? Only sleep? Disquieting thoughts? Uncontrolled grief? A crack has appeared in the heroic explanation.

Fritz Simon was a young Jewish soldier, a Zionist, and a German patriot. He was proud that so many Zionists had rushed to Germany's side in its hour of need. As his letters make clear, however, Simon's patriotism was never uncritical, and as the war continued, his doubts finally reached frightening proportions. In January 1918 he wrote to a friend:

> You will remember that I have often told you that one is at ease as long as one is at the front, and does not see or hear about life at home. This is most important for the fighter at the front, who can never be understood by a non-soldier. I always refuse to follow these thoughts to the end, because they are too depressing, and all of you have accused me of pessimism for the last three-and-a-half years. People suffer very much, but it only makes them complacent in bearing their suffering. All sense seems to be lost. Madness is triumphant. The best years of our lives pass and only disappointment remains. Nowhere is there a chance of redemption. . . .
>
> It is sometimes impossible to understand. The people, or their responsible or irresponsible leaders, are at a dead end with no way out. So, they fight on and on in the hope of making up for all the immense sacrifices which they all are bearing. The stake grows day by day, and with it, the fear of an undecided outcome. . . . Consider the phrases of the German nationalists. How unbearable.[26]

"Nowhere is there a chance of redemption." The heroic ideal was based on the reality of redemption; if there is no redemption, the heroic can have no meaning.

Once vibrant words can lose their power. In Leonard Frank's anti-war novel, *Der Mensch ist gut,* a young wife learns that her soldier-husband has sacrificed himself on "the altar of the Fatherland." "Sacrificed on the altar of the Fatherland. Al-tar of the Father-land. She tasted the words with her tongue, gazed into the distance, tried to imagine the Altar of the Father-land. She couldn't do it."[27] Franz Marc, the artist, reported a similar feeling in a letter to a friend, dated October 18, 1915:

> Something I feel, even among good comrades: you can't make yourself understood anymore; almost everyone speaks another language. There is nothing sadder, more maddening, than talking about the war, but you can't talk about anything else. It's like a conversation in a madhouse, entirely made up. No one fully believes in the reality of his interests and his connections with the world—"after all, there's a war on." And the war itself is an insoluble riddle, that the human brain, to be sure, thought up, but can't think out, can't think to the end.[28]

Disillusionment is too simple an explanation of what was happening. As

magic words lose their power, the world becomes incomprehensible and uncontrollable. Some people become lost in the resulting chaos, others desperately search for new symbols, still others repeat the shattered old formulas ever more frantically. Harmony disintegrates into cacophony. People discover they no longer speak the same language. Harangues replace conversation, and words like "betrayal" and "lies" fly through the air. The result is not disillusionment, but a bitterly painful sense of dissonance, of *Zerrissenheit*.

II

Zerrissenheit, a painful sense of torn-ness, of strife, of contradiction, is a constant in German history. There is scarcely a commentary on German culture which does not discuss the "two Germanys," Weimar and Potsdam, idealism and militarism. The patriots of the early nineteenth century mourned the division of Germany into a collection of feuding states and yearned for a unified nation. Answering Ernst Moritz Arndt's question, "Was ist des deutschen Vaterland?" (what is the German Fatherland?) was much more complicated, however, than Arndt's 1813 poem indicated. German-speaking Europe was divided by region and religion, and also, like the Americans and the English, divided by a common language: the score of German dialects were, and are, virtually unintelligible. The unified German nation of 1871 did not include all German-speaking peoples, and within the Reich, divisions of class, sex, and ethnic background were acute. At the turn of the century, the generational conflict, especially between fathers and sons, was intense. None of these divisions was unique to Germany, but they were especially marked there. The constant appeal to patriotic unity reflected a continual dread of division. The pervasive sense of antagonism was the root of a profound anxiety and produced a longing for a unity that would finally abolish contradiction.[29]

The explosion of joy which greeted the outbreak of war in 1914 was largely the result of the conviction that at last division had been overcome. The Emperor's vow, "I know no political parties, I know only Germans,"[30] quickly became the most famous remark the loquacious Wilhelm ever made. Capitalist and worker, Jew and Christian, officer and enlisted man embraced in common purpose. At long last, concord had overcome *Zerrissenheit*. Or so it seemed.

The heroic metaphor played an important role in these emotions. Everyone was called to be a hero, and anyone could be, for the essence of the heroic was the surrender of "narrow," "partisan" interests in the name of the common good. Self-abnegation, Werner Sombart constantly stressed, was the heart of the heroic.[31]

The fracturing of the heroic metaphor was both symptom and cause of the disintegration of wartime unity. Suffering was not equal; many suffered, a few did not. Farmers angrily resisted forced confiscation of their products, and workers demanded an end to inflation, shortages, and poor housing. Soldiers grew suspicious of civilians. The sutures that had closed the old wounds burst asunder, and by 1917 as confidential reports on home-front morale make clear, the country seemed to have disintegrated into a score of warring camps.[32]

Alice Salomon, a social worker, warned in 1916: "If at least an external equality in suffering is not created, if those who have given up their best and dearest are not given at least a sense of the unity and fraternity of the entire nation—then the war will leave behind a heritage of bitterness and strife (*Zerrissenheit*)."[33] By the end of the war, Salomon's worst fears had come true. There was class war, and there were secessionist plots. Rightists and leftists planned coups. Between 1919 and 1923, the country was in a state of virtual civil war. "Betrayal" became the most frequent word in the political vocabulary, though who had betrayed whom depended on one's perspective. Jews and Communists, the right screamed, had betrayed the army; opportunists, the Communists shouted, had betrayed the working class; officers, monarchists cried, had shamefully betrayed their Emperor; and the Emperor, republicans proclaimed, had betrayed his people. At the center of these bitter divisions was the inability to understand and describe the war, an inability to comprehend everything that had happened, a failure to develop symbols on which even a minimum consensus could be reached. This discord over symbols, of course, reflected profound social and economic contradictions that have been analyzed elsewhere.[34] A result of social tension, emotional conflict in turn exacerbated social tension. Arguments about the design of the flag and whether officers should wear epaulets were passionate. Because the nation was profoundly torn, there could be no consensus on national mythology. Because there was no national mythology that could explain the meaning of four long years of mass violence, there could be no social unity.[35]

Two rituals from the middle years of the republic demonstrate both the failure to comprehend mass death and the nostalgia for the heroic explanation. In the spring of 1924, the national government decided to organize a memorial service to honor the war dead. The service was scheduled for the following August, the tenth anniversary of the war's outbreak. The Prussian Minister of the Interior was skeptical about the project. Only recently, he pointed out, a furious debate had raged over the design of the republic's flag. A memorial service might only rekindle old tensions and spark new ones.[36] The Reich Minister of the Interior, Karl Jarres, who was in charge of the project, explained that the whole purpose of the service was to enhance national unity: "The service has nothing to do with politics. The government hopes that the entire population, every section of which sacrificed in the World War, will take part in the service, without consideration of political or economic antagonisms."[37]

The memorial went ahead as scheduled. On a fine Sunday, August 3, 1924, crowds in the capital filled the Königsplatz, the square in front of the parliament building. A catafalque, shrouded in black, stood before the Reichstag. A nearby banner read "To the living spirit of our dead." The delicate flag problem was solved by placing an imperial flag on one side of the catafalque and a republican flag on the other. A military honor guard stood watch. Shortly before noon, a chorus sang Max Bruck's "Heldenfeier," hero's celebration.

President Friedrich Ebert made a short speech. He must have been moved by the occasion, for he had lost two sons in the war. Only in self-defense, he told the crowd, had Germany taken up arms, and despite everything, German unity had been preserved. It was now the duty of the living, a duty the coming generation owed the dead, to preserve the nation. In this way, the president concluded, "the spirit of the dead will live in us all, in the entire German people." He then placed a wreath before the catafalque, the chorus sang the sentimental soldiers' song "Ich hatt' einen Kameraden," and cannons boomed out a military salute.

The plan was that two minutes of silence would begin precisely at noon, and for an instant everything was still. Then the crowd exploded. Some people, Communist agitators, the *Berliner Montagspost* reported, began shouting antiwar slogans, and some began singing the "Internationale." At that, others in the crowd angrily struck up "Die Wacht am Rhein" and other patriotic songs, and the chorus, in desperation, tried to drown out the chaos by singing the national anthem. Pushing came to shoving and fists began flying. By the end of the day, there had been a score of arrests, and one policeman had been stabbed.[38]

Little more than a year later, in November 1925, another memorial for the dead took place. The Red Baron came home. Richtofen had been buried with military honors by the British; the French had exhumed him and reburied him in a larger cemetery. In 1925 the Richtofen family decided to bring the body home, and the project quickly became a national event.

The train from France bearing the Red Baron's body crossed into Germany on Tuesday, November 17, 1925, and on its mournful way across the nation toward Berlin, thousands of people turned out to watch it pass. In Frankfurt/Main, veterans from the nationalist *Stahlhelm,* the republican *Reichsbanner,* and the Jewish *Reichsbund jüdischer Frontsoldaten* formed an honor guard to meet the train. A band played "Ich hatt' einen Kameraden," and a lone biplane circled overhead.

When the train pulled into the Potsdam Station in central Berlin on Wednesday night, November 18, a huge crowd was waiting despite the cold and dark. The next day, an endless stream of people filed past the coffin in the Gnadenkirche. The funeral was held on Friday, November 20. President Paul von Hindenburg, in his field-marshal's uniform, headed the official delegation. Soldiers beat muffled drums and led a riderless horse in the procession to the Invaliden Cemetery. The grave soon became a shrine, visited by the curious and the melancholy, anxious for even this symbolic tie to the ideal hero.[39]

Some years later, Manfred's brother Bolko reflected on the meaning of the funeral: "Not all of the hundreds of thousands who gave their lives for Germany, and who were laid to rest in foreign soil, could be brought home. And so, the thousands of people who streamed to greet our Manfred saw him as the representative of the self-sacrificing German hero, and honored in him the sons and brothers who had given themselves for the Fatherland."[40]

The return of the Red Baron demonstrates the extraordinary resilience of the heroic ideal, despite everything. For a moment, it seemed that the heroic could again, as in 1914, provide a common store of hopes and values. Certainly it was a wish of the *Deutscher Offiziersbund,* one of the major organizations of former officers. As an article in the Bund's journal explained:

> The German army returned home in 1918 after doing its duty for 4-1/2 years, and was shamefully received. There were no laurel wreaths; hate-filled words were hurled at the soldiers. Military decorations were torn from the soldiers' field-grey uniforms. Now, after 7 years, a lone soldier comes home, an officer like those in the olden days. He finds a Germany different from the one his brothers found in 1919. Then, the poison from the strife instilled in us by our enemies had robbed us of our wits. We were desperately sick, and in our feverish insanity, we did not even know who we were. Now we have returned to our senses.
>
> . . . Let us reckon as the last service of the young hero, that he was able to unify his people, at least briefly. . . . Welcome home, Manfred von Richtofen.[41]

In light of the events of the year before, however, it was clear that restoring the heroic to its central mythic function would be no easy matter. The very yearning for unity testified to the pain of Zerrissenheit. The mass mourning for the Red Baron, then, was more than a reaffirmation of the heroic. Mixed in the mourning was not a little nostalgia for the time when the heroic had meaning, and grief that the heroic was gone. The Red Baron was home, but the Red Baron was dead.

Otto Dix, "Wounded Soldier." (Photo: VEB Verlag der Kunst, Dresden)

CHAPTER 2

The Aesthetics of Violent Death

"Lieb Vaterland, magst ruhig sein, / Fest steht und treu, die Wacht am Rhein." I think I shall hear these words ring in my ears to my dying day. The whole life in the Germany of today seems to move to the rhythm of this tune. Every day troops pass by my window on their way to the station and as they march along to this refrain, people rush to the windows and doors of the houses and take up the song so that it rings through the streets, almost like a solemn vow sung by these men on their way to death.

—Evelyn, Princess Blücher,
An English Wife in Berlin

Violence touched everyone in Europe during the Great War, but its effect on war victims was especially intimate. Violence indelibly scarred crippled soldiers; death had invaded and exploded the lives of wives and children. After the war, a vast amount of war victims' energy was directed toward comprehending what death had done to them, toward enclosing the experience of violence and death in some sort of symbolic system. To understand what happened to the war victims, death in the Great War must be examined more closely. This chapter will focus on the experience of soldiers; a later chapter will examine the experience of wives and children.

Death was encountered from two drastically different perspectives. There was, first, death as an objectively measurable event, death as described in the army's bulletins and reported in the newspapers, death transformed into lists of names, columns of figures, autopsy reports, death as an administrative, managerial affair. There was also another death, death as it surrounded soldiers, struck them down, and tore them apart. This second death was an intimate, private experience. It was reflected in diaries and letters and in war fiction and poetry. It must be described not through statistics but through images, not through abstractions but through concrete metaphor. This chapter will deal first with the objective phenomenon and then with the subjective trauma.

I

When the Great War finally ended, no one, certainly not the belligerents, had any idea what it had cost in human lives. Some countries, Italy, for example, simply did not have the bureaucracy needed to keep track of all the dead. In Russia, the disintegration of the army, the revolution, and the turmoil of the civil war made maintenance of accurate statistics impossible. None of the governments knew exactly how many men had died; so many men were involved in the war, so many had been killed quickly, or had simply disappeared, that figures published after the war were full of error. Still, approximate numbers can be given.

The Great War lasted fifty-two and a half months. Roughly 9,500,000 soldiers, from all nations, were killed,[1] which comes to about 181,000 deaths per month, or about 6302 deaths every twenty-four hours. After the war, part of the armistice day ritual was to recalculate the human cost of the war.[2] These costs haunted Europe during the 1920s. Film historian Paul Monaco, for example, writes that French films of the period were filled with blood, because northern France was soaked in blood.[3]

Which nation suffered most depends on the standards used. Germany had more dead than any other belligerent. Serbia suffered the most dead as a percentage of population. Of the major powers, France experienced the most casualties relative to population. The Central Powers lost fewer men than the Allies; for every 1000 soldiers lost by the Central Powers, the Allies lost 1344. The table below, which follows Boris Urlanis, summarizes some of the losses.[4]

War dead, per 1000

Country	Men mobilized	Men aged 15–49	Total population
France	168	133	34
Germany	154	125	30.8
Britain	125	62	16
Russia	115	45	11
United States	27	4	1.1

In Germany, casualty lists were normally published daily, except Monday. The lists included names of the dead and wounded, as well as prisoners and the missing.[5] Reading through the seemingly endless lists became a national obsession. They were compiled by Germany's four war ministries, in Prussia, Bavaria, Württemberg, and Saxony. After the war, a single casualty office, the *Zentralnachweisstelle für Kriegerverluste,* was created; the office and its records were obliterated in an Allied bombing raid in World War II.

Casualty lists were never accurate. By the time units had forwarded names through channels and the war ministries had compiled the lists, the situation of the men had often changed. Missing men turned up; men reported dead were found to be alive. Ministries were swamped with requests for information from anxious relatives. Pre-printed postcards could be obtained, at least in the bigger cities in Germany, and deposited in special collection boxes for transmission to the authorities, who responded with another pre-printed postcard.

Germany's fundamental statistical problem was simply size. The nation had mobilized about 13.2 million men, more than any other belligerent. About 15.6 million men were eligible for military service, that is, between 17 and 50 years of age, and about 85 percent of them were mobilized.[6] Not everyone was in the army at the same time; usually the armed forces were about 6–7 million men strong. Nevertheless, virtually all the men in Germany born between 1870 and 1899 were at one time or another, swept into the military.

Between 1914 and 1918, the field army averaged about 5 million men; the other 1–2 million soldiers were in rear areas. The actual number of men in the field army, calculated from August to August, was: 1914/1915—4.6 million; 1915/1916—5.3 million; 1916/1917—5.8 million; 1917/1918—4.9 million.[7]

Units lost about 3 percent of their strength per month to all causes. The typical monthly breakdown was 2.4 percent of unit strength wounded, 0.4 percent killed, and 0.4 percent missing. Each year, then, the army lost about a third of its men.[8] Most of the wounded and sick eventually returned to duty, but the dead, missing, and captured needed to be replaced. Records on the captured were fairly accurate, but unfortunately, the army never had exact figures on the number of dead and missing.

Urlanis argues convincingly that some 2,037,000 German soldiers died during the war. The adjusted official death total, as of December 31 of each year, was:

1914	142,502
1915	628,445
1916	963,501
1917	1,271,573
1918	1,621,034
1919	1,718,608
1920	1,842,459
1933	1,900,876

As of 1933, there were at least 100,000 men still missing, and 34,836 sailors who had died but were not included in the statistics. About 1,185 colonial troops had been killed. If these additional 136,021 men are added to the 1,900,876, one arrives at Urlanis' estimate of 2,037,000 deaths.[9]

The total number of wounded can only be guessed. The problem is complicated by the fact that whenever a man was injured he was included on the casualty report, so that a man injured twice was counted as two separate "cases." Dr. Otto von Schjerning, the chief of the Army Medical Service, reported in 1922 that there had been some 4,211,469 wounded.[10] The 1934 *Sanitätsbericht* divides casualties as[11]

casualties	5,587,244
died in the field	772,687
died in the hospital	289,053
recovered	4,525,504 (of this number 74.7% returned to duty).

Somewhere around 4.3 million men were wounded but survived. In summary, German casualties in the Great War were:

dead	2,037,000
wounded	4,300,000
missing or prisoner	974,977

Again, it must be stressed that these figures are at best estimates.

The dead made up about 15.4 percent of all men mobilized, and about 19.4 percent of all the men who had served at one time or another in the field army. Of some 15.6 million males born between 1870 and 1899, about 13 percent died in the fifty-two and a half months of the Great War.[12]

From a military perspective, deaths never reached unacceptable levels. In the twelve months of the 1870/71 war with France, 45,610 German soldiers were killed. The German army then included about 1.4 million troops, so the death rate was about 3 percent. During the Great War, the death rate was only about 3.5 percent.[13] The level of violence in the later war was greater, but defenses were much more sophisticated. It was not the percentage of death that was so shocking in 1914–1918, but its scale.

On the average, 465,600 German soldiers died each year of the war. The first year was the worst and in that year the Eastern Front was deadlier than the Western in terms of losses as percent of unit strength. The total number of dead and wounded was always higher, however, on the Western Front. From August 1916 until the end of the war, deaths in the east declined rapidly. The opposite happened in the west.[14]

In August 1914, casualties were 12.4 percent of unit strength, and in September, 16.8 percent. Even during the battle of Verdun and the final offensive in France, losses never reached these percentages again. In the east, the heaviest losses relative to troop strength occurred in the last months of 1914, during the Polish campaign, and again in the 1915 summer campaign.[15] Virtually all of the 2.03 million dead were from the army; only about 34,836 were sailors.

It is obvious, but very important, that all these dead were young and male. The war radically polarized sexual and generational roles. Combat and violent death were almost exclusively a young-male experience. Between 1870 and 1899, about 16 million boys were born; all but a few served in the military, and some 13 percent were killed. Certain year groups were devastated. A comparison of 1910 and 1919 census figures reveals a demographic catastrophe. Year groups 1892–1895, men who were between 19 and 22 when the war broke out, were reduced by 35–37 percent.[16]

The dead remain anonymous; who they were and what their social background was cannot be calculated accurately, though precisely this question was furiously debated after the war. Some extrapolations are possible. The *Bund erblindeter Krieger,* the association of blinded soldiers, took a poll of its members in 1926, and the results offer some information concerning soldiers' social positions. The blinded soldiers described their prewar occupations as follows:[17]

Occupation	Number	Percentage
professional officer	13	0.5%
professional noncommissioned officer	16	0.6
teacher, higher civil servant, artist	79	3.1
merchant	46	1.8
white-collar worker	354	13.9
agricultural worker, farmer	486	19.1
craftsman	678	26.6
industrial worker	300	11.8
other worker	449	17.6
domestic worker	82	3.2
student	38	1.5
no occupation given	6	0.3
TOTAL	2547	100

Other studies reflect a similar occupational breakdown.[18] A more precise analysis of soldiers' social backgrounds would of course be most valuable, but the data available do not permit one to be constructed. During the republic, there were fierce battles about which social class had sacrificed the most, but no foolproof claim can be based on casualty figures.

The ethnic backgrounds of the dead soldiers was also hotly debated. A 1917 army survey had implied that Jewish Germans were not really sacrificing for the Fatherland. After the war, the Jewish veterans' group, the *Reichsbund jüdischer Frontsoldaten,* was determined to demonstrate the extent of Jewish German Patriotism. The *Reichsbund* carefully collected the names of dead Jewish soldiers and proved that over 12,000 Jewish Germans had given their lives for the nation. About 1 percent of the prewar population was Jewish, and about the same percentage of the dead were Jewish, so it appears that Jews were killed in proportion to their percentage of the population.[19]

The vast majority of the dead were, of course, enlisted men. Of the 1,822,545 dead counted by General Constantin von Altrock in 1921, only about 53,323 or 3 percent were officers. Enlisted men accounted for 96 percent and the remaining dead were doctors, civil servants, or colonial troops. But although the vast majority of the dead were enlisted men, the percentage of deaths among officers was higher than among enlisted men. According to Altrock, there were only about 226,130 officers in the army during the war, which means that 23 percent of the officers were killed, whereas about 14 percent of the enlisted men were killed. Regular officers had the highest death rate; about 25 percent of them were killed during the war.[20]

According to wartime tactical manuals, junior officers were to lead by example. When the whistle blew, the young lieutenant was to leap from his trench, shout "Hurrah!" and lead the charge. By and large, that is what junior officers did, and they died in droves.[21] Virtually all of the officers killed, about 96 percent, were captains or below. Only two field-marshals died during the war, one of disease, the other assassinated by a Bolshevik. This does not mean that senior officers were cowards; it does mean that battle death was a generational experience, something younger officers shared with younger enlisted men, and something older officers did not endure. In addition to the high percentage of junior officers killed, the casualties among regulars deserves emphasis. As shown above, losses among regular officers were appalling. The Great War devastated the German officer corps.

Not all deaths were combat-related. In the German army there were some 294 murders; 5,106 suicides; 13,470 accidental deaths, 55,899 deaths while prisoner of war, and about 166,000 disease-related deaths. Lung disease was the most serious medical problem (47,000 deaths), followed by influenza (14,000 deaths) and typhus (11,000 deaths).[22]

Some weapons played little role in killing German soldiers. Deaths caused by bayonet were rare. Poison gas, one of the newest weapons, killed about 3,000 German soldiers.[23]

Small arms, specifically massed rifle fire, had been the greatest killer in previous wars. In the Franco-Prussian War, 91.6 percent of casualties among German soldiers were caused by infantry rifle fire, and only 8.4 percent by artillery. This ratio changed drastically in the Great War, despite the introduction of the machine gun. According to autopsy reports, 58.3 percent of deaths were caused by artillery, and 41.7 percent by small arms.[24] Artillery fire reached great intensity during the war. For example, between 24 and 29 June 1916, some 50,000 English gunners (a force the same size as Wellington's entire army at Waterloo) fired 1,500,000 rounds into German positions near the Somme, positions measuring about 14 miles by 1 mile. One million shells were light, anti-personnel explosives. The remaining half-million shells ranged from 35-pounders fired by 4.5-inch howitzers, to 1,400-pounders fired by 15-inch howitzers. These half-million shells alone comprised some 12,000 tons of steel and explosive.[25]

Another characteristic of artillery fire was its total impersonality. In previous wars, gunners had to see a target to shoot at it, which meant that the target could shoot back. By 1914, guns could be placed several kilometers behind the front, and gunners fired not at men, but at map coordinates. The gunner never saw the men he was firing on, and the men being killed did not know where the guns were that were killing them.

II

The heroic metaphor provided a meaning for the killing. A dead hero was not simply flung into a pit but was solemnly buried among his comrades after an elaborate ritual. A hero was not torn into raw flesh and did not scream like an animal. He died neatly and usually had time to utter a last noble phrase. The dying hero was a staple of home-front propaganda, and some war literature, such as that of Walter Flex, reflects a decent and inspiring death. But it was hard to find such a death as the war went on.

Ernst Jünger, who served throughout the war as a front-line officer, was wounded a score of times and received many decorations. He was a prolific writer and wrote obsessively about his war experience. This is the way he described the dead.

> . . . what good does it do to cover them with sand or lime, or to throw a tent-half over them, in order to escape their black, bloated faces. There were too many. Everywhere, shovels struck something buried. All the secrets of the grave lay open in a grotesquerie worse than the most lunatic dream. Hair fell in clumps from skulls like rotting leaves from autumn trees. Some decayed into a green fish-flesh, which gleamed at night through the torn uniforms. If you stepped on one of these, you left behind phosphorous foot-prints. Others dried into lime-covered mummies. Elsewhere, flesh fell from bones like a reddish-brown gelatin. In humid nights, the swollen cadavers awoke to a ghastly life, as gas, sputtering and whispering, escaped from the wounds. The worst was the bubbling mass of countless worms which oozed from the corpses.[26]

Masses of worms oozing from cadavers is not a heroic image, yet it is representative of the imagery in the war literature.[27] Death was mysterious and inexplicable. The war was often described as a "storm" or a "hurricane" not because it was like a natural event, but because it was extraordinary and unpredictable. Kat in Remarque's *Im Westen nichts Neues* and Wammsch in Beumelburg's *Die Gruppe Bosemüller* were veterans of a score of battles, and their deaths were random and pointless. Other deaths were equally unpredictable, but far more violent. Men were torn limb from limb, bodies were flung through the air, the earth crashed and quaked, the very air hissed and screamed. Death also played ghastly tricks. In *Die Gruppe Bosemüller* a man in a second assault wave grabs his face and screams. He is unharmed, however. A soldier in front of him had been shot in the head, and the soldier's brains had spattered in the face of the man who had screamed. Later he too is killed.[28]

At the front, men lived in caverns in the earth and prowled at night. Trenches were often no more than 50 to 100 yards apart, and one could hear the enemy whispering on the other side of no-man's-land. The dead, the war literature reports, were everywhere. Accidental exhumation was a common occurrence, and ordinary things became sinister. August Stramm, killed in action in 1915, wrote in "Patrouille,"[29]

> Stones threaten
> Windows grin betrayal
> Branches strangle
> Mountain bushes rustle quickly
> Scream
> Death.

The living often seemed dead and corpses sometimes seemed to be alive. Jünger wrote:

> If, after such days, the front-soldier marches through some town behind the lines, in a silent, grey column, bent and tattered, then his stare freezes even the most thoughtless activity of those care-free people back there. "Like they were taken out of a coffin," someone whispers to a girl, and he shivers, when touched by the emptiness of those dead eyes.[30]

These nightmarish examples could be expanded endlessly. But Paul Fussell is quite right to insist that such descriptions hardly represent "reality." They are, as he argues, representative of a specific mood, a particular way of seeing.

Death in German war narratives is grotesque.[31] It is grotesque not simply because in some "objective" sense death was ghastly. To Walter

Flex and to those soldiers who could still cling to the heroic metaphor, death might be painful, but it was never grotesque. Death seemed utterly insane to many soldiers because the charm with which they had been equipped to tame death, the heroic metaphor, no longer worked. With no symbolic key to the meaning of violent death, many soldiers perceived death as something inexplicable and incomprehensible. Freud's observation bears repeating: the war had shattered previous conceptions of death, but no new conceptions of death had appeared. The result was the grotesque.

If so many soldiers perceived death as grotesque, how did they react to this perception? The experience of three soldiers shows three different reactions.

Jünger struggled to re-mythologize death. His self-chosen, postwar mission was to modify the heroic metaphor so it would correspond to industrial war. In his narratives, the insanity of war was accepted. His writings offered no political or social analysis, but instead focused on war as a return to true human nature. Jünger did not deny the grotesque; he aestheticized it. The experience of horror was an artistic pleasure and violence was a source of self-transcendence. Violent death was a revelation of the truth that, in a savage world, only martial values could provide meaning.[32]

For Ernst Toller death was also a revelation but of a different sort. An enthusiastic volunteer in 1914, he had seen dead soldiers frequently, but he had not really seen them. One day he unearthed a corpse by accident and suddenly the disjointed words "a-dead-man" became the charged phrase "a dead man."

> A-dead-man. . . . A dead man. And suddenly, as darkness is divided from light . . . I grasp the simple truth "man"—which I had forgotten, which lay buried and trapped—unity and oneness. A dead man. Not: a dead Frenchman. Not: a dead German. A dead man. . . . And at this moment, I know that I had been blind, because I had blinded myself, now I finally know that all these dead, French and German, were brothers, and that I am their brother.[33]

Toller organized a band of young veterans to protest against the war; violent death had provoked him into a defense of life.

A similar scene occurs in Remarque's famous novel *All Quiet on the Western Front*, but the results are different and more typical. Paul, the protagonist, kills a Frenchman with his hands, and for hours he shares a shellhole with the corpse. Paul is overwhelmed by guilt. Like Toller, he recognizes that he has murdered not an abstraction, but a fellow human being.

Red Cross workers tending a wounded soldier, Champagne, France, July 1918.
(Photo: Bundesarchiv Koblenz, Federal Republic of Germany)

When Paul returns to his lines, however, he recovers from his experience. Killing, he learns, is unavoidable; after all, "war is war,"[34] and who can change it? He becomes an efficient and ruthless killer. Like Jünger, Paul does not kill out of hatred, but unlike Jünger, he does not infuse his killing with a warrior's ethos. He is finally transformed into an automaton, a living-dead man, and his own death is anticlimactic; he was psychically dead long before the bullet hit him.

Most soldiers, unlike Jünger, could not accept death's embrace and, unlike Toller, they could not escape its embrace. Instead, they tried to survive by clinging to a net of emotional compromises, and the result was psychic death.

The dead finally escaped the need to confront death; it was the living and especially the wounded who had to confront it. Disabled soldiers faced a desperate problem. Touched by grotesque death, they discovered to their horror that they had become the grotesque. Robert Jay Lifton noted a similar experience among survivors of the atomic attack on Hiroshima. They had been touched by a death they felt was "bizarre, unnatural, indecent, absurd." Writes Lifton, "After any such exposure, the survivor internalizes this grotesqueness as well as the deaths themselves, and feels it inseparable from his own body and mind."[35]

German aid station in northern France, immediately behind the line, between Saint-Quentin and Laon, March 1917. (Photo: Bundesarchiv Koblenz, Federal Republic of Germany)

CHAPTER 3

Wounds, Disease, and Insanity: The Soldiers' War

A hospital alone shows what war is.

—Erich Maria Remarque, *All
Quiet on the Western Front*

In December 1914, a group of soldiers accompanied by a nurse visited one of Berlin's better theaters. The soldiers were recuperating from battle wounds. One man's leg had been amputated shortly before; the stump was not completely healed and his pants leg was flecked with blood. After the performance, the nurse gathered them together and distributed candy and cigarettes. Two fashionably dressed ladies stood a short distance away and gawked at the soldiers. One of the women who had been staring at the amputee whispered to the other: "God, isn't that disgusting! They could have left that one behind!" The soldier who reported this incident to *Vorwärts* said that only the intervention of the nurse prevented him from giving vent to his rage.[1]

The story illustrates the tensions that plagued wounded soldiers. Tensions between soldiers and civilians, between men and women, between the sick and the healthy, between the suffering and the comfortable, fissured the soldiers' lives. The image of the nurse distributing treats to her charges, like a school teacher passing out prizes to her wards, represents still another dimension of the soldier's life: heroes reduced to sick children.

The wounded soldier's alienation began with the injury itself, which radically altered his emotional as well as physical condition. Then came the entry into the new environment, the world of aid-stations, hospital wards, and therapy rooms, an environment that some never left. Most men did leave the hospital, however, and entered the third phase, recuperation, a complex attempt at both physical recovery and social re-integration. This chapter focuses on each stage of this strange new world.

I

Men were killed and wounded primarily because they were struck by various types of projectiles. A projectile, such as a bullet, kills and wounds according to the law of kinetic energy: $F = mv2/2$. The force of a projectile is the product of its mass and half the square of its velocity. Thus, a small object that is traveling at great speed strikes a target with tremendous impact. The small stone flung by David killed Goliath because of the law of kinetic energy. The musket and, later, the rifle were great advances over the spear and bow because exploding gunpowder can throw a projectile faster than the human arm or the bow string. By 1914 bullets could travel at great velocity.

The British Lee-Enfield Mark III rifle was probably the deadliest small arm used during the war; the French and German rifles were roughly equivalent. The rifles fired a bullet of about 9 millimeters, with a mass of approximately 150 grains. When the bullet was fired, it traveled about 2,500 feet per second.[2]

A bullet's energy depends on a variety of factors. Besides speed, a bullet's yaw, its shape, and air drag affect its striking power. Fired a long distance, a tumbling bullet loses speed and impact, but at close range a tumbling bullet can do more damage than a smoothly flying bullet. In the jungle of wire around the trenches, tumbling bullets were common.

A bullet's speed, however, is the most decisive factor. A bullet of 150 grains that strikes a thigh with an impact velocity of 2500 feet per second traverses 8 inches of bone and tissue in 0.00033 seconds. In the process, some 1330 foot-pounds of energy are released.[3]

This sudden release of energy is the most destructive result of a wound, even more destructive than penetration. Some 1330 foot-lbs. absorbed in 0.00033 seconds is the equivalent of 7200 horsepower; one horsepower is the energy expended in lifting 550 pounds one foot in one second. The result of this great burst of energy is that a body part literally explodes.

For this reason, head wounds were usually fatal. Muscle was torn and bone was fragmented but softer body parts, such as the brain, disintegrated when struck by a bullet. Doctors were stunned by this "hydro-static effect." Though it was not a new phenomenon, few doctors were familiar with it. In the first months of the war, many doctors were convinced that the British, whose rifle fire was especially deadly, were using explosive bullets or dum-dums. Gradually doctors discovered the real reason for the appalling nature of gun shot wounds.[4] And single wounds were rare. Small arms fire, particularly machine gun fire, was so intense and troops were often so congested that men were usually wounded several times simultaneously.

It was artillery however, that was the great killer. More than 50 percent of fatal wounds were caused by artillery fire.

When a shell explodes, it creates a sudden change in air pressure. Compressed air at the epicenter sweeps outward at tremendous speeds. It was part of the lore of the front that the concussion from even a mortar could do very strange things. In *All Quiet on the Western Front*, Paul Bäumer sees the effect of high explosives:

> At several places there are tremendous craters.
> "Damn, something's hit that," I say to Kat.
> "Trench mortars," he replies, and then points up at one of the trees.
> In the branches, dead men are hanging. A naked soldier is squatting in the fork of a tree; he still has his helmet on, otherwise he is entirely naked. There is only half of him sitting there; the bottom half, the legs are missing.
> "What's that?" I ask.
> "He's been blown out of his clothes," mutters Tjadin.
> "It's funny," says Kat. "We've seen that several times now. If a mortar gets you it blows you clean out of your clothes. It's the concussion that does it."[5]

However, the blast effect was not the worst part of artillery fire. Artillery shells were designed to shower projectiles, and the shells came in a wide variety. Shrapnel consisted of hollow shells that sprayed pellets on detonation. But the speed of pellets was comparatively slow, and except at very close range, shrapnel was usually not deadly. The deadliest kinds of shells were those designed to fragment on detonation. Pieces of jagged steel the size of a human hand or smaller than a needle flew through the air at tremendous speeds, and these fragments caused ghastly wounds.

A surgeon submitted observations about shell fragments to the war department:

> The power of these bits of iron is particularly violent. Even the smallest fragment rapidly penetrates the body and causes the most unpredictable damage; the larger fragments cause frightful destruction of bone and tissue. Healing these irregular, jagged wounds is complicated by the fact that they are frequently dirty, and even more by the fact that most are penetration-wounds, which means that a large area of the wound is deprived of blood and hence subject to gangrene. This gangrenous condition in turn induces substantial wound discharge, infection, bleeding and putrefaction . . .[6]

Autopsy reports reveal that head wounds were the major killers (47 percent of the deaths) followed by chest wounds (20 percent of deaths). Most cadavers had suffered multiple wounds. Wounds to the left arm were very common, apparently because when a right-handed man fired his rifle, he exposed his left arm.[7]

After-effects of wounds were equally lethal. Infection and loss of blood often resulted in death. Particularly deadly, however, was shock. When a man was struck by a projectile, his entire body was affected. The nervous and vascular systems worked irregularly. High amounts of hydrogen appeared in the blood. Breathing was irregular, the skin became pallid, lips turned blue, and body temperature dropped. Sometimes there was vomiting or loss of consciousness.

Emotional reactions varied widely. Some men reacted to their injuries with dullness and apathy, others with panic. The most common reaction was surprise. Lieutenant Wilhelm Hoffmann was directing his platoon in October 1914, when suddenly he could not see. A tiny shell fragment had struck the side of his head, directly behind the eye. The fragment instantly destroyed the optic nerves of both eyes, but initially, there was no pain, only amazement.[8]

Soldiers sometimes felt a sense of invulnerability, a conviction that others would be killed but they would survive. They often experienced a feeling that their bodies were somehow separate from their "real selves." Franz Marc wrote on May 25, 1915: "I see myself entirely objectively, as if it were some stranger riding, speaking, etc."[9] The protagonist in A. M. Frey's novel *Die Pflasterkästen* comments: "It's always the same, always this stupid, incorrigible confidence that makes the whole war possible: it can't hit me!"[10] Because of this "incorrigible confidence," there is surprise when they are struck down. Later in the same novel, a doctor is wounded and the protagonist remarks: "And even though he must have had severe pain, the expression of surprise in his eyes, surprise that such a thing could happen, was greater than any sign of pain."[11]

Fear came after surprise. The screams of the wounded in war narratives are often screams not of pain but of terror. Wounded soldiers desperately asked doctors where they had been hit, and the sight of their own blood and their sudden immobility frightened them.

For the first time in warfare, combat injuries were greater causes of casualties than contagious disease. German doctors were proud of having brought disease under control; it had been the soldier's worst enemy.

Still, disease remained a major problem. Army doctors treated more than 19 million cases during the war, in the following fourteen categories:[12]

Case type	No. of cases, 1914–18	Percent of total
combat wounds	4,807,568	24.7
stomach/intestinal disorders	4,138,384	21.3
dermatological disease	2,605,738	13.4

Case type	No. of cases, 1914–18	Percent of total
contagious disease	1,785,718	9.2
lung disease	1,728,241	8.9
orthopedic injuries	1,325,647	6.8
"other"	652,185	3.4
heart/circulatory disorders	461,560	2.4
injury to reproductive organs (excluding venereal disease)	356,227	1.8
eye disease/injury	350,604	1.8
ear disease/injury	337,543	1.7
neurological disorders	313,337	1.6
"for observation"	288,199	1.5
venereal disease	283,313	1.5

Note the extremes of this table. After battle injuries, the most common medical cases were stomach or intestinal disorders, not ordinarily thought of as war injuries. The cause of stomach disorder is often difficult to find; it can be caused by poor diet or by excessive anxiety.

Venereal disease was the least common medical problem. This was not because cases were unreported; doctors were scrupulous in investigating. Indeed, such careful medical attention is probably the reason venereal disease was a minor problem.

Disease and wounds drastically altered the soldier's world, and more trouble awaited him. Of no further use to the army, he was carted off into the complex and mysterious world of the hospital.

II

The hospital ward became the injured soldier's new world; he was surrounded by its odors and enclosed in its hygienic walls. All disabled soldiers were separated from the army eventually, but thousands never left the medical world.

Entering it was no easy task. Getting from the front to the aid-station was the most hazardous part of the journey. Medical corpsmen led the sick and injured to the aid-stations. The corpsman needed unusual strength to pull a wounded man to safety as well as courage to help the wounded when everyone else was scrambling for cover. Corpsmen wore red-cross armbands which made them illegal targets, and the enemy rarely shot at corpsmen deliberately. The armband did not make corpsmen immune to stray bullets or artillery fire, however.

Early in the war, dogs were used to sniff out wounded soldiers, but dogs rooting around in no-man's-land tended to draw fire, and their use was quickly abandoned. Anticipating an above-ground war, the army had equipped corpsmen with stretchers, but the rigid stretchers were useless in the zig-zag of the trenches. The tent-half became the corpsman's indispensable tool. It could be used as a kind of travois; it could also serve as a shroud. Automobiles were used later in the war to move men from aid-stations to hospitals, but for the wounded men, riding in the springless, hard-rubber-tired vehicles was agonizing and frequently fatal.[13]

The wounded man's first stop was the battalion aid-station, located near enough to the front to provide emergency service but far enough back to be out of the range of small arms. The first selection occurred here. Men with minor wounds were treated and sent back to their units. Dying men were set aside to die. Men with serious injuries were given emergency care, tagged, and prepared for shipment to the rear. The wounded "all have a tag on their chest, like a crate being shipped on the railroad. On the tag is confirmation from the aid-station that the person has been wounded, is being transferred to a field hospital . . . and that he has received a tetanus shot. The tag must be signed by a medical officer."[14]

Behind the aid-station, the medical system extended through the rear area and to nearly every town and village at home. Field hospitals were attached to divisions, larger hospitals were controlled by rear area commanders, and hospitals at home were under the command of deputy commanding generals.[15] At home too were many special hospitals, such as Dr. Silex's School for the Blind in Berlin, Dr. Kraepelin's psychiatric hospital in Munich, and the Düsseldorf Clinic for facial wounds. Through this complex system, the injured man was shipped, examined, tagged, loaded on to hospital trains and unloaded into ambulances, all the while unconscious or semi-conscious, and in every case, unable to control what was happening to him. Others made the decisions. His uniform was replaced by a hospital gown. Mysterious terms were inscribed on the bit of blackboard above his bed. What to eat and when to defecate, when to get up and when to lie down, were all controlled by benevolent but alien forces. He was wheeled here, shipped there, bandaged and unbandaged, dressed and undressed, cut open and sewn back together, and through it all, he was, unavoidably, an object. Only gradually was the wounded man able to assert himself again.

III

The first major transports of wounded reached Germany in the fall and winter of 1914; subsequently, trainloads of sick and wounded arrived daily. Meeting the trains became an important activity for civilians. As the men were unloaded from the trains, crowds stood around them and gawked. Perhaps a friend or a loved one would be on board, or there would be something novel to see. Soldiers hated being stared at. *Vorwärts* chided its readers for hanging about the Berlin stations as if they were waiting for a show.[16] "Dr. Owlglass" wrote a sarcastic poem about the "concerned public" who flocked to see the wounded.[17]

> . . . and there is the dear public,
> they gossip and nearly twist their heads off staring,
> as if monkeys and camels were coming,
> as if it were a carnival.
> They crowd around the stretchers—
> the old human beast likes blood,
> wants to "see something" and only "means well"

Some of the wounded could return to a nearly normal life, but it was hard work. Walking with crutches was exhausting and awkward, and artificial limbs were nearly as tiring and painful as crutches. It was worse to lose an arm than a leg. To help arm-amputees, the army distributed a pamphlet, written by a man born with one good arm. The pamphlet was full of practical advice: wear boots, not shoes with laces; have coats with large pockets and little hooks to hold gloves or a hat; learn to use knees and mouth when getting dressed, and so on.[18]

Recuperation was especially difficult for blinded men, although there were not very many of them, since almost any kind of head wound was fatal. By the end of the war there were no more than 3,000 blinded veterans. Initially, they were totally helpless and even after retraining, their autonomy was severely restricted. They had to learn many things: that sounds are complex, that people often shout at the blind as if they are deaf rather than blind, and that, when a blind person is accompanied by someone, people usually speak only to the sighted person. They learned too that the blind still dream, and that in their dreams, the blind can see.[19]

The majority of disabled men were neither amputees nor blind. In 1924, when the government finally collected data on disabled veterans,[20] it tried to describe the nature of the veterans' injuries. The effort was futile. Of some 720,931 veterans, the injuries of only 16 percent could be classified; the rest were simply classified as "Other." The injury breakdown was as follows:

Injury	Number	Percent
blind	2366	0.3
tubercular	41,688	5.8
insane	5410	0.8
loss of		
1 leg	44,657	6.2
1 arm	20,877	2.9

Injury	Number	Percent
2 legs	1264	0.2
2 arms	136	0.02
"Other"	604,533	84.0

Most disabled men did not have obvious injuries. They had stomach disorders, trouble moving; they did not have ghastly wounds. Other studies re-enforce this impression. In Aachen, for example, 2,275 disabled veterans were treated through the local social insurance office. While over half had some orthopedic difficulty, only about 15 percent were amputees.[21]

The disabled veteran was a staple of Weimar's art and literature. In paintings by Grosz and Dix, crippled men are often central, grotesque figures. In Andreas Latzko's story "Home Again," a veteran of the Austro-Hungarian army returns to his village. He had been shot in the face. At the train station, a former girl-friend is working.

> John Bogdan saw her, and his heart began to beat so violently that he involuntarily lingered at every step. Would she recognize him . . . ? His knee joints gave way . . . his hand trembled . . .
>
> How do you do?
>
> How do you do, the woman rejoined. He encountered her eyes, saw them widen into a stare, saw them grope over his mangled face, and then quickly turn in another direction, as if she could not bear the sight. He wanted to stop, but he noticed her lips quiver and heard a murmured "Jesus, Son of Mary," as if he were the devil incarnate. And he trotted on, deeply wounded.[22]

Most of the wounded soldiers did not have terrible wounds, but the veterans' wounds that appear in art or literature are horrible. When authors who had been wounded themselves, like Remarque or Alverdes, write about wounded men, the pictures they present are particularly frightful.

In Alverdes's 1929 story *Die Pfeiferstube,* the three main characters have been wounded in the throat. Small silver tubes were inserted in their throats to ease their breathing, and when they breathed, the tubes whistled softly. So, they were nicknamed "the whistlers." One day, while exploring the hospital, one of them finds himself in the blind ward. Because he can scarcely speak, he cannot explain who he is. He is shocked and frightened. The blind, meanwhile, sense that someone is staring at them, and they are furious. Slowly, though, the whistler and the blind soldiers realize that they are not strangers, but comrades.[23]

Although many of the disabled did not have grotesque wounds, they felt, nevertheless, that they had become outsiders. Living for long periods in the hospital, wearing hospital gowns, and spending the day in a chair or bed served to isolate them. The disabled soldiers were seen to be, and felt themselves to be, freaks. Two veterans in Remarque's *Der Weg zurück* talk about what the war had done to them. "We seem to have turned into first-rate bogey men," one soldier says. His comrade adds, "We smell of blood, that's what it is. . . ." Later in the novel, two other veterans talk about everything that had happened to them. Ludwig stares at Georg and says, "I think we're sick, Georg, we have the war in our bones." Georg nods and responds, "We'll never be free of it."[24]

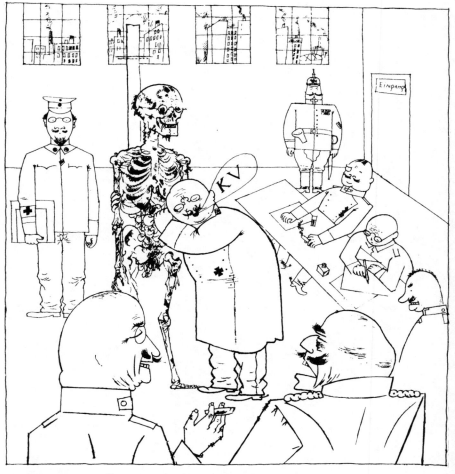

George Grosz, "The Faith Healers." The doctor is pronouncing the skeleton "kriegsver-wendbar," fit for duty. (Estate of George Grosz, Princeton, N.J.)

CHAPTER 4

The Medical Solution to the War Victims Problem

The primary source, from which ever new infectious material flows into the outer world, the chief producer of disease carrying agents is . . . the sick person. In him can exist thousands of infectious agents: the causes of diphtheria and meningitis; influenza and whooping cough bacteria; typhus, dysentery and cholera germs; tuberculosis and leprosy bacilli; malaria plasma; protozoa causing trypanosomiasis; spirochete causing syphilis and recurring fever; amobae causing tropical dysentery as well as organisms causing ancylostomiasis.

—*Weyl's Handbuch der Hygiene,* 1918

A peculiar debate took place in the Prussian state assembly in June 1919—peculiar even for that time filled with violence and confusion. It focused on psychiatry. With few exceptions, doctors had refused during the war to acknowledge shell-shock as a legitimate war disability. Some delegates denounced doctors for preventing men driven insane by the war from receiving pensions. The doctors' defenders retorted that the debate was absurd. Disability was a scientific, not a political question, they argued. Doctors were experts with years of study behind them; whether a man had a war-related disability should be left to the medical experts. An independent Social Democrat ridiculed that argument. So-called experts, he said, constantly make judgments to please the political powers. "For example, you all know perfectly well, that up until 9 November the most famous professors assured us that it wasn't so bad to have no food. Actually, they said, it was really good to have so little to eat; that way you didn't have to go to Kissingen or Karlsbad to go on a diet!"[1]

Although the debate accomplished nothing, it does raise an important question. Doctors dominated the lives of the war victims. They not only prescribed the disabled soldiers' treatment; they also decided whether an injury was war-related, which, of course, determined whether a man could get a pension. How did the doctors go about resolving the intractable war victims problem?[2]

At the beginning of the nineteenth century, doctors were barely distinguishable from barbers or, for that matter, wizards. The village doctor was a person of low status and sometimes ill repute. Medicine was dominated by romantic conceptions of life forces and vague powers—ideas that were more of philosophical interest than of practical value.

But in the middle of the nineteenth century, medicine in Western Europe dramatically changed. Young scientists, typically sons of the middle class, insisted that medicine must be made a positive science; it must borrow the methods of physics and become objective, mathematically precise, and rigorously experimental. The faith of these scientists was unbounded; they were convinced that through medicine, the wonders of science could heal all human ills.

Rudolf Virchow is the most representative of these reformers. A polymath, of remarkable energy and passionately dedicated to improving the lot of the poor, Virchow described medicine as the total science. For him medicine was the basis of all the other disciplines, since it concentrated on the biological person. Anthropology, sociology and philosophy were merely subdivisions.[3]

Virchow's dreams of sweeping social reform engineered by benevolent physicians were never fulfilled, but the changes in medicine were far-reaching. Medicine in Germany flourished. Virchow and such contemporaries as Koch and Ehrlich, became world famous. The social position of doctors in Germany soared. Medicine became a privileged profession. Doctors had their own standards of admission to their guild, their own journals, their own professional jargon, and their own costume and code of conduct. Even the most obscure village practitioner considered himself, and was considered by his patients, to be a "man of science."

The number of physicians in Germany increased by more than 100 percent between 1876 and 1909, from 13,728 to 30,558. In 1876 there were 3.2 physicians per 10,000 citizens; in 1909, there were 4.8. The medical system grew rapidly. In 1877, there were 2357 hospitals in Germany, an average of 24.6 for every 10,000 people; in 1910, there were 4805 or 63.1. In 1877, doctors treated about 472,000 patients; in 1910, the number of patients was 24,197,000.[4]

As in most of Europe, doctors in Germany were recruited from the upper strata of society, particularly from the educated bourgeoisie; unlike most of Europe, German doctors were generally not private entrepreneurs but civil servants. They were affiliated with a public institution or, as in the case of military doctors and university professors, they were employees of the state.

In 1914, there were 33,031 doctors in Germany, of whom 200 (0.6 percent) were women. Nearly 80 percent were mobilized for military service. There was always a chronic shortage of doctors; by 1918, the shortage had grown to 30 percent. During the war, 1,819 doctors died of injury or disease, and 2,218 were wounded.[5]

Many doctors possessed great technical skill, and in some specialties their accomplishments were outstanding, particularly in orthopedics. Before the war, opportunities for orthopedic specialists were limited, but with the coming of the conflict, the demand for orthopedists' skills soared. Working closely with engineers, orthopedists designed an impressive variety of artificial arms and legs.

The principle of design was efficiency, not aesthetics. There was no point in trying to copy the human arm; it was the arm's use-value that had to be reproduced. Through a complex network of straps and hinges, the artificial limb could do many things normal limbs could do. (One concession to fashion was allowed: clerical workers were issued a screw-on "Sunday hand," made of wood and covered with a glove, whose purpose was purely decorative.)

In February 1916, the *Verband Deutscher Ingenieure,* the German Association of Engineers, sponsored an artificial arm contest. A total of 82 arms were submitted and put on display for three months. In the end, the engineers did not award a first prize, but second prize went to the "Jagenberg arm," which consisted of "two metal rods joined by a ball-and-socket joint which can be turned in any direction, a grip of the well hand sufficing to fix or loosen it. It is fastened to the stump by a tight-fitting leather cuff. With the arm is furnished a set of 20 attachments suitable for all the ordinary operations of life. . . .[6] By the end of the war, orthopedists, with the assistance of engineers, had developed some 30 different types of arms and 50 types of legs.

Photographs testified to the success of orthopedic engineering. A typical photo showed an amputee at work in a factory or shop deftly manipulating tools with his mechanical hands.[7] The reconstruction of the human body, based on principles of engineering, was medicine's most dramatic achievement during the war.

II

Psychiatrists were far less successful. The first task of medical analysis—classifying and labeling symptoms—was extremely difficult for psychiatrists during the war. A grab-bag of maladies, from tremors and tics to depression and mania, were simply diagnosed as "war neurosis." The subdividing of war neurosis into specific neuroses provoked considerable confusion.

The debate about the origin and treatment of war neurosis was particularly sharp between the conventional psychiatrists and Freudian psychiatrists (psychoanalysts).[8] Critics of psychoanalysis pointed out that Freud's theories on sexuality failed to explain shell-shock; men broke because of bullets and bombs, not because of some unresolved sexual dilemma.

Freud and his allies conceded that the relationship between sexuality and war neuroses was unclear; nevertheless, they argued, war neurosis confirmed the validity of the psycho-dynamic approach.

According to the Freudians, war neurosis demonstrated the psychological origin of behavioral disorders. Like peace-time neuroses, war neuroses were the outcome of inner conflict, which rages only in part at the conscious level; symptoms, such as tics and depression, were efforts to resolve this conflict.

The analysts believed that war neuroses arose when the ego was threatened by forces it could not control. While these might be unresolved sexual problems, they could also be the obvious dangers of military life. The war literally threatened to destroy the ego, and, faced with annihilation, it escaped into neurosis.[9] Neurotic symptoms served to remove the soldier from danger in a way more likely to be condoned than mutiny or desertion. This did not mean that the man was malingering; the truly disturbed soldier was quite unaware of the psychological causes of his illness. It was the analysts' general position that the neurosis was narcissistic; libido became detached from the outer world and rushed to the defense of the weakened ego. This explained the soldier's abstraction from the outer world, his childlike absorption with himself, his hypochondria. At the same time, the unconscious realization of the ego's fundamental weakness and vulnerability produced depression and melancholia.

A peculiar aspect of the psycho-dynamic explanation of war neuroses was the argument that neurosis was a sign of health. Neurosis, analysts maintained, is a way of avoiding psychosis; it is an effort, however inadequate, to resolve psychic difficulties. Neurotic symptoms are attempts at self-healing.

Psychoanalysts vigorously advanced their arguments. At a 1918 international conference on psychoanalysis, held in Budapest, war neurosis was discussed in detail. Working in psychiatric hospitals, analysts such as Karl Abraham and Ernst Simmel attempted to demonstrate the validity of the Freudian approach. Nevertheless, the vast majority of psychiatrists rejected the analysts' arguments.

Despite their difficulty in understanding war neuroses, however, there was a broad consensus among conventional psychiatrists about the origin and treatment of behavioral disorders. Such disorders, they said, are essentially neurological malfunctions that can have internal or external causes. Certain external causes, head wounds or infections, for example, can disrupt the nervous system and result in abnormal behavior. But most psychiatric difficulties, they believed, have internal causes, frequently hereditary in nature.

Dementia Praecox (schizophrenia) was a favorite diagnosis among convential psychiatrists. In their view, shortly after adolescence, some young males experience a serious disruption of the nervous system, which is due to organic disfunction and results in withdrawal, inability to work, and, finally insanity. Why the nervous machinery broke down, the doctors could not explain, but they were convinced that the breakdown could not be caused by an external experience such as war.[10]

The case of mailman Wilhelm S. illustrates how such views affected victims of war neurosis. Wilhelm, a hard-working, dependable mailman, was called up in 1914. What he experienced during his service is not recorded, but by 1916, he was acting very strangely. He began to complain of a variety of aches and pains. He recited poetry and passages from the Bible and warned of a coming Last Judgment. His behavior became so bizarre that the army discharged him and sent him back to his old job, but his poetry and scriptural recitations prevented the other mailmen from doing their duty. Wilhelm S. was incarcerated in a mental hospital and finally declared to be insane.

After the war, Wilhelm's relatives applied for a pension for him. But a government doctor rejected the application. A pension was "not justified." Undoubtedly, the doctor wrote, this was a case of dementia praecox, and there was "evidence" of hereditary insanity—the mailman's sister exhibited abnormal behavior. Besides, the doctor concluded, if war could cause lunacy, Germany would have a generation of lunatics on its hands. Since there was no such crisis, it was clear that war could not cause mental breakdowns among otherwise normal people.[11]

The statistics, the psychiatrists maintained, support their conclusion that war did not cause breakdowns. Only about 313,000 cases of neurological disorders were treated during the war, less than 2 percent of all the cases treated. In the 1924 census of disabled veterans, only 5410 were classified insane.

But more than medical considerations was involved in war neurosis; there were moral questions, too. Suppose the doctors' figures were accurate, that the vast majority of men adapted themselves to mass killing with the help of doctors and psychiatrists. Was that not lunacy? Were not the doctors, who convinced soldiers to return to the front, themselves lunatics or worse? After the war a number of writers asked precisely these questions. In his 1926 memoir, *Wir sind Gefangene,* Oskar Maria Graf presents himself as a Schweik figure who is finally released from the army as a "war neurotic." It is clear, however, that not Graf, but the generals and doctors and all those who kept on killing were the real neurotics.[12]

After his revelation that the enemy was his brother, Ernst Toller actively opposed the war. The army wanted to court martial him, but Toller's family managed to have him committed to an insane asylum instead. Even the famous Dr. Kraepelin, according to Toller, could not cure his "illness." How, Dr. Kraepelin demanded, could Toller dare to challenge Germany's just war aims? It was precisely people like Toller who were responsible for the failure to capture Paris! The professor's face reddened, Toller remembered,

> with the pathos of the manic political-agitator. He tries to convince me of the necessity of pan-German policies. I learn that there are two types of sick people: the harmless ones who lie in cells with bars on the windows and no handle on the door and are called "insane." The others, the dangerous ones, argue that hunger educates people, found societies "for the defeat of England," and are allowed to lock the harmless ones up.[13]

The difficulty was that certain types of behavior were clearly "abnormal," but defied diagnosis. Graf, Toller, and people like them were certainly not normal soldiers, but it was hard to describe them as "insane." What was wrong with them? Their problem, the psychiatrists explained, was a lack of "will-power."

Will was a basic component of every doctor's diagnostic model. Most insisted that health and recovery ultimately depended not on medicine, but on the patient's character, and specifically, on his or her willpower.[14] Soldiers suffering from every kind of malady were inundated with literature exhorting them to exert their will.[15] Probably the most extreme statement of this attitude can be found in the work of the medical missionary, E. G. White, whose book, *In den Fussspuren des grossen Arztes,* had gone through eight German editions by the outbreak of the war. God, White writes, intends everyone to be healthy. Sickness is a result of violating God's law; disease is a sign of a weakness in moral character.[16]

Doctors were usually more circumspect, but they too reminded soldiers that willpower was the key to recovery. A hospital poster announced that everyone could return to work again, "if only he has a strong enough will." The poster, however, also stated that the soldier "must take care to carry out the doctor's orders exactly."[17]

Of course, recovery often does depend on the patient's attitude and courage. Moreover, the stress on will conformed to the prevailing conviction that rewards and punishments were related to personal virtue, and that, in the end, the good prospered and the bad suffered. It conformed also to the heroic ideal, for the hero transformed the world through his courage and iron will.

Will, however, took on a peculiar meaning among doctors. It did not mean asserting one's own opinion against that of the doctor. Will was not what Ernst Toller displayed. Fighting the doctor, as Toller did, was a sure sign of a lack of will. Will meant imposing on oneself the regimen the doctor ordered. In effect, it was a demand that the patient surrender his will—akin to the political ideology in which the highest expression of life was surrendering it for the good of the nation.

There was an even more troubling aspect to the emphasis on will. Since recovery was a matter of willpower, if the patient did not recover, it was his own fault, not the doctor's. Blaming the victim is a device hardly unique to German doctors, but it played a most important part in the complex relationship between physicians and their soldier-patients. From the doctor's perspective, the patient was a noble hero to be helped, but also a potential recalcitrant who had to be disciplined. The doctor's task, then, was both to control illness and to control the patient.

III

The most spectacular medical advances in Germany were in the field of epidemiology of which hygiene was the chief tool. Robert Koch, Virchow, and others demonstrated the direct link between hygiene and disease. Virchow was tireless in his promotion of urban sanitation and in publicizing the need for waste disposal and personal cleanliness. Hygiene became a public concern in the rapidly growing cities of the late nineteenth century. Scores of voluntary societies were organized to champion public health.[18] Medical metaphors became embedded in everyday conversation. Words like "infection," "fever," and "parasite" were used to describe all manner of phenomena. Such terms did not originate in the late nineteenth century by any means, but all the discoveries in hygiene gave such terms a scientific flavor, and evidence of the link between parasites and disease gave them an added frightfulness. Since relatively few people understood the complex relationship between parasitology and epidemiology, these terms also had a certain mysterious, sinister, loathsome quality about them.[19]

A major fear of army doctors in 1914 was that parasites would run rampant and the resulting epidemics would destroy the armed forces. Periodic outbreaks of typhus were common on the Eastern front; in 1915, typhus nearly destroyed the Serbian army. Doctors were particularly concerned about the trench system; it was the type of environment they had campaigned against for years. The trenches were infested with rats, mice, flies, mosquitoes, and lice.

Soldiers in the trenches were plagued with lice. After an initial disgust, however, they came to accept their guests with a certain equanimity. "Lice," Arnold Zweig wrote, "like superior officers and Fate, are beings of a higher order; you may struggle against them, but you must, to a more or less degree, come to terms with them."[20] However, body lice worried doctors, for among other diseases, they carried typhus.

Doctors used a number of weapons to combat lice. Peasants in the east were deemed primary carriers and soldiers were warned to stay away from them. The slang term for Russian prisoners of war was "lice," and an anonymous poet claimed that it was impossible to stay clean in "the land of lice."[21]

Immunization was another weapon in the doctors' arsenal, used to combat typhus and other contagious diseases. Doctors used a great amount of serum during the war. Between 1914 and 1919, they administered a minimum of 200 million immunizations, which is about 15 per soldier.[22] When disease scares occurred, it was not unusual for entire regiments to be immunized and reimmunized.

In 1915, a weapon to fight lice appeared, which the soldiers called the "louseoleum." It was a large, portable fumigation station. A variety of chemicals and soaps were used by medical personnel to clean several hundred soldiers a day. Russian prisoners were run through the louseoleum before being shipped to camps in Germany. German soldiers had to have a louseoleum stamp in their papers before they could go on leave.

In 1915, a Society to Purchase Louseoleums began raising money in Germany. A fund-raising letter, signed by Prince Hans zu Hohenlohe-Oehringen, explained: "As is well known, our troops in the east are plagued by vermin. These vermin carry contagious diseases, particularly typhus. To meet this threat, and especially to prevent the spread of disease to Germany, troops must have the opportunity to bathe and disinfect their clothing."[23] The society collected enough money to purchase several louseoleums for the army.

The society is interesting because it represents an attitude that had developed among civilians about soldiers. At the beginning of the war, there was a comic aspect to the plague of insects. One popular present for Christmas 1914 was a powder called "Nick-o-louse." As the war went on, however, the fun faded, and civilians began to fear the soldiers as carriers of disease.

Part of this fear is rooted in the taboo that surrounds the hero. He does things and goes places normal people do not, and wartime prose warned that combat would set soldiers apart from civilians. For example, in 1916 the bishop of Speyer wrote, "After the war, a clear line will divide those who were there, from those who were not. The millions now in the combat zone, who have endured bloody battle, will say for years to come: "We were there . . ."[24]

Freud, in his 1915 "Thoughts on War and Death," argued that this taboo is directly related to the act of killing. Soldiers become identified with actions that are normally prohibited, and the soldiers become outcasts, at least briefly. As Freud wrote: "Savages . . . are far from being remorseless murderers; when they return victorious from the war-path, they may not set foot in their villages or touch their wives until they have atoned for the murders they committed in war by penances which are long and tedious."[25]

Soldiers were also associated with the violation of sexual mores. They were particularly identified with venereal disease. It was common knowledge that this disease had been a serious medical problem in the Franco-Prussian war.

In 1915, Social Democrat Rudolf Wissell, warned health insurance officials that the nation faced a serious peril. "This concerns the grave danger to the public health from venereal disease, an indirect consequence of the war . . . It is, I am sad to say, a frightful fact, that among our soldiers, the number of cases of venereal disease has risen significantly, especially in the west."[26] He later said that 33,538 German soldiers, the equivalent of an entire army corps, had been put out of action between 1870 and 1871 because of venereal disease.[27]

Doctors, however, insisted that venereal disease was not out of control. One doctor calculated that venereal disease among rear-echelon troops remained at peacetime levels, while venereal disease among front troops was actually lower than peace-time levels;[28] and venereal disease was the least common medical problem during the war.[29]

But the doctors' comments were largely ignored by the civilian population, and not infrequently by other doctors, so that the image of the diseased veteran became fixed in even the expert imagination. After the war, venereal disease increased in rural communities, and for some, it was self-evident who the infectious agents were. One doctor wrote: "The distribution [of venereal disease] had changed markedly, in so far as there were significantly more cases reported in rural areas and small towns (return of not-fully-cured soldiers!)."[30]

At first, the soldier had been a hero; by the end of the war, he had become something else. He was lice-ridden and violent, and he was sexually uncontrolled and possibly diseased. For the soldier, this image did not bode well for a warm welcome back home. The situation was further complicated by a grim discovery the soldiers made when they finally got there: home was already filled with victims of the Great War.

Käthe Kollwitz, "Widow." (Ralph Jentsch, Munich)

CHAPTER 5

Widows and Orphans

So, how many women are there then? Two million, maybe, who sit in their rooms and, like me, think of their dead husbands. Look out the window, and think of their dead husbands. Do the dusting, take care of the kids, knit the socks, do the cooking, go to work, and think of their dead husbands, of their dead husbands. Go to bed at night, and think of their dead husbands.

—Leonard Frank, *Der Mensch ist gut*

Among German war victims, there were as many civilians as there were soldiers. The wounds of the civilians were less obvious than those of the veterans, but they were no less deep. The veterans' fate can be reconstructed in some detail, but describing what happened to widows and orphans must rest more on speculation and imagination because there is no comprehensive study of the experience of civilian war victims. However, social workers periodically counted widows and orphans and occasionally someone collected their stories, and these two strands of evidence reveal the general pattern of their lives.

I

When they talked about their past, war widows recalled a predictable, orderly pattern. They did not remember political events or battles or the Kaiser's speeches; they remembered the details of their own lives. What they spoke of first was the time before the war, when they had been young. No matter what troubles their families had experienced, the women recalled their childhood as a peaceful and happy time.[1]

During the war, statistics were collected on widows in the IVth Army Corps, an area in central Germany. According to these statistics: 90 percent of women widowed in the first year of the war had been married fewer than 10 years. Over half (58 percent) of the 1914 widows had been married fewer than four years. They were young women. Almost all of the widows (97 percent) were under 40 years of age, and two-thirds (68 percent) were under 30.[2]

In the years immediately before the war, these young women and their husbands were beginning their families and planning their futures. Most of the 1914 widows in the IV Corps area (97.9 percent) had children; one or two usually, though a few had more. The children, of course, were only infants in 1914. Of the children orphaned in 1914, 76 percent were under 6 years of age, and 53 percent were under 3.[3]

The young families lived in modest circumstances. Most of the husbands (65–70 percent) were industrial workers, about 13 percent were in agriculture, and 10 percent were in trade. Their incomes were low. In 1913 a skilled worker earned about 1500 marks a year, and an unskilled worker, about 1000 marks.[4] Three out of four husbands killed in 1914 had pre-war incomes of less than 2000 marks. One in five earned between 2000 and 3000 marks per year; few (4 percent) made more than 3000 marks. In the IV Corps area, most families lived in small towns: 62 percent lived in communities of fewer than 10,000 inhabitants; 22 percent were in towns having between 10,000 and 100,000 inhabitants; and only about 15 percent lived in cities of over 100,000 inhabitants.[5]

The years before the war were full of plans, the women remembered. They spoke of the optimism they felt, the pleasure at finding a better apartment, or the hope that their husbands might find a better job—perhaps as craftsmen or even as self-employed shopkeepers.

A wife's role was clearly defined.[6] Kaiser Wilhelm outlined the role in terms reminiscent of the heroic metaphor:

> . . . our women . . . should learn that the principal task of the German wom-an lies not in the field of assemblies and associations, nor in the achievement of supposed rights, with which they can do the same things as men, but in quiet work in the house and in the family. They should bring up the younger generation above all else to obedience and respect for their elders. They should make it clear to their children and their children's children that what matters today is not living one's life at the expense of others, achieving one's own aim at the expense of the Fatherland, but solely and exclusively commit-ting all one's mind and strength to the good of the Fatherland.[7]

However, there were a number of trends that might well have disturbed the Kaiser. There was a small but vocal women's rights movement,[8] and an increasing number of women were working outside the home. In 1882, women made up about 30.7 percent of the workforce; by 1907, the percentage had climbed to 35.8 percent.[9] This trend continued despite the fact that women earned considerably less than men for comparable jobs. In March 1914, for example, women's wages were about 44 percent of men's wages.[10]

In addition, the German family was becoming smaller. In 1900, a couple after 19 1/2 years of marriage averaged 4.1 children; by 1910, the average had dropped to 3. (By 1935, the average had plummeted to 2.1.)[11]

However, marriage remained a popular institution, and the number of divorces scarcely changed. In 1871, 58.3 percent of German females were unmarried. In 1900, the percentage was 57 percent, and in 1910, it was 56.5 percent. In 1871, 0.2 percent of females were divorced; by 1910, the number was only 0.3 percent.[12]

The widows remembered their marriages with affection. Talking wistfully about their lives with their husbands, they would suddenly interrupt themselves, saying ". . . and then came the war." The simple phrase recurs regularly in the widows' narratives. It is as if the war were a tear in the very fabric of time.

The widows did not remember the outbreak of the war with joy, but the old photographs of August 1914 seem to tell a different story. They show young women cheering as their young men left for the front. Perhaps later events shaped their memories or the old photographs do not tell the entire story. What the women remembered feeling that summer was fear. When one man told his wife that he just had to volunteer, she cried. She said later: "[I told him] 'it's all right if you want to volunteer. I want to be brave like the other women. But come home again.' With a shout of jubilation he took me in his arms, but my heart was so heavy." She accompanied her husband to the train station on the day he left. "My husband and I walked hand-in-hand without speaking. I couldn't say anything or I would have cried, and I didn't want to make his departure hard."[13] The departure was a typical element of the widows' narratives. The date, the time of day, the weather, and what was said, became indelible memories.

For civilians, the war was an exhausting and enervating experience. It became worse as months dragged on into years. For many, the worst experiences occurred during the British blockade.

Before the war Germany was a major importer of goods. The nation imported all of its cotton, three-fifths of its copper, three-fourths of its oil, half its phosphatic fertilizer, half its barley, about half its meat, and a quarter of its milk products.[14]

Since most of these imports arrived by ship, Germany was extremely vulnerable to a naval blockade. Only one power could conduct a blockade effectively, and that was Britain. Instead of working for smooth relations with Britain, however, the German government consistently clashed with the English. The blockade was in a sense the appropriate penalty for years of mismanaged foreign policy.

It took some time for the blockade to take effect. But by 1917, Germany had no cotton, tin, nickel, platinum, or rubber, and copper and cotton were in very short supply. And there was hardly any food.[15]

The government bungled the distribution of food supplies, and the war itself devoured resources at an incredible rate. By the "turnip winter" of 1917/1918, many people of this once wealthy nation were reduced to grubbing for roots. Food, milk, coal—everything—had run out. At first, the shortages resulted in strange, almost comical incidents. Evelyn Blücher, an Englishwoman who had married into a famous Prussian family, spent the war years in Germany, most of them in Berlin. In her diary for "Sep.–Oct. 1916," she wrote:

A friend of mine wanted to buy some woolen underwear, and her experiences are typical of war-shopping now in Germany. She saw what she wanted in a shop and went in. The girl who attended her was very obliging and got everything ready, but when the bill was made out, she turned to my friend and said, "Where is your *Bezugsschein* (permit of purchase)?" "Oh," said my friend, "I have none." The girl told her it was a trifle, and that she would reserve the goods for her until she had obtained one; she need only go to the police station. Off went my friend, and when she arrived at the police station, they told her to go to a stationer's, and get a form which is filled in as a kind of control when one moves about. So she departed and returned with this form. "What shall I write on it?" she asked. The answer was, your name, your age, where you were born, what subject you are, and last, but not least - not how much material do you want, but what faith do you profess? My friend filled in all this, whereupon the official stamped her paper, which meant that he guaranteed for the truth thereof, and then sent her off to the place where she might receive the permit. This was a good walk from where she was, and she decided to go the next day. When she got there at 4 o'clock in the afternoon, she was told the office was only open from 8 to 1 o'clock. Patiently, she trudged home, to start again next day. When she arrived this time, she was asked what the permit was to be for. "For three pairs of combinations," she told the official (there are no discrete secrets from officials in war-time). "What!" he exclaimed. "You want three pairs? You cannot have more than two, one to wear while the other is in the wash!" Shopping becomes a strange thing when controlled by Prussian officialdom.[16]

An indication of Germany's crisis was the drastic drop in caloric intake. An adult needs about 2000 calories a day. By the middle of the war, average caloric intake for adults had dropped below 1500 calories and in the winters of 1916/1917 and 1917/1918, some adults were averaging less than 1000 calories a day.[17]

The most obvious result was drastic weight loss. Women who had weighed between 50 and 59 kilograms before the war lost as much as 10 kilograms; those who had weighed between 60 and 69 kilograms lost up to 14 kilograms. Many women lost up to 25 percent of their pre-war body weight.[18]

In addition, the quality of the German diet deteriorated. Meat, milk, eggs, and other staples disappeared from the market. The following table shows rations of various foods as a percentage of prewar consumption.[19]

Food	July 1916–June 1917	July–Dec. 1918
meats	31 percent	12 percent
fish	51	5
eggs	18	13
lard	14	7
butter	22	28
cheese	2	15
vegetables	14	7
sugar	48	82
potatoes	71	94
vegetable fats	39	17
cereals	52	48

The result, of course, was an increase in disease and death. The figure for women's deaths, per thousand females over one year of age, rose as follows:

1913	10.9
1914	11.2
1915	11.8
1916	12.3
1917	14.1
1918	17.8

Between 1914 and 1918, the increase in the death rate was about 67 percent. The influenza epidemic of 1918–19 was the leading cause of death among women, followed by sicknesses associated with cold and hunger, such as pneumonia and tuberculosis.[20]

The social disruption during the war was profound. Fathers, sons, and brothers left their families. Schools had to be reorganized when male teachers went into the service. As skilled workers left for the military, thousands of women and adolescents rushed into the labor force; yet at the same time thousands of workers became unemployed as entire sectors of the economy were closed down. And prices soared.

Worst of all for the wives was the endless waiting. Mail was a constant source of frustration. Families worried when letters did not arrive as expected. Mail was slow at best; the post office was often overwhelmed. To reduce mail volume, the government encouraged the use of postcards.

Shopping trips and travel plans were arranged around the letter carrier; the first question on arriving home was about the mail. Often soldiers tried to establish a routine so that mail reached their families at the same time each week or month, and if the little brown post card did not arrive when it was supposed to, the worry at home was almost unbearable.

The letter carrier naturally assumed an extraordinary importance during the war. By 1916, most letter carriers were women or old men. Their job was hard. Letters addressed to soldiers were sometimes returned, stamped "Dead—Return to Sender," which was a brutal way for anyone to learn that a man had been killed. Letter carriers quickly learned to recognize the official notifications of death or injury and sometimes, anticipating the news in the letter, they became upset, so that the sight of a distraught letter carrier was the first sign that something awful had happened. To avoid this, letter carriers were instructed to delay delivery of "suspicious" letters and contact a postal official or a clergyman.[21]

Women often knew of their husband's death before the news officially came. Some had dreamed about their husband's death. "You might laugh at me because of this," a widow wrote, "but my husband and I had promised each other, that if one of us died anywhere in the world, without being able to tell the other, the one who died would still somehow contact the one still living." This woman had a dream about her husband: ". . . as he came closer, I awoke with a terrible scream, since what was staring at me was a death's head." Later she learned that only hours before her dream her husband had been killed at the front.[22]

Widows' memories were filled with such prophetic dreams, and whatever their psychological "explanation," they suggest the often devastating psychic strain on the women, which often aggravated or caused physical illness. The woman who reported this dream later suffered a nervous breakdown.

Virtually all of the widows whose stories have been recorded tell of heart trouble, stomach pains, or some kind of physical decline, usually after learning of their husband's death. The combination of psychological suffering and declining living conditions meant that the widows were, at least temporarily, physically disabled and this became an important factor in the demands of the war victims' movement.

The age of women who became widowed increased during the war, as is shown in the IV Corps area.[23]

Widow's age	1914	1915	1916
17–20	3 percent	1.5 percent	1.1 percent
21–29	65	51.6	45
30–39	29	41.4	46

The reason for the increase is that as the war went on, older men were called up. The result on the home front was insidious. Older widows usually had more children than younger widows and thus were less able to leave home and find work.

When the news came that their husbands were gone, the widows' first reaction was usually withdrawal. "If only I could get away somewhere," was the common response.[24] There were very practical reasons for this. Everything was in short supply in the cities; it was better to live in the country where one might still find food. Widows needed both the emotional and financial support of parents and relatives. Yet, in Rohrbeck's sample, moving from town to town was rare. Of the 1914 widows, 12 percent moved; of the 1915 widows, 9 percent moved; and of the 1916 widows, 6.7 percent moved.[25]

Wherever they lived, the widows were faced with a storm of troubles. Upset, confused, and often terrified of the future, they were prime targets of every sort of thief and criminal. Agents swarmed around them, offering to arrange pensions, sell monuments, and even set up new marriages, all for a fee, of course.[26]

Even the wives of living soldiers faced a grim economic situation, and were generally unable to put aside any money from their husbands' miniscule army pay. In acute cases of need, the government might supplement the wife's income, but such support was equally miniscule. The following is an estimated weekly food bill for a four-person working-class family; for purposes of comparison, the April 1914 bill is assigned the index value of 100:[27]

October 1913	7.96 marks	—
April 1914	7.93	100
October 1914	8.85	111
April 1915	11.05	139
April 1916	14.43	182
April 1917	14.90	188
February 1918	16.67	210
October 1918	17.60	223

A private earned about 15 marks a month, which usually went for his personal needs. In 1916 a wife might be eligible for a monthly government payment of 15 marks, plus an additional 7.50 marks a month for each child.

Of course, the food bill dropped when the husband went off to war, but even if the bill were halved, government support could scarcely pay for the groceries. How were wives to buy clothes, pay the rent, and take care of other basic needs?

Local social service agencies provided some help, as did churches and private charities, but the wives' situation remained desperate. When a husband was killed, the government support stopped, and the pension did not begin until months later. And the pension, when it finally came, often provided less support than the wife had received when her husband was alive.

Thousands of artisans, clerks, skilled workers, and white collar workers had rushed to join the army, and had accepted the sharp drop in income as a patriotic sacrifice. When the husband was killed, the wife's pension was not based on his prewar income, but was tied to his rank. A skilled worker in 1913 would bring home between 120 and 150 marks per month.[28] In 1916, the widow's pension was:

private's widow	33.30 marks/month
corporal's widow	41.66 marks/month
sergeant's widow	50.00 marks/month

For each child there was an additional 9 marks per month.[29] Even with help from charities and churches, widows faced catastrophe.

To pay the bills, widows took odd jobs. Thousands tried to set up little shops in their homes, although even before the war, a shopkeeper's economic prospects were limited. Others took up piecework, such as laundry or sewing, or they cleaned other people's homes. What they earned from such jobs did little to ease their financial burden.[30]

The death of her husband forced a woman to be autonomous, often for the first time in her life. At the same time, living with parents, or working in a subordinate job, only reemphasized dependency. "It has become the war-widows' fate," a widow wrote, "almost without exception, to have to make due with subordinate, dependent positions, because of their lack of job-training. To women who have learned to take their lives in their own hands, this makes their lives doubly hard."[31]

Children generally became the focal point of the widow's life. Having to take a job outside her home, a woman wrote, ". . . was especially hard for me, because after my husband's death, my child was all that made my life worth living."[32] Yet, a certain wistfulness, even resentment, enters the women's testimonies when they talk about their fatherless children. Without children, they could find a good job, or continue their education. Now widowed, a woman wrote, "I had to make a new beginning, I had to begin a new life in which suddenly I was alone, burdened with the great responsibility for a child's fate."[33]

By 1917, two elements had evolved from the experience of widows that were important in the development of the war victims' movement. One was a rage that drove women into public protest. The other was an urge for solidarity that widows felt with their "sisters." The war taught widows that they had interests that separated them from men, but which at the same time brought women and men together with each other.

II

Most war orphans were infants when their fathers were killed, and the impact of the war on them can only be inferred. Central institutions in the child's life were shattered by the war. The family was disrupted not only by the prolonged absence of the father and older brothers, but also by the chronic worry and illness of the mother. Not infrequently, the mother too was forced to leave the children temporarily while she sought employment. Schools were also disrupted when male teachers went into the army. Together with this social dislocation was the ever worsening health problem.

One surprise was that the infant mortality rate did not increase during the war. Possibly, since the overall birth rate dropped, more resources were devoted to the smaller number of infants. Or perhaps the very extremity of living conditions encouraged adults to be especially careful of babies. The war did, however kill slightly older children in significant numbers.[34]

Children's death rate (1913 = 100)

		1914	1915	1916	1917	1918
Boys,	5–10	106.4	142.9	129.3	150.3	189.2
	10–15	107	121.7	128.5	154.2	215
Girls,	5–10	101.4	142.2	133	143.8	207.3
	10–15	104.1	128.3	131	152.9	239.2

Not only did girls generally have a higher death rate than boys of comparable ages, but the increase in the death rate was higher for girls than for boys. Why? Without further evidence, one can only guess. It may be that boys and girls endured the same hardships, but that girls proved more vulnerable. Or, it may be that boys and girls did not endure the same hardships, that in the distribution of scarce resources, little girls received less.[35]

Children's physical deterioration during the war was obvious. They were underweight by as much as 8 to 12 percent. They did not grow normally; average height by age declined by 3 to 4 percent. Rickets, a disease associated with malnutrition, was common, and polio increased among teenagers. Ordinary childhood diseases did not increase significantly, but stomach disorders, such as vomiting and cramps, were common, and there was an increase in tuberculosis. Nervous disorders were frequent; for example, an "enormous increase" in bed-wetting was reported among school children.[36]

The war pervaded the lives of children. They were mobilized into varied patriotic activities and were frequently handed patriotic literature. When asked to write poems or essays about the war, children parroted current patriotic language. Rituals connected with *Nagelsäulen* were particularly popular. Children, as well as adults, were urged by patriotic groups to contribute to scores of war charities, but simple contributions should be accompanied by some outward gesture, pamphlets suggested.[37] Thus, a town, or private group, would set up a plaque or pillar, a *Nagelsäule,* and contributors would be given a nail in exchange for their contribution. The nail was pounded in, and all the nails formed a design. The most famous *Nagelsäule* was a giant wooden statue of Field Marshal von Hindenburg in Berlin, but every town had its own designs. (A handsome *Nagelsäule* still stands next to the cathedral in Mainz.)

Each school or class had its own *Nagelsäule* project. The children, in turn, stood in front of the class, submitted their contribution, made a little patriotic speech and, sometimes with the teacher's help, drove in a nail. The completed object, a map of Germany perhaps or a slogan, was then placed in the school, and photographs were taken, with the teacher and pupils proudly standing by their class creation.

In the immediate post-war months, children were involved in the intensely emotional prisoner- of-war issue. The allies had demanded that the Germans release all their prisoners after the armistice, but the allies refused to release the prisoners they held until Germany agreed to a peace treaty. There were rumors in Germany that the prisoners would be held forever or they would be used as slave labor. Dozens of associations sprang up to raise money to buy clothes and food for the prisoners, and one source of money was the pennies of children. Teachers collected the children's contributions and announced in class which child had contributed and which had not.[38]

In 1915, the Society for School Reform in Breslau collected children's drawings, poems, and essays about the war. According to the Society, the work was done freely, and teachers did not dictate what the children were to do. Although the material is from only a few schools in Breslau and was done in 1915, when conditions at home were still relatively good, it at least gives a glimpse into children's lives during the war.

Before the age of 10 or 11, boys and girls showed little difference in their perceptions. Their drawings were of genderless stick-figures, their poems and essays tended not to distinguish between war and non-war. Poems to "O Hindenburg, O Hindenburg," quickly drifted into the more familiar rhythmic pattern of "O Tannenbaum, O Tannenbaum." To one 11-year old girl, the most important part of a victory celebration was that it involved a school holiday.[39]

After the age of 10 or 11, however, a marked break appeared in the perceptions of the girls and boys. Boys demonstrated a passion for, and an amazing mastery of, military minutiae. Their drawings emphasized violent action, with abundant gore. Their identification with their soldier-fathers and brothers was intense. Of course, boys played at being soldiers, but they also collected maps, military photos, and pictures of war heroes, such as Baron von Richtofen. Albert Speer recalls that as a child, he sometimes slept on the floor so that he could share the suffering of the soldiers at the front.[40]

A curious boy-father relationship developed. No longer was the father at the front simply "father"; he became a mythic, superhuman figure, and a boy was expected to model his behavior on this distant, idealized, and frightening father.

In Ernst Glaser's 1928 novel, *Jahrgang 1902*, the young narrator does not want to attend a school his father has chosen. From the front, the father writes home: "If our youth do not understand that we only wish the best for them, if they contemptuously reject our concern for them, and start living according to their own ideas—then they simply are not worthy of their fathers, who daily out here risk their lives for their children." The effect of this letter on the young narrator and his mother was devastating.

> We were shocked. That was the Voice of the Front. That was the voice of those men, who once had been our fathers, but who for years had been distant from us. They stood before us, strange, frightening, omnipotent, with black shadows, overwhelming like a monument. What did they know of us? They knew where we lived, but what we looked like, what we thought, that they no longer knew.

Yet, in the end, the boy and his mother obey. As the boy explains: "They were better than we were. After all, they were risking their lives. We submitted. . . ."[41]

Girls seemed to experience the war in a totally different way. Their poems, drawings, and essays in the Breslau collection are melancholy and introspective. They concentrate on death and suffering. The war's "ruth-less attack on the love-relationship of the family filled their souls . . . Again and again, appears the same theme: death of the soldier and the grief of his loved ones, but in always new, extraordinarily diverse man-ifestations . . . many poems concern the soldier's grave—a theme which frequently appears in the girls' sketches."[42] While sons tried to be heroic like their fathers and brothers, daughters mirrored the worry, grief, and passivity of their mothers.

Yet this is not the entire picture of girls during the war. The crime rate for all women soared during the war; the figure for women's convictions per hundred men's convictions are as follows:[43]

1910	19
1913	19
1915	36
1917	54

The greatest increase in crime occurred among young women, who were often involved in crimes against property, such as theft. Following is a comparison by age groups of women convicted between 1911/13 and 1917.[44]

Age of women	Change between 1911/13 and 1917
under 15	+ 90.9 percent
15–18	+ 54.9 percent
19–21	+ 63.3
22–25	+ 54.7
26–30	+ 13.4
31–40	− 8
41–50	− 8.5
51–60	− 6.1

These statistics confirmed the fears of adults about the impact of the war on young people. Clearly, the war was not teaching them traditional values. Newspapers and academic journals frequently presented reports about young women and men growing up without supervision and engag-ing in immoral acts.

Many solutions were proposed for this "youth problem." Para-military training was encouraged for boys, not only to prepare them for the trenches, but to teach them discipline and respect for authority. Such training had only limited success as the following order from the Deputy Commanding General, XI Corps, makes clear:

The right spirit cannot be present in a group of young men who go out to drill singing, but then come back with cigars in their mouths, looking for bars, and girls with whom to waste time. The proper spirit is also missing, when young people show discipline while drilling, but otherwise behave in an uncontrolled and improper way.[45]

Towns imposed curfews and prohibited the sale of tobacco and alcohol to minors. Some observers were convinced that movie theaters had a sinister influence on youth and demanded strict censorship of films. Despite all these measures, disorderliness increased. In December 1915, for example, a county official wrote to his superior: "It seems that mothers, whose husbands are in the army, cannot raise children . . . properly. Despite repeated police warnings, which have been printed in all the newspapers, the incidence of youthful crime has increased not insignificantly."[46] A social worker wrote in 1920, that as a result of the war, children were "insolent, headstrong, intolerant, . . . and deceitful."[47] The children seemed transformed, in the eyes of their parents; the war had turned them into violent strangers.

„20 Jahre nach meinem Tod
will ich aufstehen aus meinem
Sarge, um zu sehen, ob Deutschland in Ehren vor der Welt
bestanden hat oder nicht!"
Bismarck

Wenn einst Bismarck's Geist
durch sein bedrängtes Land
geht — findet der eisern
Kanzler ein eisernes Volk

Daß er es finde, sorge dafür
Hilf auch Du,
daß Dein Volk bestehe

Zeichne die Kriegsanleihe!

This advertisement for the war bond campaign appeared in the *Berliner Illustrirte Zeitung:* " 'Twenty years after my death I will arise from my coffin to see whether Germany stands in honor before the world or not!' —Bismarck. If the spirit of Bismarck should visit his besieged nation—would the Iron Chancellor find an iron people? It's up to you! Help your people: Buy War Bonds!" (Photo: Ullstein, Berlin)

CHAPTER 6

Political Prophylaxis:
The German Welfare Tradition

It would be good simply to hold fast to the principles already laid down by Bismarck.

—Dr. Hugo Schäffer

This comment, made by Hugo Schäffer when he succeeded Paul Kaufmann as president of the National Insurance Office in 1924, reflects nostalgia in hard times. In that year Germany was recovering from unprecedented political and economic turmoil. Inflation had raged. Civil war had repeatedly burst into flame. Political terrorism had been epidemic. Understandably, then, the old days of the empire seemed "good" indeed. The memory of Bismarck and the values he represented seemed to be an anchor in troubled waters.

Bismarck and the empire were more than memories during the war and the republic; they were a living presence to everyone but children. Kaufmann, the retiring president, had begun his civil service career when Bismarck was chancellor. Schäffer had begun his only a few years after Bismarck's retirement. Virtually all of the civil servants in the republic's government had been trained during the empire, and their values were imperial. This chapter will investigate some of these values and explain how they shaped the prewar welfare state—a necessary examination, since the war victims' program developed in the cocoon of the prewar welfare system.

Human thought, Max Black has observed, moves from metaphor to algebra. At the basis of every value system is a root metaphor, a conceptual archetype, which asserts some fundamental proposition about human beings, nature and society. Thought technicians, to use Victor Turner's phrase, translate this metaphor into a logical order, into algebra, but this later algebra rests on the prior metaphor. What was the root metaphor of German social welfare?[1]

I

In April 1872, Bismarck wrote a letter to Kaiser Wilhelm I in which he diagnosed Germany's domestic ailments.

> The so-called International is only one of the manifestations, if currently the most striking manifestation, of the disease afflicting the entire civilized world. This disease has as its cause the fact that the property-less classes, their self-confidence and demands for the pleasures of life increasing, struggle to satisfy these demands at the expense of the propertied classes. To cure this disease, repressive measures are not enough. A cure can only be achieved through the gradual effect of progressive education and experience, and the most diverse legal and economic measures. Such measures would be designed to eliminate the hindrance to productive work by the property-less classes. At the same time, so long as this curative process is not complete, it is the duty of government to protect society from violent attacks on property. Mere police measures are not sufficient. It is not just a question of keeping out foreign agitators, since the disease exists here at home and is not the result of contagion from abroad. The important point is not just to observe and uncover preparations for violent attacks, but also to have the means with which to punish. For this purpose we require appropriate laws . . .[2]

What is striking about this passage is the imagery. To defend property, the government must cure a "disease." According to Bismarck, society is like a living organism. Each part is dependent on other parts, and if the social organism is sick, medicine, however bitter, must be taken to return the organism to its natural functioning. This concept of society is hardly unique to Bismarck. However, its implications for the German welfare system are important.

The biological metaphor depoliticizes the question of social welfare. Politics involves the clash of interests in which no single interest has a monopoly of wisdom or power. Debate, compromise, and argument are the stuff of politics. But there could be no negotiation between doctor and patient. Bismarck and his heirs no more expected or tolerated objections from their citizens than did doctors from their patients.[3]

Therefore, demands for reorganization of property rights are not matters of political debate. They are symptoms of a sickness. People who make such demands are ill, and are infectious agents. Society is a single organism, not an arena of competing factions, and the body politic must be immunized from such infection. Diseased portions of the organism must be cured for their own, as well as for the organism's, good.

The cure in this case obviously would not be to re-distribute wealth, but to stabilize the existing distribution of wealth. The cure would protect the property-owners and put the property-less back to productive work. Once they went back to work, their jealousy of wealthier classes would end, for they would learn that wealth was not the result of exploitation but a reward for virtue. Once they learned to help themselves, they would be immune to the various socialist diseases. These concepts of self-help and the return to productive labor were central to the welfare measures adopted by Bismarck.

But many people concerned with preserving the status quo were not convinced that Bismarck's prescription would protect wealth. Who would pay for Bismarck's cure? Industrialists warned that any increase in wages, pensions, or health insurance would have to be passed on to consumers in the form of higher prices, and such price increases would dampen demand at home and price German products out of the international market.

Defenders of Bismarck's program insisted that improved worker morale, increased loyalty to the state, and a decrease in the socialist appeal would be well worth whatever cost employers had to pay, and, defenders argued, much of the expense would be borne by the workers themselves and taxpayers in general.[4] Furthermore, they said, the program was economically rational and would enhance productivity and profitability. An American commentator stressed the efficiency of social insurance: "Germany hates waste in any form. She has taught the world the value of the by-product. This is one of her contributions to industry. Other countries have adopted her methods of industrial salvage, but none of them . . . has followed her example in the working out of a programme for saving the waste of human lives which the mill and the factory produce."[5]

Another defender argued in 1913, that social insurance would lead to healthy workers who would work harder, and affluent workers who would increase the domestic market for German products. In addition, he continued, an expanded social welfare system would yield important social-hygienic results, particularly a reduction in tuberculosis, alcoholism, and venereal disease. Thousands of social burdens, therefore, would become productive members of society.[6]

The argument for the economic rationality of Bismarck's social policy, however, is not convincing. The social insurance program diverted funds to the economically nonproductive, such as the injured and the elderly. Other legislation was designed to support such groups as shopkeepers and the great East Elbian landlords precisely because they were not economically viable. Furthermore, the social policy was based on political rather than economic decisions; it was based on the judgment that expenditures were the price to be paid for social stability. Social welfare was thus an alternative to social reform.[7]

The algebra of the Bismarckian social insurance system was based on the laws of 1883, 1884, and 1889. In 1911, the regulations were encoded in a single mammoth piece of legislation, the National Insurance Law.[8] Workers were guaranteed a portion of their pay if they became ill and a pension if they were permanently disabled or too old to work. Costs were divided among the insured, the employer, and the state.

This division produced constant bickering. Employers alone were responsible for contributions to the accident insurance fund. Employers and employees contributed equally to the larger disability and retirement fund with the state making a small contribution. Employees paid for two-thirds of the sickness insurance fund, and employers paid the remaining one-third. Employers frequently complained that the insurance costs were devouring profits. Employees retorted that employers passed costs along to consumers, or deducted costs from wages, so that profits actually were untouched.[9]

Administration of the system was complex. A hierarchy of committees supervised the insurance funds. The committees included worker and employer representatives, chaired usually by a civil servant. The small National Insurance Office in Berlin, directly subordinate to the Chancellor, did not administer the system, but rather supervised what was in effect a self-administering system. An elaborate hierarchy of Insurance Courts resolved disputes. The courts were composed of tribunals, chaired by professional jurists, who were assisted by lay judges representing workers and employers. Major issues were resolved by the National Insurance Court in Berlin, whose president also headed the National Insurance Office. A network of hospitals and other facilities, funded by the insurance system, provided medical care.

The insurance system was governed by a body of law so complex that only highly trained civil servants could understand it. Rules were established for every conceivable illness and for every possible type of insured person. The chairman of the Association of German Guild Cooperatives, spoke of the National Insurance Law, with its 1,805 paragraphs, as "a labyrinth for me, but, as I have observed, the lawyers around me consider it sheer bliss to wander about in this maze."[10]

The benefits of the insurance system reflected the fundamental needs Bismarck had outlined—the need to preserve the existing social order, to protect the interests of the propertied, and to return workers as quickly as possible to productive labor.

This is the way the sickness insurance worked: After three days of illness, an insuree became eligible for medical care and for payments that equaled 50 percent of the prevailing day-laborer's wage. The benefits were obviously designed to keep insurees from starvation, while discouraging them from staying on the pension rolls. Clearly, there was little incentive to try and live on sick benefits.

After 13 weeks, a person still unable to work but not permanently disabled became entitled to accident insurance. Again, benefits were tied neither to specific injury nor to a minimum income but to a person's income level. The Accident Insurance Law prescribed that, for the duration of the disability, an insuree was entitled to two-thirds of his or her normal income. Once declared permanently disabled, or at age 70, a person came under the Disability and Retirement Law, and the benefits received were linked to the person's income. Thus, for both long-term disability and retirement, laborers, for example, were guaranteed something that approximated a laborer's income, and artisans were guaranteed something close to an artisan's income. The aim of these long-term benefits was obvious; as far as possible, people had to be kept within their class.

Disability, then, was not an absolute but a relative term, and defining disability sorely taxed lawyers' imaginations. A section of the Disability and Retirement Law, for example, described disability this way:

> Benefits are awarded to those insurees . . . who are disabled for a long period . . . Disability is to be recognized when the insuree, as a result of his physical or mental condition, is no longer able, through his own power and ability, to earn at least 1/6 of the income which he had earned, on the average, over the previous five years . . .

A section of the Accident Insurance Law defined disability as follows:

> The insuree is entitled to benefits amounting to: 1) 2/3 of the previous yearly income, in cases of complete disability (full pension); 2) that percent of the full pension which corresponds to the percent of reduction in earning-capacity (partial pension).

The key, then, in determining long-term benefits was calculating the impact of an injury on a person's ability to stay in his or her social position. Loss of a right hand might mean little reduction in earning capacity to a migratory laborer, who therefore could receive a small pension. However, the same injury might severely impair an artisan's livelihood, and consequently, the artisan could receive a substantial pension.

Suspicion that this cure was worse than the disease persisted, however, and debate about social insurance flared up repeatedly in the years before the war.[11] Critics argued that the insurance system contributed to a weakening of worker morale, encouraging workers to claim injury where none existed; the system, in effect, provided an exit from the industrial world, and workers were rushing to use the exit; and once on a pension, workers became dependent and lost any sense of autonomy or personal responsibility. Moreover, critics said, the system was infested with the very people it wa designed to combat: socialists, union bureaucrats, and various political radicals; from their positions on the insurance committees, these people could expand their influence and affect political decisions. What's more, insurance raised worker expectations and encouraged rather than defused worker demands.

But these are not simply objections raised by the systems' opponents; they reflect some of the complex results of social insurance that reappeared in the war victims' program and in other types of social welfare, such as military disability.

II

Military disability laws were not part of the Bismarckian system, but legislation governing disability paralleled the social insurance laws. Indeed, what is striking is the extent to which the disability laws reflected not only military concerns, but also the ideas of civilian social welfare theorists.

The military disability laws, which date from 1906 and 1907,[12] were designed to cover professionals and draftees, as well as soldiers' dependents. Rank played a critical role. Precise income levels were established for various ranks, and the disability laws guaranteed that a soldier did not fall below his designated income level. The Officers' Pension Law, for example, prescribed the following minimum yearly incomes: captains, 2400 marks; first lieutenants, 1800 marks; and second lieutenants, 1200 marks. If an officer with a disability pension did not reach these minimums, he was entitled to an additional allowance.

Widows' pensions were also tied to military rank; for example:

Husband's rank	Yearly Pension
Field grade officer	1500 marks
Company grade officer	1200 marks
Senior non-commissioned officer	300 marks
Junior non-commissioned officer	200 marks
Common soldier	100 marks

Pensions were thus used to buttress the military hierarchy. If two soldiers had the same injury, the soldier with the higher rank received the higher pension. In 1916, for example, the yearly pension for a 100 percent disabled soldier was: for a private, 540 marks; for a corporal, 600 marks; for a sergeant, 720 marks; and for a sergeant-major, 900 marks.[13]

Pensions were controlled by the military agencies. Each war ministry (in Prussia, Württemberg, Bavaria, and Saxony) had a pension section; so did the Colonial and Naval offices. All the administrative processes were controlled by the military. Complaints, for example, were processed through military channels, and judgment was rendered by boards of officers. The procedures were administrative, not judicial. There was no argument but merely requests, followed by approvals or denials. Only in unusual cases were civilian courts involved in the process. Administering the system was no burden to the prewar military, since the number of persons receiving military disability pensions was miniscule.

Although the laws were designed for the military, they reflected current thinking on disability compensation. Earlier military disability laws had focused on the actual injury, and had used vague verbal formulations to describe the soldier's condition. The 1906/07 laws were, like workers' compensation laws, much more scientific, as if war were a colossal industrial accident. Disability was defined in terms of economic productivity. According to the Soldiers' Disability Law, to determine the level of disability, a soldier's pre-military occupation had to be considered. As in the civilian laws, soldiers with identical injuries might well receive different pensions, depending on their prewar incomes. The military disability laws thus supported both the military hierarchy and the civilian hierarchy.

Like the worker's pension, a soldier's pension could be fine-tuned to his particular needs, through the addition of a variety of special allowances to his basic pension.

The military disability laws received little attention before the war; by the middle of the war, however, politicians, welfare experts, and millions of ordinary citizens were passionately interested in the way military disability pensions worked, and almost everyone was unhappy with the system. The recurring demand, as the next chapters show, was that the military pension system be merged with the existing social insurance system— that injured soldiers be treated as if they were injured workers.

III

There were two peculiarities about the prewar German welfare state. The first was the extent to which "sozialpolitik" was a matter of vehement public argument between 1871 and 1914. The problem of integrating an increasingly assertive and self-conscious working class into the authoritarian state plagued politicans and academics of all ideological persuasions. Reform—whether as an antidote to revolution, as the first step toward social revolution, as a dangerous subversion of the social and political order, or however else it was seen, was the topic of debate among Germany's social theorists. In the years before the war, people like Max Weber, Rosa Luxemburg, and Werner Sombart, groups like the *Verein für Sozialreform,* and, of course, politicians like Bismarck devoted themselves to the task of defining and analyzing the ends and means of social policy.[14]

The second peculiarity was that the state played a very small role in the welfare state. Donald McMurtrie, describing Germany's war victims' care program in 1918, noted that social services in most cases were not administered by civil servants, but by a bewildering collection of volunteer groups.[15] At the local level especially, volunteer groups were the backbone of social welfare.

Labor unions, church groups, fraternal organizations—all had their own welfare funds and projects. The most important social service agencies were the reform societies created after 1871 by women. As respectable organizations, these middle class groups had access to money and power while smaller or more radical groups did not. To a great extent, they monopolized the delivery of social services, and they thought in Bismarckian terms; they would heal the entire society by caring for its diseased parts.

The sudden flourishing of these groups (described in Chapter 4) was a response to obvious social problems. Cities were unsanitary, and crime, venereal disease, and prostitution were rampant. But the reform organizations did more than respond to immediate problems. They helped satisfy the increasing demands of women for some measure of political and social independence. Middle-class women devoted themselves enthusiastically to social reform, in part because morality and charity were socially defined as women's concerns. Women could expand their activities in these areas without directly confronting male-dominated institutions. At the same time, women could claim that if political rights were tied to state service, they certainly were serving the state and thus were entitled to greater political rights.[16]

In fact, from the state's perspective, the women's groups were beneficial. They provided a nondisruptive outlet for women's energies and a means of combating serious social ills, all at minimum cost to the state. The groups were also important agencies of social control. They helped discipline society and bring wayward citizens into conformity with proper moral standards.

The *Berliner Frauenbund,* organized in 1893, was a typical example of the reform organizations. Its 1915 yearly report, outlined the *Frauenbund's* hopes:

> . . . it is not enough to save the endangered and fallen girls; rather it is the task of the German woman to purify our people again, to clarify judgments about moral right and wrong, to combat the so-called double morality, and everywhere to combat frivolity and apathy in the condemnation of sin - great is its power, and earnest must our struggle against it be.[17]

The purpose of the multitude of reform groups was to identify society's ills and apply the medicine that would return society to purity and health. This social therapy, however, was riddled with contradictions.

IV

Social policy is a complex interaction between revolution and integration. In the Bismarckian welfare system, workers were integrated into the political order through a web of committees and benefits. While votes for the Socialists increased, the radicalism of many socialist leaders declined. July 1914 seemed to prove that Bismarck's cure had taken; in the crisis, millions of German workers rushed off to defend the state, and labor unions vowed to cooperate with employers in the war effort.

But Bismarck's welfare system had raised worker expectations. What workers' parents had accepted as natural was considered intolerable during the war. The assorted committees gave workers sources of patronage, administrative experience, and positions from which to exert influence. If 1914 demonstrated the extent to which the working class had been integrated into the society, 1918 showed just how fragile that integration was.

The burst of social reform had mobilized thousands of women and had vastly expanded the "woman's sphere." An example of the potentially radical aspects of this movement is clear from the 1915 yearly report of the *Berliner Frauenbund*. The organization's aim was not simply the care of "fallen" women; it was nothing less than the moral regeneration of the entire society. The attack on the double morality, that is, the different standards of sexual behavior for men and women, directly questioned sexual roles and male dominance. This conservative, women's group had profoundly radical ambitions for the entire nation.[18]

Such peculiar outcomes of Bismarck's plans should not be surprising, given the contradiction and evasion characteristic of Wilhelminian society. A "social imperialist" analysis of Bismarckian welfare policies stresses the manipulative integration of workers into the authoritarian, militarist, imperialist state. Social welfare and imperial expansion were both, from this point of view, tools of social stabilization. Such an analysis has much to commend it, but it tends to ignore the limitations and blunders of the Bismarckians. Consider again Bismarck's 1872 memo to the Emperor. Bismarck refers to a "self-satisfied," selfish set of people eager to enjoy themselves at other people's expense. Anyone familiar with the Germany of 1872 might well think that he means the *Gründerprunk* of the period—the ostentatious, hedonistic materialism of the assorted speculators and promotors who made a killing in the Reich's early economic boom. Bismarck mentions these people not at all, however, and attributes this materialism to workers, union organizers, and leftist militants. One suspects that not a little projection is at work here.

Social peace was Bismarck's goal. But social peace required that the people remain peaceful. As a means to that end, simple oppression was both costly and provocative. It would be far more effective if the lower classes in particular would police themselves; individual self-repression was far more effective than repression from outside.

But how does one convince people to repress themselves? Bismarck emphasizes education, law, and the economic system. Implicitly, he calls for "self-control," for "will-power," and thus reveals himself to be a typical Victorian, or rather Wilhelminian, looking to "character" as a source of stability in the very unstable world of high capitalism.

In that world, work could also be a source of order, according to Bismarck. But he apparently does not think that the workers did "productive" work. Factory workers and coal miners were not really workers; presumably, the indirect producers, the property owners whom Bismarck wants to protect, were the "productive" workers.

And yet, even this point is not really clear, for Bismarck evades a discussion of capitalism altogether. The Chancellor recognizes that there is a serious danger of instability in his society, yet he ignores a major source of instability. Could capitalism play any role in this growing social discord? Or could the egoism of the upper classes? Or the lack of opportunity for workers and women and Jews and most Catholics and many others in the new Reich? Could the absence of genuine democracy anger people who would benefit from expanded democracy? Bismarck addresses none of these questions in his prescription for the cure of the nation's ills. To be fair, of course, one must recognize that Bismarck could not discuss everything in his brief note, but to be accurate, one must recognize that in this note at least, Bismarck is not so much a master manipulator as a confused and evasive late-nineteenth-century bourgeois; here at least, he is not a Machiavellian but a Wilhelminian.

This is important for social as well as for biographical reasons. Bismarckian organized benevolence was designed to guarantee social peace. It partly succeeded, but because it consistently avoided or evaded many of the crucial problems of German society, it could at most scotch the sources of discontent, not kill them. This refusal to confront real problems was cause of trouble enough in peacetime; it was the reason for a systemic crisis in wartime, as the next chapter will show.

George Grosz, "You can be sure of the thanks of the Fatherland." (Estate of George Grosz, Princeton, N.J.)

CHAPTER 7

The Administrative Solution to the War Victims Problem, 1914–1918

"You can be sure of the thanks of the Fatherland!"
—Government slogan

In the winter of 1914/15, the trains that had carried singing heroes to battle the summer before, returned home bearing a cargo of broken men. The longer the war went on, the longer the trains became; for Leonard Frank, the hospital train was the central metaphor of the war because it brought the frightfulness of the war home.[1]

Soldiers were killed and wounded so quickly that it was difficult for the government to keep track of the casualties. Casualty lists were published almost every day, but it was forbidden to publish running totals of casualties, and the government was never sure what the precise statistics were. Figures published after the war, however, demonstrate the war victims' population explosion.

According to the official Army Medical Report,[2] the estimated numbers of cases treated during the war were:

	Wounded	Diseased	Total
1914/15	1,579,023	4,513,215	6,092,238
1915/16	1,398,281	5,706,370	7,104,651
1916/17	1,303,322	5,491,044	6,794,366
1917/18	1,406,311	5,787,674	7,193,985

Dr. Schjerning wrote that about 90 percent, or 24.3 million, of the cases treated resulted in the soldier's returning to duty,[3] leaving some 2.7 million with some kind of permanent disability.

In 1923, before any census of war victims was completed, the Labor Ministry estimated that dead soldiers were survived by about 533,000 widows and 1,192,000 orphans.[4] The German welfare state, unable to cope with this vast number of people, underwent profound changes between 1914 and 1918.

Throughout these changes, the deeply conservative bureaucracy, molded in Bismarck's image, insisted that it was not "political" but "above politics," not "partisan" but benevolently "patriotic." And these claims affected the approach officials took to the war victims issue.

The leading groups in any society define their own interests as everyone's interests. In Prussia-Germany, "society" consisted of agrarians and selected industrialists, and the cultural machinery, the churches, universities and official art, reproduced and distributed the elite's values. Contradictory values were by definition "anti-social," "unpatriotic," and "selfish."[5] The problem, of course, was that German "society" did not represent German society. There were multitudes of Germans whose interests did not correspond to those of East Elbian landlords or steel and coal barons. Since these other values were defined as "anti-social" and since there were no customs or institutions, or even language, that permitted and simultaneously moderated conflict, this other Germany had very few ways to express, let alone assert, itself.

Silencing critics did not, of course, resolve critical conditions, and the more Germany's leaders ignored or evaded dissent, the worse dissent-inducing conditions became. The more exacerbated conditions became, the greater the impulse to protest, and the more intense the resort to repression. Politics became a murky, mysterious, endlessly frustrating and incipiently violent business. Nearly everyone, the elite as well as the elite's critics, longed for concord.

In 1914, German civil servants saw themselves as the agents of concord, the scientific managers of the organized benevolence that would disarm the angry and hysterical politics. This was no easy task, however, especially when it came to the war victims, as this chapter will show.

I

At first, it seemed that voluntary activity would heal the wounds of war. Such activity was encouraged by the government, not only because it was cheaper than spending tax money, but because it was a way of generating feelings of solidarity, national unity, and patriotism. New associations blossomed in the first months of the war, including associations to care for the refugees from East Prussia (which the Russians had briefly raided), and groups dedicated to sailors' welfare and troops of specific regiments.[6] The older social reform and patriotic groups also mobilized their resources.

Enthusiasm was contagious. Thousands of young women volunteered as nurses. Public collections of items to be sent in "love packages" to soldiers at the front were major social occasions. In the small town of

Niederheimbach on the Rhine, for example, the following items were collected in October 1914:[7] "Shirts; underwear; jackets; socks; wrist-warmers; knee-warmers; wool blankets; table cloths; pillows; gloves; handkerchiefs; suspenders; pocket knives; wallets; tobacco; pipes; chocolate; envelopes; pencils; post-cards; soap; candles; playing cards; ear muffs; one bottle of strawberry soda . . ."

But voluntary activity proved to be no solution. As shortages grew at home, enthusiasm for patriotic rallies waned. By the last year of the war, people had all they could do to keep from starving. A local official reported to a provincial president in November 1917: "Public opinion has become a stomach question. . . . Interest is devoted almost exclusively to obtaining food, and political issues inspire little interest. Consequently, participation in the recent local elections, and in other public events has been extraordinarily small."[8]

Near the end of the war, conditions became so desperate that soldiers began sending supplies home from their own meager stores. Such reverse voluntary care provoked hard feelings, since officers usually had something to send to their families, but common soldiers did not. The chairman of Limburg County in Hessen reported in October 1918 that he was flooded with complaints about officer's families receiving packages from the front, while families of common soldiers received nothing.

The multiplicity of benevolent groups created great confusion. Some crippled soldiers and widows were overwhelmed by attention, while others were ignored. Who each group was responsible for was seldom clear and attempts to match needs with appropriate groups sometimes reached near comic levels. For example, Sebastion Beyer, who had been severely injured early in the war, required constant medical attention. But the only facility near his home that could have provided care was an institution for the elderly and indigent, and he objected to being placed there. Local welfare officials hit upon a solution. The man was single, but his brother, who had been killed in action, had been married. Why couldn't Sebastion marry his widowed sister-in-law? That way the soldier would get a full-time nurse, the woman would get a husband, and the government could cancel one widow's payment.

The army officer who reported this incident insisted that such situations were common and, he added, they deeply angered disabled soldiers.

Beyer and with him the ill, the tubercular, the lame, all raise the same question: Is this the Thanks of the Fatherland, that as a result of war injury, they are locked up with the local poor and people from the streets? The people and the soldiers find this sort of care absolutely unworthy.[9]

The unscrupulous took advantage of such confusion. Merchants offered goods made by "genuine" disabled veterans; others hired cripples, some of whom were not veterans, to troop door to door peddling merchandise. Beggars donned second-hand uniforms and camped out in train stations, exposing frightful injuries they claimed had been suffered in the defense of the Fatherland. Police throughout the country waged a losing battle to keep the beggars under control. Beggars were especially troublesome in the large cities, of course. Evelyn Blücher wrote in her diary in December 1918: "A new feature in Berlin is the number of beggars one now sees everywhere. All the blind, the halt, and the lame of Prussia seem to have collected here."[10]

Some schemes were complex. For example, Louis Donner, a Russian Jew who had emigrated to Germany, specialized in raising money for right wing, anti-Semitic causes. Once a contract was signed, Donner produced brochures, posters, and small armies of door-to-door fundraisers. From the funds raised, Donner received a generous portion. His business flourished in the immediate postwar period, and though he was repeatedly sued by government agencies, his profits remained substantial.[11]

Some who exploited the war were dishonest; others were simply opportunists. Shortly before the war, a speculator by the name of Hans Jacober purchased a castle near Nürnberg. He renovated the ancient structure and advertised it as an ideal health resort, but no one wanted to buy it. Thus he found himself with a renovated castle and mounting debts on his hands. Then came the war. Jacober rushed to the Bavarian War Ministry and offered to sell the castle as a patriotic sacrifice; it would be ideal for the unfortunate injured soldiers, he claimed. The Bavarian government was not interested. The indefatigable Jacober invaded every office in Munich with proposals, but the government turned them all down. Unloading his castle became an obsession with Jacober. He wrote to the Prussian War Ministry; he complained to the Kaiser; he accused the Bavarian officials of hard-heartedness. When Jacober was called up for military service, he was sure that this was in reprisal for all his "generous" gestures. Finally, in 1919, when new officials appeared in revolutionary Munich, the inexhaustible Jacober, claiming that he had always been a revolutionary at heart, offered to sell the regime his castle. The revolutionaries declined the offer. At this point the file ends, with Jacober still in possession of his castle.[12]

The problem of corruption, however, was overshadowed by the war victims crisis. As early as the spring of 1915, the dimensions of the crisis were clear. Many men had been killed and their widows were faced with ruin. Something had to be done.

II

In March 1915, representatives from the Bund der Landwirte and the Hansa Bund presented a report to the deputy War Minister, General von

Wandel. Members of the "free professions," such as craftsmen, teachers, and lawyers, were especially penalized by the military disability laws, the report stated. When these men were killed at the front, their survivors received a pension based not on the men's respectable civilian income, but on their ridiculously small military income. The report concluded: "In cases where the deceased had an income greater than that of the ordinary laborer, his survivors suffer a severe economic loss."[13]

In the May 1915 budget debate, Representative Meyer reported on conclusions of a parliamentary panel that had investigated the military pension system. Linking pensions to military rank was, in the committee's opinion, the source of serious trouble. Therefore, Meyer said,

> it is certainly a good thing, that some 58 economic associations under the leadership of the *Bund der Landwirte,* and the *Hansa Bund* have pointed out this serious problem. They have also made the suggestion that in the future, military rank should not be the basis for calculating the pension, but rather the individual's civilian income. The committee and the government unanimously agree that this suggestion is fully justified.[14]

Speaking for the conservatives, Count von Westarp echoed Meyer: "There exists the real danger," he said, "that the wife and children will be driven out of their social position and that they will sink into the proletariat. Thus, it is our opinion, that in calculating the pension, not only the military rank, but the civilian income, should be considered."[15]

Although Social Democrats disagreed with Westarp on nearly everything, they agreed with him on this point. Virtually every issue of their *Vorwärts* denounced the grievous plight of widows; they had to be helped, the Social Democrats insisted. And disabled soldiers had to be provided with an income related to their prewar income.[16]

What were the results of all this pressure for something to be done? For one, the welfare system was rapidly bureaucratized, as nation-wide organizations eclipsed or absorbed local volunteer groups. Second, the problem was ideologically rationalized; by 1918, there was, among government officials at least, a set of principles governing pensions. Finally, the problem was slowly nationalized, as, much to its distaste, the government learned that it would have to do something about the millions of war victims.

In 1915 and 1916, volunteer organizations and political figures began to define the war victims problem as a national problem. There were practical reasons for this. Often soldiers were treated in hospitals away from their homes, and local officials thus became responsible for nonlocal people, and pensions received by disabled soldiers, widows and orphans came from the national treasury, making the financial problem a national one.

In addition, there was a widespread conviction that care should be standardized; soldiers and survivors in poor parts of the nation should not receive care inferior to that received by people in more fortunate areas. Furthermore, it was believed that inefficiency and duplication of effort could be avoided through national coordination. In March 1915, Representative Giesberts, a Social Democrat, argued in the Reichstag, that the creation of a central authority should not be a partisan issue. A year later, Joachim von Winterfeldt, a conservative civil servant, who became a key figure in war victims' care, wrote: "A central office must be created, which can develop unified standards of care."[17]

People involved in private charity felt the same urgency, and slowly national bureaucratic organizations emerged. In April 1915, for example, the German League for Private Charity sponsored a convention in Berlin on the care of widows and orphans. The delegates agreed to form a single national committee to coordinate care for survivors, the Working Committee for Survivors' Care. At the committee's first session two months later, 19 groups were represented, including the German Red Cross, the Free, Christian-National, and liberal unions, the Society for Social Reform, and the League of German Women's Associations; the national and Prussian state governments also sent delegates. The delegates agreed on three principles to guide the care of survivors: widows and orphans were to be kept in their prewar social position; the memory of the heroes would be kept alive in the coming generation; and honoring the survivors would be a way of honoring the defenders of the nation.[18]

The Working Committee published material designed to standardize care, and in 1918, it merged with a government-sponsored foundation that raised money for needy survivors.

Existing groups that already possessed a national structure also became concerned with the war victims problem; among these were labor unions, which were primarily worried about insurance funds. The enormous number of injured soldiers and needy widows would quickly exhaust existing funds, union officials warned.[19]

The unions were in competition with the state for influence over workers and their dependents. The Saxon Minister of the Interior, for example, wrote to subordinates in September 1915 that government offices, not unions, should take care of survivors. "The Interior Ministry places the greatest stress on not forcing soldiers' dependents to turn to labor organizations for help. Rather, every effort must be made to win back popular respect for local governmental authorities, respect which they certainly deserve."[20]

In the unions' view, the participation of labor and management was essential in solving the war victims' dilemma. Writing for the Free Unions, Gustav Bauer stated, "This task can only be satisfactorily solved if labor and management work in the closest possible way with the public authorities." The unions were convinced that management was trying to use the vast pool of disabled soldiers as tools to depress wages, Bauer wrote. Disabled soldiers were so badly off that they would work for almost nothing, and thus they would reduce overall wage rates. "Disabled veterans must not be used to depress the wages of healthy workers."[21]

While volunteer groups and labor unions defined the problem as a national one, the state and national governments were reluctant to do so. From the beginning of the war, national and local governments attempted to solve the war victims' problem through volunteer action. Early in the war, delegates from labor and management had formed committees to resolve economic disputes and encourage war production, and this type of organization became the model for war victims' care. Typically, the committees involved representatives from labor, management, church groups, schools, charitable associations, and government. Curiously, disabled soldiers and widows were usually not represented on these committees.

Although the stress was on volunteer action, the level of state involvement increased during the war. Cities and regions developed their own programs.[22] In Bavaria, for example, the State Commission for War Victims' Care held its first session in April 1915. As well as representatives of charitable groups, veterans' association, labor, and management, the commission included civil servants; its chairman was the Bavarian Minister of the Interior. Similar bodies were created throughout Bavaria. Though these committees had no judicial, legislative or executive authority, they tried to coordinate the rehabilitation of disabled soldiers and the care of needy survivors.[23]

In Prussia, on the other hand, the state government rejected any major involvement. A Commissioner for War Victims' Care was named for Prussia, but his job was to ferret out fraudulent charities. War victims' care was left to provincial authorities. Each of Prussia's provinces established an office for war victims, which usually was affiliated with other social welfare offices and advisory panels like those in Bavaria.[24]

In the rest of the country, state action varied from the Bavarian model to volunteer action. In Saxony, for example, the government established a public corporation to raise money for war victims. Württemberg, like Bavaria, had a state advisory committee, with a series of subordinate local committees. Smaller states formed joint organizations and the city states had their own special war victims' care associations.[25]

At the national level, the government avoided facing the war victims problem with all the vigor it could muster. The army, not surprisingly, had little interest in becoming involved in social welfare; it had all it could do to win the war. Moreover, Berlin was mindful of regional sensibilities. Germany was a federal state, and each state fiercely guarded its autonomy. The main reason the national government avoided the issue was that it knew how enormous the problem was and how limited its resources were.

As pressure to improve care for war victims increased, however, the issue became a frequent topic of debate. A conference on disabled soldiers and survivors was held in the Reich Office of the Interior in February 1915. Two members of the Prussian Interior Ministry argued: "It cannot be denied that a pension measured only according to military rank produces a very small compensation. The solution, however, is not to be found in raising pensions, as, for example, the Hansabund suggests. It would be much nobler to return the war invalid to society as a productive member of economic life." Another participant noted that his superior had "no doubt" that the Reichstag would present him with "a great number of proposals concerning war victims' care. He will have to respond to all such proposals that, in view of the financial burden of the nation, which grows every day, any increase in costs above those already required by law is simply out of the question."[26]

As pressure for action grew, however, the national government undertook a number of stop-gap measures. Support payments to soldiers' wives were increased. Foundations were established to collect donations for needy war victims. The Reich distributed to the states some 10 million marks to help war victims. The Reichstag passed a pension-capitalization law in July 1916, which permitted war victims to receive part of their pension as a single cash payment. (Such a payment was authorized, for example, when a pensioner intended to purchase a home or open a business.) However, none of these measures came near to solving the problem.[27]

The most important event in terms of war victims' policy during the early part of the war was not any action taken by the national government, but the creation of the institution that became the center for such policy, the National Committee for War Victims' Care, the *Reichsausschuss für Kriegsbeschädigten- und Kriegshinterbliebenen-Fürsorge*. The committee was a peculiar hybrid: a voluntary organization, organized and administered by professional civil servants. It had no authority to formulate policy, yet its decisions determined government policy toward war victims. Essentially, the National Committee provided a mechanism by which the national government could be minimally involved in war victims' care.

Joachim von Winterfeldt, the governor of Brandenburg, was instrumental in forming the committee. In the spring of 1915, he invited all Prussian provincial officials involved in war victims' care to a conference in Berlin, and at the meeting he expressed his determination to provide some coordination in war victims' care. Subsequently, Winterfeldt and Freiherr von Welck, the Saxon official charged with war victims' affairs, organized a national conference on the subject. The conference opened in Berlin in September 1915, with delegates from throughout the nation in attendance (Bavaria did not send representatives, but later endorsed the conference's decisions). The delegates unanimously agreed that, while the delivery of care had to remain a local task, a national coordinating body was essential. The result was the creation of the National Committee, with Winterfeldt and Welck as co-chairmen.

The committee's most important task was the publication of a journal called *War Victims' Care* (*Die Kriegsbeschädigten- und Kriegshinterbliebenen-Fürsorge*), which became the forum for expert debate on war victims' policy. The editor of the journal was a young civil servant named Anton Kirschensteiner, and for the next decade and more, Kirschensteiner helped shape the lives of the millions of war victims. He was a Bavarian who had gone through the rigorous legal training required of German civil servants. Following brief military service, he had found a career in the field of social service management. When the war broke out, Kirschensteiner was working in the Bavarian Interior Ministry; in 1916, he was appointed editor of the National Committee's journal.[28]

In the pages of *War Victims' Care*, Kirschensteiner and other experts sketched the administrative solution to the war victims problem. The following disclaimer appeared in the journal's first edition: "As a scientific journal, this publication is directed to professionals in the field of war victims' care, not to the war victims themselves."[29] The distinction was important. The question officials posed themselves was not "what do war victims want?" but "what should be done with war victims?" It was not that the National Committee disdained the concerns of the victims; it was simply that, in the Committee's view, victims could add little to the insights of medical experts and state officials.

The fundamental concern expressed in the journal was the need to put the disabled men back to work, and no one challenged the urgency of this need. The journal was filled with suggestions, which were often ingenious.[30]

The goals of the pension system were also developed in the pages of the journal. An important article in the first issue, written by Dr. Franz Schweyer of the Bavarian Interior Ministry, outlined the consensus that was repeatedly reaffirmed in the pages of *War Victims' Care*. A pension, Dr. Schweyer wrote,

is not compensation for military service. A pension is compensation for any economic disadvantage the disabled person suffers in his civilian position . . . The same pension clearly cannot be awarded for the same injuries, or simply to persons having the same rank; that would merely plunge everyone to the same low social position. This compensation can only be based on the principle that each person be assisted in staying in the social position he occupied before the war . . .

Care for war victims is a freely undertaken public duty. It is guided by principles of efficiency, and its aim is to protect the veteran or survivor from need, and as far as possible, to help secure their future . . .

A pension is certainly not any type of legal restitution for injury for which the nation is obliged; war victims' care is simply a question of war-time social welfare. This point cannot be stressed enough . . .

No one can demand that a pension free him from all responsibility to engage in work; indeed, the duty of veterans to work must constantly be stressed.[31]

These points were central to the evolution of war victims' care and therefore deserve re-emphasis: the aim of the pension system was to keep people in their prewar social position; there was no legal right to a pension; and a pension did not free a person from the responsibility of work. These principles were the basis of wartime and postwar pension policies.

Thus by 1916 both a local structure, and an ideology for the care of the victims of the war had emerged. It remained for the national government to act.

III

The national government, however, adamantly refused to make the problem its own. The reason was a fundamental contradiction between political need and economic reality.

From the summer of 1917 until the end of the war, a running battle raged between officials in the National Finance Office and officials in the War Ministry and the National Interior Office. Civil servants in the latter two offices were convinced that action was essential; they urged adoption of amended pension laws that would base pensions on prewar income and thereby substantially increase the pension rates. In response to such demands, Count von Roedern of the National Finance Office wrote to the Chancellor: "In my opinion, amendments to the pension laws must be made dependent on the financial condition of the nation after peace has been concluded. . . . I cannot accept responsibility for imposing a burden of billions on the nation."[32]

A joint commission was established in the summer of 1917 to consider the entire pension issue. Worried about home-front morale, army representatives urged that some gesture be made to satisfy the increasingly restless war victims; at least, they argued, draft amendments to the three pension laws should be presented to the Reichstag. But representatives from the Finance Office refused to even consider the issue until the war was won.[33]

The commission met periodically throughout the fall of 1917, without reaching any agreement. Finally, in December, War Minister von Stein wrote to the head of the National Finance Office and urged cooperation: "I consider the question of a rapidly increased program of care for veterans and survivors so politically important, that financial considerations cannot be the determining factor."[34] But von Roedern was not moved: "I cannot justify any action when the number of persons eligible for pensions is totally unknown. Financial obligations for the future cannot yet be fixed, particularly when there is no idea where the funds will come from to cover these obligations."[35]

By the spring of 1918, the National Interior Office was drawn into the debate. A Dr. Wallraf of the Interior Office wrote to the Chancellor:

> I agree with the Minister of War that the rapid presentation of draft amendments to the pension laws . . . is essential. If we do not introduce this legislation, we can assume that the Reichstag, which has repeatedly requested such reform, will write up legislation on its own . . . Such an action would not only be a blow to the prestige of the government, but the danger would also certainly exist that any amendments written by the Reichstag would include demands which the government is unprepared to accept.[36]

In the end, pension rates were slightly increased in the summer of 1918,[37] but neither the Reichstag nor the government attempted to develop a reformed pension system, not because of inefficiency or indifference, but because the contradiction between political necessity and economic reality paralyzed the political actors. The war had devastated German society, and millions of war victims were demanding action. The war, however, had shattered the German economy; by 1918, Germany was bankrupt. Faced with this fundamental contradiction, the national government did nothing.

A month before the war ended, the army did take one significant action. It established a network of veterans' offices. Each Deputy Commanding General created a veterans' office at corps level, and each corps office established subordinate offices as needed. At last, a framework for a national veterans' affairs system had been established. It was none too soon, for by the fall of 1918, war victims were in open rebellion.

Otto Dix, "War Cripples." (Photo: VEB Verlag der Kunst, Dresden)

CHAPTER 8

The War Victims Rebel,
1916–1919

> The thanks of the Fatherland comes to 67.80 marks a month!
> —War victims' slogan

In March 1916, Deputy War Minister von Wandel wrote to the director of the National Interior Office that home front morale—critical to the war effort—was sinking fast. People were demanding peace and de-nouncing inflation, shortages, and poor housing. A vigorous effort to gain public enthusiasm for the war effort was essential, General von Wandel wrote. "It should be made clear that the peace movement will only pro-long the war . . . and how unreasonable it is, to complain about little things, and forget the daily sufferings and self-sacrifice of the troops in the field . . . All the anger about the burden of the war must be diverted from conditions at home, and re-directed against England and its allies."[1]

But this effort was unsuccessful. In 1917, a study of home front morale conducted by the Bavarian War Ministry reported: ". . . when people talk about hate, they mean hate directed against those people who live better than they do, and have more to eat, they don't mean hate for the English or French; the disintegration of the people into little groups, and ultimate-ly into individuals, who try to get by at the expense of everyone else, is continuing." Especially disquieting, the report continued, is the pro-letarianization of people of small or fixed incomes: "The state is blamed for all this, and no statesman should doubt that this economic fall of millions of people must automatically lead to political radicalization over the long run."[2] Bitterness, not patriotic self-sacrifice, was the fruit of the war, and the longer the war went on, the greater the bitterness became. Resentment could be read in the faces of hungry women staring at wealthy patrons enjoying themselves in comfortable restaurants. It could be heard in the shouts of farmers who refused to surrender their products to government officials. It could be heard too in the chants of workers who refused to work and marched through the streets demanding an end to shortages, inflation, and the war.

Germany was not the only nation besieged by crisis. In 1917 there were mutinies in the French army, and in the same year the tsarist rule in Russia collapsed. The war destroyed not only lives and property; it ruptured whole societies as well. This chapter focuses on one aspect of this social explosion—the rebellion of Germany's millions of war victims between 1916 and 1919.

I

The reaction of widows to the war cannot be separated from the overall reaction of German women. The war drastically affected women's lives. Hundreds of thousands of women entered the labor market, and millions of wives were faced with the desperate struggle of trying to manage their families alone. The result was that the war radicalized German women and drove them into public protest.[3]

Germany's defeat would come about through a womens' revolution Gertrude Atherton had predicted in her 1918 novel, *The White Morning*. An American, Atherton had lived in Germany for a number of years before the war and based her prediction on her personal experience.

German women, Atherton wrote, were on the verge of rebellion even before the war. The women in her novel bitterly attack German men, and they vow never to marry. The war, planned and conducted by men, proved their stupidity and brutality; humanity would have to be saved by women.

Gisela, the novel's heroine, organizes a secret network of women and tells her co-conspirators: "The German women altogether are restless and dissatisfied. They were promised a short and triumphant war. They are daily more skeptical of promises. They have suffered death in life . . . They have suffered too much at the hands of men."[4] On the appointed day, women all over Germany arise, seize barracks and government buildings, and proclaim an egalitarian republic. Gisela commandeers a fighter plane, and in the novel's apocalyptic ending, buzzes Munich, strafing the last male defenders of the old regime.

Atherton's novel may seem fantastic, but there were some underpinnings of truth to it. Conditions at home by the middle of the war were impossible. Women and men workers joined together in the mass strikes of 1917 and 1918, which directly contributed to Germany's political collapse. Equally the tasks of everyday life, such as finding food and clothing, contributed to political radicalization.

Finding the necessities of life meant standing in endless queues. Evelyn Blücher recorded in her diary:

> May 1916.
> The butchers' shops were closed for two to three weeks . . . vegetables were not to be had; butter almost unknown; whilst soap had become so scarce that regulations were enforced forbidding white dresses in some parts of Germany . . . Long processions of women waiting for hours before the butchers', grocers', and bakers' shops gave rise to the name of the "butter polonaise." These women often got up in the middle of the night, to be first on the scene. . . .[5]

When goods suddenly ran out, the women often exploded in anger. In November 1915, Blücher noted that butter suddenly disappeared from the shelves of some Berlin shops and women stormed down Unter den Linden shouting "Peace!"[6]

In July 1917, the Magistrat of Frankfurt/Main reported to the provincial minister-president a picture that was typical:

> Popular feeling, especially among workers, was not so peaceful as last month, above all, because of the complete lack of potatoes, the continuing shortage of vegetables and fruit, and the constant price increases. The mood was partly depressed, but also partly very excitable. This was especially clear, for instance, when during a distribution of grain to the poor, innumerable women stormed the food distribution point. Around the middle of the month, there were absolutely no vegetables to be found, because of the drought, and there were countless incidents in the markets and in front of the shops, when people who had waited in line for hours, had to go away empty-handed. The disappointed people expressed their dissatisfaction in the most vigorous of terms, and even uttered threats. . . .[7]

At the same time, war widows, whose everyday lives were marked by exhaustion and deprivation, slowly became conscious of themselves as a distinct group. The simple fact of being a single woman with small children to support set the widow apart in a society that held the patriarchal family as a social ideal. A peculiar fact about the widows' experience, however, was that despite this idealization of marriage, most widows never remarried. At the end of the war, there were about a half-million war widows. About 200,000 of them, or 40 percent, remarried between 1919 and 1924. After that, the number of widows on the pension rolls remained remarkably stable. In 1924, 364,950 widows were receiving pensions; in 1928, the figure was 359,560; in 1930, it was 362,190; and in 1931, 360,930 women were receiving widow's pensions. Between 1924 and 1931, then, the number of widows on the pension rolls declined by only about 1 percent.[8]

Why did not more widows remarry? An obvious reason was that the war had devastated their generation; men they might have married had been killed. There was also a financial disincentive to remarriage: when a woman remarried, she lost her pension. In addition, some women saw themselves in terms that did not necessarily include marriage. Their self-definition came from their ties not to men, but to other women. In their accounts, widows often remarked that the support of their "sisters" was critical both to their economic and psychic survival. "How often," a widow wrote, "have widows told me, that they have far more trust in another woman, than in a man, because men simply cannot have the same understanding for the many sufferings of a soldier's widow."[9]

In 1932, Martha Karnoss, a leading organizer of war widows, summarized the widows' experience:

> The basis of our organization, is something unique, an experience that frightfully disrupted our entire lives and at the same time bound us together with our disabled comrades . . . Many wars have come and gone, many wars have swept through Europe and Germany. They have all brought great pain and suffering; an infinite number of tears have been shed, and a quiet heroism has been displayed by survivors, a heroism which will be forgotten by coming generations. For the first time, however, the World War forced women to face their common fate, forced them to overcome their sufferings themselves, and work together to help their sisters . . .
>
> Women before the war were in general politically uneducated. They were used to depending on men, who today, just like before the war, are alone the legal heads of their families. Political activity was something for the man alone. His voice and his opinion set the tone for the family. . . .
>
> It was only after the return of the veterans, that the widow really became aware of how different her situation was from those families which had a husband and father. . . .
>
> Economics was critical. The widow first learned this when she found herself in competition with men in the labor market. Only then did the widow realize how inadequate her pension was; only then did she realize that many others shared her situation, and it was only then that she united with people facing similar problems in an effort to improve her economic condition. . . .
>
> The war educated us, and now we began to place our demands before the state.[10]

In placing their demands before the state, the war widows found allies in the organizations founded by disabled veterans. Women, eager to promote their rights as women and widows, joined with men, determined to preserve their special status as disabled veterans. Their alliance was rooted in a common rebellion against broken promises and intolerable conditions, and it was one of the most unusual social movements in Weimar Germany.

II

Soldiers were not immune to bitterness and resentment. Their anger, however, was diffuse; it was directed at multiple targets. Front soldiers generally hated staff officers. Even the most patriotic resented the pomposity and luxurious living conditions of rear-area officers. Friedrich Lehmann, an ardent patriot and future National Socialist, wrote: "I know how the men complain about the food the officers have in their clubs; on practically every latrine wall you find 'Same food, same pay—the war would be over in a day!'"[11]

The relationship between junior officers and men in the army was relatively close, so long as there was no great discrepancy in food and housing. In the navy, however, tension between officers and men was acute. Germany's surface fleet sat out almost the entire war, and morale aboard the ships was disastrous. This situation had serious political consequences, for the riots that led to the final political collapse in 1918 began in the north German ship yards.[12]

Front soldiers also hated civilians, who, a refrain in soldiers' letters went, could never appreciate the soldiers' sufferings. A regular element of every war-experience novel was the encounter with the people at home and the soldier's realization that communication with nonsoldiers was impossible. Virtually all civilians were despised. Some soldiers denounced nationalist saber rattlers. Others criticized defense-plant workers who were comfortably at home, enjoying fat salaries, while soldiers died. Still others attacked pacifists and socialists, who seemed to denigrate the soldiers' sacrifices.[13]

Soldiers also hated the army. In postwar literature, veterans castigated the army and all its works. Tucholsky's essays, Graf's memoir, and Zweig's novels are examples of such antimilitary literature. Indeed, antimilitary stories were basic to the proletarian literature of the 1920s.[14]

Wounded soldiers, hospitalized at home, shared the multiple resentments of soldiers, as well as the bitterness of civilians. They also had a series of specific angers, their own pool of outrage. The *Heimatschuss,* the "million-dollar wound," was a soldier's most prized possession. Every soldier hoped to be wounded seriously enough to be shipped home and to get a pension, but not so seriously that he was totally disabled. Once men had their Heimatschuss, they seemed to feel that they had done their duty, and that the army should heal them, but also leave them alone. The army was quite aware of this attitude. In 1914, army officers opposed permitting job counselors to speak to recuperating men until the men had been formally discharged; even such a minor breach of the army's control over its troops, the officials apparently believed, could have serious consequences.[15]

The army's fears were not unfounded. Discipline was difficult to maintain in the hospitals. There were, to be sure, no mutinies or mass rebellions, but there was chronic shirking, non-cooperation, and even passive resistance. A major headache for medical officers were civilian schools. Many soldiers, as part of their rehabilitation, were sent out of the hospitals to civilian-run vocational schools. Not infrequently the soldier-students, once beyond their sergeant's sight, would simply wander away and end up in establishments that had little to do with vocational training. Dr. Hans Bernstein, of the Württemberg contingent, devoted much of his handbook on rehabilitation to devising methods to keep track of peripatetic soldiers. Whenever a man left the hospital, Dr. Bernstein advised, he should be issued some sort of identification paper, which would have to be stamped both on departure and on arrival at the proper destination. In addition, authorities should take careful attendance, and signatures should be scrupulously examined, because soldiers sometimes actually forged teachers' signatures. Progress reports should be maintained as well, and the precise status of every soldier had to be monitored frequently.[16]

The army was desperate to keep men on active duty. Even amputees could perform rear-area duties and thereby relieve healthy men for duty at the front. Soldiers were deeply suspicious of doctors' enthusiasm for declaring a man "k.v.," that is, *kriegsverwendbar,* or "fit for duty." Although doctors were anxious to demonstrate their healing skills, soldiers were none too enthusiastic about being healed quickly if that meant returning to the trenches, and they were sure that doctors were conspiring with the generals to ship men out even before their wounds had healed.

Dr. Theodor Brugsch, in late 1918, was instructed by his superior in a Bucharest hospital to accelerate the number of men declared k.v.

> When I said to him, in the Club: "Sir, you must not be surprised at the unhappy results, since these old soldiers, some of whom have been in the army for four years, simply have no desire to go to the Western Front. They pretend

to be sick as long as they possibly can."—Then he was furious. Completely misunderstanding the situation, he had expected every last one of them "to answer the call of the Fatherland in this hour of need." That was out of the question. For example, when I said to one of the convalescents that he was k.v. and was being sent back to the Front, then his inner resistance was quite tempermentally expressed. It was a resistance that even disciplinary measures could not repress.[17]

Evelyn Blücher recorded a similar scene:

August 1918. The soldiers are embittered at the way they are treated in comparison with the officers, and the country is overrun with invalids with grievances. Wounded men refuse to consent to operations, which might heal an injured limb, on the ground that they would then be sent back to the Front, and they have no intention of going there.[18]

Being discharged from the army only added to the injured man's outrage. Being free in a bankrupt economy was no treat. No job, decent medical care, or pension was the common lot. Even healthy veterans had a hard time finding employment. Soldiers often turned to the state for help, but the state could do nothing. In February 1919, for example, three brothers, Georg, Willy and Otto Klapproth from Dortmund, sent a neatly handwritten, four-page letter to Chancellor Philip Scheidemann in Berlin. "We were five brothers," the letter began, ". . . one fell on the field of honor, and another was severely wounded and released from the service." The three brothers were unemployed and had been supported by their parents who could no longer take care of them. "It was through giving our all for the Fatherland that we have ended up in this condition, while people we know, who were never in the army but always were deferred, have fine jobs. For us veterans, it makes things doubly bitter when we see such things. We, on the other hand, were constantly at the Front, and have always done our duty." Now, the brothers continued, there seemed to be no place for them. Although they had been trained in business before the war, they would take any job and would go anywhere.

Two weeks later they received a postcard from the Chancellor's office, stating that their letter had been forwarded to the Interior Ministry. Later, the Ministry replied in an unsigned postcard that, regrettably, there were no jobs available.[19]

During the war, there had been a labor shortage, but within the first months of the peace, the percentage of unemployed leaped from zero to 8 percent, or about 1 million workers. The labor situation had improved by the end of 1919, however, in part because women workers were fired and no longer counted as unemployed since, presumably, they were back at home.[20]

Still, it was extremely difficult for disabled people to find jobs. Even the churches were hesitant about accepting the disabled as seminarians. The Catholic Church discouraged such men from studying for the priesthood because a physical disability would prevent fulfillment of a priest's responsibilities. Prospects seemed equally bleak in the Protestant churches. Before a disabled or disfigured man could serve in a parish, a Protestant official wrote, the "sensibilities" of the parishioners would have to be considered.[21]

The veterans' offices, which the army finally established in 1918, offered little help. Either officers tried to run them as they would have run a rifle company or they showed no interest at all in the social work the offices were supposed to do. Frequently, the only one who knew what was going on in the veterans' office was a corporal, who seldom received the support of his superiors.[22]

A major cause of bitterness among disabled soldiers was the Auxiliary Service Law of December 1916, which was designed to mobilize the labor force for the war effort. Crippled soldiers were to be included in this effort. The National Committee for War Victims' Care was opposed to putting disabled men in defense plants, since such jobs were dead-ends; after the war, the defense plants would be reduced in size, and the men would have to be retrained. However, given the seriousness of the situation, the committee urged officials to help put disabled men to work in war industry. But the men refused to cooperate, and for good reason. A pension was based on disability. If a disabled veteran went to work in a factory, the government would declare the man recovered and snatch away his pension. From the disabled veterans' perspective, the Auxiliary Service Law was a pretext to rob them of what was rightfully theirs. The government denied any such intention, but the disabled soldiers felt that the government was lying. How many disabled veterans were put back to work under the 1916 law is not clear, but from government circulars, it appears that soldiers' cooperation was nil.[23]

Disabled soldiers' complaints were not always so precisely focused. They were angry, but it was sometimes hard to say why. Little things often assumed great importance. In one hospital, blinded soldiers were taught to play musical instruments. After they were discharged, the men complained, they were denied use of the instruments, but who could afford to buy a piano or violin of his own?[24]

The "discharge suit" was another source of complaint. When a man was separated from the service, the army, in cases of need, issued him civilian clothes, a "discharge suit." But material for such suits, like everything else in Germany, became scarce, and discharge suits ceased to be issued. For the soldiers, the suit had an obvious practical importance; symbolically it was even more important. After all they had been through, it seemed to the soldiers that the army owed them at least a suit.[25]

Women who took "men's" jobs was another source of bitterness. A basic demand of disabled veterans was that women be excluded from the labor force as quickly as possible to make room for men, and this demand was forcefully expressed.[26]

> Among other things, the Reichsbund has assumed the task of combating the intolerable competition of women workers, clerks and temporary workers, especially in government jobs. . . . There can be no question that the disabled veterans—who have endured so much suffering for the good of the entire nation, who for the rest of their lives will endure physical and emotional pain—there can be no question that the demands of the disabled veterans are absolutely justified. Above all, in our opinion, the government authorities are obliged to ensure the livelihood of the disabled veterans. This duty must be fulfilled; it is a matter of national honor. The women civil servants and workers, often poorly trained and only hired as temporary workers anyway, must take second place behind the disabled veterans.[27]

The whole area of veterans', and particularly disabled veterans', relationships with women was charged with diffuse but intense anger. During the war women were civilians and, as such, targets of soldiers' hostility; the constant fear of the soldier at the front was betrayal by his wife or lover at home. Among veterans and especially among the disabled, a hostility to women was palpable in the immediate postwar years. The disabled felt emasculated, and were fearful that as cripples they could never depend on a woman's love. This fear is dramatically expressed in Ernst Toller's play *Hinkemann*, whose protagonist is a kind of archetypical disabled veteran, an absurd and grotesque figure who is betrayed by his wife.[28]

By 1917, soldiers on leave and those convalescing in hospitals were actively opposing the war. Reports on home front morale complain that soldiers on leave were spreading subversive rumors and that disabled soldiers were participating in protest marches.

In a secret report, the War Ministry in Berlin directed the Deputy Commanding Generals to watch for soldiers on leave who might be spreading subversive propaganda.

Reports concerning the distribution of pamphlets from the Front are increasing. For example, a soldier on leave brought home a number of pamphlets which he intended to distribute among the civilian population. The pamphlets were entitled "You poor Germany," and "We will build a new Germany." They were signed "the Committee." The soldier on leave expressed the opinion that such materials are produced in great numbers and regularly brought home and distributed among civilians. The prosecution of this particular soldier has begun. The High Command has taken appropriate measures regarding this problem in the field army.

This is brought to your attention in order that you take the appropriate steps to prevent distribution of such subversive literature.[29]

In Bavaria, disabled veterans played a leading role in a number of protest marches in the summer of 1918. In July, for example, a crowd of about 1,000 people, many of them women and adolescents, marched on the town hall in Hof. They shouted down officials who tried to talk to them, and they demanded improved rations and working conditions. An official reported to the Interior Ministry in Munich:

I would not want to fail to take the opportunity to report that also in the case of this disturbance, as elsewhere, soldiers on leave and disabled soldiers were the chief troublemakers. The scene this morning could have been avoided, had not a group of disabled veterans, including two so-called "shiverers," repeatedly simulated nervous attacks, and thereby excited the women.[30]

On August 14, 1918, a crowd of between 3,000 to 4,000 women gathered on the Marienplatz in Munich, and marched to the royal palace. According to the police:

In the crowd were numerous wounded soldiers. In general, they behaved in an orderly fashion, and did not actually take part in the demonstration. They were repeatedly asked to leave the Marienplatz, which, however, they did only very slowly. In any case, the repeatedly observed presence of wounded soldiers in such situations is extremely troubling and disruptive.[31]

A letter that the Interior Ministry prepared for the War Ministry in August, urging that something be done about the soldiers, noted the touchiness of the problem:

It is clear that even the simple presence of wounded soldiers makes police action very difficult. I need only think of the serious consequences which would result if a wounded soldier were trampled by police horses or sustained some other injury. The disturbing nature of so-called "shiverers" in these circumstances has been clear from events in Ingolstadt and Hof.[32]

In August 1919, the commander of the I Bavarian Army Corps reported that agitators were in rural areas, plotting to overthrow the government in Munich. Most of the "agitators" were Independent Social Democrats, but "the actions of communist disabled veterans intensifies this subversion."[33]

Though anger and resentment was at first disorganized, ominous developments had, from the state's perspective, begun as early as 1916. In the spring of that year, the first formal organization of war victims had appeared. Over the next two years, the millions of war victims began to pool their resources, and the welfare question began to take on definite political overtones.

III

"Only we know, no one else." This line from Paul Alverdes' 1929 story *Die Pfeifferstube, The Whistlers*, expresses the central emotion of the war victims. The "whistlers," men who have been wounded in the throat, "loved one another. Not that they would ever have said so, or ever have been sentimental with each other. But every time, when one of them would be rolled away on a stretcher, which often happened, to go under the knives and prongs of the doctors, then the others couldn't do anything. They wouldn't want to play cards or try to talk. . . ." When a whistler was wheeled back from the operating room, his friends would come up to him and "they would nod and wink to him, which meant: 'We three know, and no one else.' And the one returning, would, through his pain, wink back."[34]

Blinded soldiers also felt a strong emotional tie with each other. In March 1916, several blinded men, recuperating in Dr. Silex's School for the Blind in Berlin, decided to form an association for blinded soldiers and their families. They called themselves the *Bund erblindeter Krieger*, the league of blinded soldiers; they were the first formal association of German victims of the war.[35] The association was part of a general trend. Thousands of war victims in the country were beginning to organize. But the question was, what form would a mass organization take?

War victims could have joined the labor unions, which insisted that they had a primary interest in social welfare and that veterans' care was a part of social welfare. Besides, union leaders argued, once a man left the army, he was first a worker and only secondarily a disabled veteran. Disabled veterans should not form their own groups, the unions insisted; they should turn toward the unions and other existing professional groups for support.[36]

But nondisabled workers were concerned about having disabled veterans join their unions. Their concern centered on wages for the disabled. If managers could hire disabled men at reduced wages, they would use disabled men to depress overall wages. Should disabled veterans, then, be hired at the same pay as healthy workers? That hardly seemed fair to the nondisabled.[37] However, disabled men insisted on preferential treatment; without it, they argued, they would never be able to keep a job. Healthy workers responded that at least the veterans had their pensions and, therefore, could more easily survive unemployment. The rivalry reached a climax during mass layoffs. After the war, for example, there were layoffs at the Spandau factories, and fighting broke out between the disabled and nondisabled over who should be laid off first. At least one disabled veteran suffered gun shot wounds in the melee.[38] As a result of such conflicts, disabled veterans turned away from labor unions.

War victims could have joined the veterans' organizations. Germany's major veterans' group, the Kyffhäuser Bund, insisted that men were veterans first, and workers or clerks or managers second. The war presented the Kyffhäuser Bund with a serious dilemma. It was, its literature insisted, a nonpartisan, patriotic organization. However, patriotism was identified with monarchism, conservative politics, and a dedication to social hierarchy, discipline, and authority. Socialists and other troublemakers were defined as nonpatriotic and excluded from the Bund. Before the war, there had been furious debates between the Social Democrats and the Kyffhäuser Bund over the meaning of "patriotism."[39] In 1914, however, millions of socialists had rushed to Germany's defense. Should these socialist veterans be admitted to the Kyffhäuser Bund? Grudgingly, then enthusiastically, the leadership of the Bund said yes. After all, admitting the socialists might actually wean them away from subversion and make patriots of them.

Not surprisingly, Social Democrats were determined to keep their members away from the Kyffhäuser Bund.[40] Moreover, even non-socialists were little attracted by what seemed to be the stuffy, rigid, old-fashioned Bund. Veterans of the Great War insisted on creating their own groups, because they were convinced that the war had set their generation apart. Even if they shared many of the political convictions of their fathers, sons who had been to the front also felt themselves to be separate from their fathers' generation.[41]

Disabled front soldiers felt themselves to be different, however, from other front soldiers. Bound to each other emotionally, with interests sometimes at odds with those of the unions, generally unattracted by the older veterans' groups, and feeling themselves distinct from other veterans, disabled veterans began to form their own groups. The word "special" was particularly important; it was, in fact, the basic reason war victims were generally uninterested in being junior partners in either unions or veterans' groups.

Disabled veterans and war widows did not see themselves as a political faction. They were above all that, above labor and management, above political left and right. Partly, this was a tactical posture: their greatest weapon was public sympathy, which tying themselves to any one faction would threaten. At the same time, it was far more than tactical. They had sacrificed more than anyone else for the common good, they were convinced. Politicians had told them since 1914 that they were special people, entitled to the "Thanks of the Fatherland."[42] War victims desperately wanted to fit back into society, but they also wanted to be recognized as unique human beings. The organizational form of their movement followed from this deeply held conviction.

In the fall of 1916, Hans Adorf, a Krupp employee, began organizing an economic association of disabled veterans in Essen. Early in the war, Adorf had taken an interest in wounded soldiers. As head of a boys' gymnastic group in Essen, he used his contacts to help the recuperating veterans. He first came to the attention of the local authorities when veterans complained that they had been misled into thinking that Adorf represented a governmental agency.[43]

Such details scarcely bothered Adorf. His press releases announced that his project had the full support of the authorities, who hastily announced that they had never even heard of Adorf. He then wrote the Kaiser and asked permission to come to Berlin to discuss the project. The letter was passed to the War Department, and a junior official met with Adorf. When he returned to Essen, Adorf declared that the Kaiser had instructed the military to fully support the creation of an association of disabled veterans; the War Department denied any such instruction. Adorf also claimed that Governor von Winterfeldt, the chairman of the National Committee, supported him. In a letter to the press, Winterfeldt angrily denied this.[44]

The position of the authorities was clear. They totally rejected the idea that war victims had any business organizing. Such an organization would come between the experts and the war victims. The latter should rest assured that the state was fully able and willing to care for them. The matter was discussed at a meeting of the National Committee. According to the minutes of the meeting:

In the meeting of the working committee, held on 16 Dec. 1916, the representatives of the social welfare offices were unanimously of the opinion, that the creation of special organizations of disabled veterans was undesirable. It was emphasized that such organizations could receive no official support. The authorities should take no position with regard to the opinions of these groups, and above all, it was stressed, that disabled veterans be encouraged to turn to the proper authorities for assistance.[45]

Adorf, however, was not discouraged by such objections. On Sunday, April 7, 1917, in Essen, Adorf chaired the first meeting of the group he had just formed, the *Wirtschaftlicher Vereinigung Kriegsbeschädigter für das Deutsche Reich,* the German economic association of disabled veterans, which was quickly dubbed the *Essen Verband* (Essen league).[46] The number of delegates to this first meeting was small; most were associates of Adorf from the Essen area. However, Adorf had been able to arrange a few minor triumphs. He had informed several conservative politicians of his plans, and they sent congratulatory telegrams, and General Ludendorff had agreed to be an honorary chairman (although later, at Winterfeldt's urging, Ludendorff declined the offer).

Adorf's contacts with conservative politicians reveal his primary motive for creating the Essen Verband. Officially, the group was neutral; its stated aim was the economic welfare of disabled veterans. But at the same time, the Essen Verband was a patriotic group, whose aim was to promote patriotism and oppose radicalism. In private letters and conversations, Adorf reiterated his hostility toward any form of radicalism. In trying to gain state support, Adorf constantly raised the specter of revolution. Socialists, pacifists, and Bolsheviks, he warned, were recruiting among the millions of disgruntled war victims. In November 1917, for example, he wrote to the Prussian Commissioner of Wartime Welfare: "It cannot be ignored, what would happen if that against which we have struggled with all the strength at our command, if the millions of war victims should drift under radical influence. But it's still not too late!"[47]

On December 28, 1917, the chairman of the Rhineland Committee on Disabled Veterans met with Adorf. Several days later, the chairman reported to the committee on the meeting.

> Mr. Adorf repeatedly stressed throughout the conversation that the importance of his group lay in the fact that it would keep the disabled veterans away from "radicalism" and "social democracy" . . . In this patriotic activity, he insisted, the group must have the support of the authorities.[48]

Adorf's ties to Krupp were close. Adorf was accepted as a member of the

Essen War Victims Aid Committee largely at the urging of Krupp officials. Adorf was also close to the Fatherland Party, which had been created by the High Command and heavy industry in an attempt to mobilize popular support for the war. In a sense, then, the Essen Verband was an auxiliary of the Fatherland Party; it was, as the Prussian War Ministry wrote, the equivalent of a "yellow union."[49]

The Bund erblindeter Krieger had been the first formal association of war victims; the Essen Verband was the second. While the Bund erblindeter Krieger restricted itself to defending the interests of blinded men and their families, the Essen Verband saw itself as a mass organization that would include all the millions of disabled veterans. This grand ambition, however, was never realized. Within two years of its creation, the Essen Verband was dead.

One problem facing the Verband was Adorf himself. He was dictatorial, unreliable, and perpetually in the bad graces of officials. Worst of all, it appeared that he misappropriated funds. Rumors spread quickly in the Verband that there were irregularities in the accounts and that Adorf had diverted contributions to his personal use. A faction of the Verband, led by some members from the Ruhr, demanded an accounting. Faction leaders exchanged secret messages and plotted to oust Adorf. The tension broke during a weekend convention in Cassel in September 1918.

At the convention, the opposition charged that Adorf was enriching himself with funds donated for the care of war victims. Adorf denied this. In the vote for chairman, Adorf lost, but his supporters on the Rules Committee invalidated most of the opposition votes and Adorf retained his seat. The opposition stalked out and formed a "free" association of disabled veterans. Adorf had won, but the Verband was in ruins.[50]

But there was another, more important reason for the Essen Verband's collapse. Adorf's warning that radicals threatened to take over the war victims was, in a way, accurate. Many disabled veterans found Adorf's support of the war intolerable. Indeed, by the fall of 1918, Adorf's superpatriotism was out of vogue. A few weeks after the Essen Verband had been created, another group had been formed, which was considerably less nationalistic than the Essen Verband, and while the Verband plummeted in popularity, this rival group soared in popular appeal. After a number of name experiments, the rival group called itself the *Reichsbund der Kriegsbeschädigten und ehemaligen Kriegsteilnehmer*, national association of disabled soldiers and veterans, and it emerged as the preeminent organization of German war victims.

The driving force behind the Reichsbund was a young Social Democrat named Erich Kuttner, who was typical of the intellectuals attracted to social democracy. He was well educated, trained as a lawyer, and active as a journalist, agitator, and organizer. In 1914, when he was 27, Kuttner volunteered for the army, and two years later, was severely wounded at Verdun. As a wounded soldier, he became involved in the concerns of disabled veterans, and as a Social Democrat, he began to fear that workers might be swept up in the conservative, anti-socialist veterans' groups. Kuttner was convinced, therefore, that socialists had to start their own veterans' groups, which would appeal not only to socialist veterans, but to all veterans. By late 1916, Kuttner was back in Berlin as an editor of *Vorwärts,* and he began trying to convince his colleagues of the need for a veterans' organization.

Kuttner was able to win over a number of friends to his ideas, all of them active in the labor movement and the Social Democratic Party.[51] Others on the political left, however, were deeply suspicious of the plan. Why, after all, couldn't disabled veterans simply join the labor unions or the Social Democrats? Union leaders particularly resisted the notion of a separate organization of veterans. Throughout the spring of 1917, *Vorwärts* was the forum for the debate on organizing disabled veterans.[52] Kuttner insisted that veterans could not be left to the right-wing veterans' groups; to attract the widest possible number of men, a veterans' group would have to be independent of political parties and unions. But the appearance of Adorf's *Essen Verband* in April 1917, made this debate superfluous. The political right was already organizing disabled veterans; the left would have to act or accept defeat.

In May 1917, Kuttner and some thirty friends and supporters held a public meeting in Berlin to announce the creation of the *Bund der Kriegsbeschädigten und Kriegsteilnehmer.* The Bund's early literature argued that the new group was politically and religiously neutral but that its demands were radical. Better care for disabled veterans and widows was the Bund's basic goal. How was this to be achieved? The entire pension system would have to be revised, and the military would have to be excluded from the system.

Who would pay for improved pensions? The Essen Verband argued that the Allies would have to pay, since they had forced the war on Germany. Therefore, a German victory was essential for the wellbeing of war victims. German war profiteers would pay, the Bund insisted. This was a shrewd tactical move; since public hostility toward war profiteers and black marketeers was intense, they were a convenient target for attack. The demand was more than a tactic, however. To care for war victims, the *Bund* demanded a major redistribution of wealth.

The *Bund's* demands would require profound changes in the political order as well. The Prussian three-class voting system was the symbol of everything the left despised about the authoritarian *Kaiserreich,* and for years, the Social Democrats had demanded equal suffrage, or at least, equal male suffrage. Kuttner, in the early Bund literature, denounced the three-class system as an insult to veterans. If men were good enough to fight for the Fatherland, they were good enough to participate in its politics. On the question of the war, the Bund did not demand surrender. It did, however, reject the annexationist demands of the right, and called for a "peace of understanding." As for the military establishment, it was to be transformed into a "people's army."[53]

By the fall of 1917, the Bund was recruiting throughout the country. Its growth was phenomenal. In June, the Bund had only 150 members; by the end of 1917, it had more than 5,000 members, and by the time of the first national convention, in the spring of 1918, the Bund, had about 25,000 members, organized into 200 local organizations.[54]

Karl Tiedt in Berlin was one of the Bund's leading organizers. He had long been associated with the Social Democrats' left wing. His sympathies were radically democratic, but he was more of a Bohemian than a Bolshevik. Like Kuttner, he was a middle-class intellectual, and he too had been wounded in the war. His Berlin organization was the largest and most active Bund local.

In the south, Erich Rossmann was the Bund's chief organizer. Unlike Kuttner and Tiedt, Rossmann had a proletarian background. His life had been dedicated to building up the unions and the social democratic organization, and he was firmly tied to the majority Social Democrats. From his home in Stuttgart, Rossmann began building the Bund organization in southern Germany.[55]

The authorities opposed the Bund. Censorship during the First World War was neither as brutal nor as efficient as in the Second, but it was still strict.[56] Political rallies and propaganda were carefully monitored, and the army repeatedly tried to prohibit the Bund's activities, but with little success. Kuttner, though disabled, was recalled to service in June 1917 and was shipped to Königsberg, apparently the most obscure place the army could think of at the time. But when confronted with howls of protest from Social Democratic politicians, the army relented and Kuttner was released after six weeks and allowed to return to Berlin. The National Interior Office advised against an open attack on the Bund; instead, it urged that military authorities support the conservative veterans' groups in their recruitment of disabled veterans.[57]

In sparring with the authorities, the Bund used a number of ruses. When recruiting was prohibited among military personnel on active duty, the

Bund changed the "soldiers" (Kriegsteilnehmer) in its name to "former soldiers" (ehemalige Kriegsteilnehmer). When the activities of the Bund itself were sharply restricted, the Bund changed its name to Reichsbund. The most serious clashes came not with the authorities, however, but with agitators from the Fatherland Party.

A score of skirmishes occurred between this party and the Reichsbund. The most famous was the "Battle of Alexanderplatz," which took place on January 7, 1918. On that Monday evening, the Fatherland Party held a rally in the Lehrervereinshaus on Berlin's Alexanderplatz. In the audience were some young veterans from the Reichsbund. Precisely what happened is not clear. Spokesmen for the Fatherland Party insisted later that Reichsbund members had heckled them. (Not so, said the organization; its members had merely made "parliamentary interpellations.") The Reichsbund argued that its members had been called "shirkers" and "deserters who had abandoned Hindenburg's colors in order to stab their comrades in the back." (The Fatherland Party later said that its speakers had not been referring to members of the Reichsbund in particular.) In any case, fighting broke out, the police were called, and the veterans temporarily retreated.

A short time later, Kuttner, through *Vorwärts,* renewed the offensive, denouncing the "shameful" attack on the disabled veterans. Kuttner organized a public rally at which veterans tossed their military decorations into a package to be mailed as a protest to Admiral Tirpitz, the leader of the Fatherland Party. This was too much for the authorities; General von Kessel, the commander of the Berlin military district, banned Kuttner from any future political activity. But who, Kuttner retorted, had more disgraced the military decorations—the disabled veterans or the so-called patriots from the Fatherland Party, who had assaulted the veterans?[58]

Kuttner's shrewdness deserves emphasis. The war had produced tension between veterans and civilians, which was evident in the various proto-facscist groups that flourished in the postwar years, and Kuttner used this hostility toward nonsoldiers as a weapon against the political right. The Reichsbund ridiculed the "arm chair warriors" and "bitter enders" of the Fatherland Party. Why, those old men had never even "smelled gunpowder"; most had never been to the front; and some of the Fatherland Party agitators were actually draft dodgers![59]

The Reichsbund's largest rally came on Sunday, December 22, 1918, in Berlin. Some 10,000 people massed at the Zirkus Busch, and then marched on the War Ministry. It was a ghastly parody of the triumphal marches of 1914. Row after row of war victims marched down Berlin's frozen streets, bundled in tatters of uniforms against the harsh Berlin wind. Trucks carrying paraplegics led the way. The blind, guided by their dogs, followed, and then came the widows and orphans.[60]

In late 1918 and early 1919, other bizarre parades took place throughout the country, and they became engraved in Weimar's literature. Leonard Frank concludes *Der Mensch ist gut* with a terrifying march through Berlin. Trainload after trainload of the maimed arrive in the city and hobble through the streets. Their leader is a man with no arms or legs, carried on a litter like a potentate. His stare draws thousands of people into a giant march for peace.[61]

Remarque, in *Der Weg zurück,* offers a particularly vivid parade:

> Slowly, a column of people comes along, in the faded uniforms of the Front. . . . Big white placards say: "Where is the Thanks of the Fatherland?" and "The War Cripples are Starving!"
>
> One-armed men carry these signs. Men follow, led by guide dogs. After them come men with just one eye, men with torn faces, with no noses, with mouths ripped and jagged, with no jaws, with holes where mouth and nose once were, men with a single red scar where once their face had been. And above this destruction, still, questioning, sad eyes stare out. After them come row on row of leg amputees. . . . Then come the "shiverers." Quietly, this group moves through the streets. . . .[62]

This silent protest was not typical of the early days of the war victims' movement, however. The war victims were angry and sometimes violent in their demands. Margarete Cordemann, a social worker, wrote:

> I often admired my male colleagues in Düsseldorf, who had to work with the disabled veterans. They had only a table between themselves and the furious men, and they would have been lost if their nerves had failed and they had shouted at the applicants or had grabbed some object to protect themselves from the infuriated veterans. . . . In individual cases it was often incredibly difficult to dissuade the disabled veterans and their families from the notion that they had been unjustly treated.[63]

On April 12, 1919, a crowd of disabled veterans threw the Saxon War Minister into the Elbe, and he drowned.[64] On April 25, 1919, a delegation from the Reichsbund met with Chancellor Philip Scheidemann. The session was stormy. The Reichsbund delegates are identified only as Bader and Foth.

> *Foth:* Everywhere in the circles of war invalids and survivors there is such bitterness that I was surprised myself. . . . You wouldn't believe how many

letters we get everyday, and when we make inquires we are always told "we're working on it." That just is no good, when its about a case that's been lying around for 4 or 5 months. There is a problem with the entire system.

Bader: You would understand why I'm so upset, if you saw everyday the suffering our comrades endure both in Berlin and in the country. Don't be surprised if some day a collossal storm breaks. You say, the financial condition of the nation doesn't permit [improvements]. That's what Bethmann Hollweg said, and that's what Max von Baden said, and that's what the new government has said since 9 November. Well, the comrades say, maybe you, Minister-President, should have done more to end the war sooner.

Scheidemann: It would be better if you don't say that outside. That was a very nasty comment.

Bader: That's always said to us outside. I have no intention of stirring people up, but we have to tell you the truth, we have to tell you what people think.[65]

In the first months of 1919, the Reichsbund dominated the movement, greeting the collapse of the monarchy joyfully, but its monopoly was brief.[66] The organization was attacked from both the right and the left. Trouble from the right was not unexpected. The German labor movement had been split for years between the socialist and Christian-national unions. Leaders of the latter had no intention of surrendering the war victims to the Social Democrats, and talks between the Reichsbund and representatives of the conservative unions stalled. The Reichsbund reported in *Vorwärts* that it had made every effort to cooperate with the right wing of the labor movement and that it had stressed the need for unity among war victims, but all had been in vain.[67]

Leaders of the Christian-national unions finally joined forces with the remnants of the Essen Verband and several smaller groups, and in September 1919 announced the creation of the *Zentralverband deutscher Kriegsbeschädigter und Kriegshinterbliebener,* the Central Association of Disabled German Veterans and Survivors. We are not dividing the war victims' movement, nor politicizing it, stated the founders of the Zentralverband. The Reichsbund is a tool of the Social Democrats; the Zentralverband, on the other hand, is scrupulously non-partisan.[68] But the Zentralverband was anything but neutral. It quickly became the rallying point for nationalist, conservative veterans, who opposed the Reichsbund's social democratic orientation.

Meanwhile, two other groups sprang up to the right of the Reichsbund. The Kyffhäuser Bund had never ceased recruiting disabled veterans, and it had met with considerable success. Officers had no intention of belonging to the same group as enlisted men; therefore, most disabled officers joined the Deutscher Offiziersbund, which had been created in November 1918.[69]

By the spring of 1919, then, there were five war victims' groups: the little Bund erblindeter Krieger; the Kyffhäuser Bund and the Deutscher Offiziersbund, which mainly represented disabled veterans and their survivors; the Zentralverband and the Reichsbund, which were both mass organizations of war victims.

The resurgence of the right was expected, but the attack from within the Reichsbund itself was a shock. The war had torn the German left apart. Prewar disputes between revisionists and radicals had been exacerbated by the long war, until finally the radicals seceded from the Social Democratic Party (SPD) altogether. Indeed, the battle between the radicals and the majority Social Democrats was one of the chief reasons for the political fragility of the republic. This division ran through the entire left, and the Reichsbund was not untouched.

In January 1919, shortly after the violent suppression of the Communist uprising in Berlin, Karl Tiedt urged the Reichsbund to break with Social Democracy. But his proposals were rejected in an uproarious meeting of the Berlin local, and Tiedt and his supporters stalked out of the meeting. A month later, Tiedt announced the formation of yet another war victims' group, the *Internationaler Bund der Opfer des Krieges und der Arbeit,* the international association of the victims of war and work. Tiedt insisted that his group was above politics, but as the word "international" in the group's name suggested, the organization was linked to the German Communist Party.[70]

The secession of Tiedt and his supporters had a profound impact on the Reichsbund. In an effort to de-politicize the organization, Kuttner stepped down as chairman and devoted himself to working in the Prussian state legislature. In a *Vorwärts* article, Erich Rossmann reaffirmed the organization's political neutrality and attacked the newly formed Communist group for its political partisanship. He concluded optimistically: "One thing we are sure of: a comrade, who goes through the social and political school of the Reichsbund will never join one of the rightest veterans' groups, nor will he ever become a reactionary hireling."[71]

In April 1919, a new group appeared, with the promising name of the *Einheitsverband,* the "unity league." It was organized in part by Leipzig dissidents from the old Essen Verband who could not support the conservatism of the Zentralverband or the social democratic ideas of the Reichsbund. Officially, the Einheitsverband was neutral, but like the other groups, it had a political orientation; it represented the liberal wing of the movement: people to the left of the Zentralverband, but to the right of the Reichsbund.[72]

There were other, smaller war victims' associations. The movement, however, was dominated by these seven groups, all of which had emerged by the summer of 1919. For the next fourteen years, these groups formed the German war victims' movement, and according to a 1921 calculation by the Labor Ministry, they represented nearly 1.4 million members. In that year the membership of each group was as follows:[73]

Reichsbund	639,856
Kyffhäuser Bund	225,382
Einheitsverband	209,194
Zentralverband	156,320
Internationaler Bund	136,883
Deutscher Offiziersbund	27,435
Bund erblindeter Krieger	2,521

IV

All the groups, with the possible exception of the tiny Bund erblindeter Krieger, were thoroughly political, yet all denied any contact with politics. In part, the protest of political innocence was an attempt to appeal to as wide an audience as possible. It was typical too of the German disdain for "partisanship," and the idealization of being "above politics," which was characteristic of virtually every political group in the country. The difficulty was that debate and dissension became intolerable. Anyone who rejected the "neutral" values of an organization was expelled or had to secede. The very search for harmony promoted endless factionalization.

More important, however, the political orientation of the groups demonstrated the survival of prewar antagonisms. The fissures in the movement followed the wider faults in the broader social foundation. Despite their common war experience and the similarity of their interests, the war victims could not form a unified or cooperative movement.

Another contradiction complicated the behavior of the seven organizations. War victims could claim to be nonpartisan because they were special; they were not just another interest group but heroes and the survivors of heroes. They felt that they were a generation set apart. Yet they also longed to be re-integrated into society.

A third contradiction was between the size and visibility of the movement and its rapid loss of political influence. Indeed, it seemed that the larger and more sophisticated the movement became, the less able it was to influence the state. In 1919, the war victims' movement was turbulent; it was in the street and in the welfare offices demanding change. The fractures that appeared soon within it certainly contributed to a decline in power, but there was another reason. During 1919, the state constructed the bureaucratic and legislative framework of the pension system. In a way, the system that finally emerged in 1920 was both a triumph and a defeat for the war victims, and later chapters will show how this was so.

Unidentified German soldiers undergoing physical therapy. (Photo: Ullstein, Berlin.)

CHAPTER 9

The National Pension Law of 1920

Disabled Veterans! Survivors! What Is the Nation Doing For You?
—Government pamphlet

Meeting in Berlin in April 1920, the National Assembly rushed through the law that millions of war victims had been anxiously awaiting. Its official name was the *Reichsversorgungsgesetz* (RVG), the National Pension Law.[1] It took effect retroactively on April 1. The law was both a beginning and an end: a beginning, since it established the legal framework within which the war victims would live for the rest of their lives, and an end, in that it represented the culmination of all the efforts to create a program for their care.

In terms of scope and cost, the National Pension Law was one of the Weimar Republic's most important pieces of legislation. No one knew precisely how many war victims there were; however, according to a pamphlet produced by the government to explain the new law:

> The scope of the law is extraordinary. About 1-1/2 million disabled veterans, 525,000 widows, 1,130,000 orphans and 164,000 parents will be cared for. Since families of war victims will share pension benefits, altogether around 5 million people will be affected by the new law.[2]

Finance Minister Bernhard Dernberg was sure that even these figures were underestimates. In April 1919, he commented sarcastically to his cabinet colleagues:

> We know from past experience that in a relatively short time every other man, if not every man, will try to grab something from the pension fund. As far as I know, disabled veterans from 1870–1871 are still collecting benefits. When I

was in the Reich Colonial Office, over 70% of the troops involved in the Herero and Hottentot campaigns received some sort of compensation, at least temporarily.[3]

No one had any clear idea what the cost of the pension system would be, but officials were sure that it would be colossal. The Finance Minister presented a grim picture to the delegates at the National Assembly.

I have requested some 1.2 billion marks for the general pension fund. Doubtless, this sum is too low. We must recognize that, just as after every war, injuries in the form of every sort of complaint and sickness only appear later. Therefore, we will probably have to increase this fund by 3 billion more marks to some 4.2 billion marks.

Still, we can hope that in the future these expenses, after they have swollen, can be reduced through the deaths of the recipients. In the next difficult times, however, we will have to reckon with frightfully increased costs.[4]

There were two components to the pension system: the administrative apparatus and the benefits prescribed by the National Pension Law, and each will be discussed in turn.[5]

I

The administrative apparatus had four parts, which had been hastily grafted together: The army's pension offices, the medical facilities affiliated with the National Insurance System, the army's pension review panels, and the local social service agencies. All of these parts were under the general supervision of the Labor Ministry. The army's pension offices had been created in the last hectic months of the war. Each of the 25 deputy corps commanders established a regional pension office, with subordinate branch offices scattered throughout the corps area. In October 1919, this entire apparatus was transferred from the military to the Labor Ministry;[6] in many cases, soldiers simply exchanged uniforms for suits and ties. By 1920, this bureaucracy consisted of 25 regional offices, 308 local offices, and some 45,000 employees.[7]

No alternative to this transfer had been considered. The radical reduction in the size of the German military establishment demanded by the Versailles Treaty left the government no choice but to take the offices away from the army. There was no serious discussion about creating a separate pension ministry. Any pension program would have to work closely with the existing National Insurance System, which was under the supervision of the Labor Ministry. Most war victims were familiar with the insurance system, and the civil servants in the system were experienced in pension and disability matters. Many Social Democrats, including those in the Reichsbund, saw in the Labor Ministry an all-purpose social welfare agency, and it seemed only logical to place war victims' affairs under its control.

The twenty-five regional offices and their subordinate offices were directly responsible to the Labor Minister; there was no separate pension section in the Labor Ministry. The section of the ministry in charge of pension legislation, headed by Anton Kirschensteiner, acted as the coordinating center for war victims' affairs.

While the pension offices managed the files of the war victims, the medical facilities of the National Insurance System provided medical care. The hospitals connected with the insurance system provided treatment, and the government reimbursed the hospitals. An independent medical system could have been created for veterans, but there had not been enough time or money.

The third component of the pension system, the pension courts, were grafted on to the existing insurance courts. Like the latter courts, the pension courts were essentially administrative panels. The president of the local insurance court was president of the pension court, and he was assisted by the professional judges and representatives of the war victims. The panel considered complaints raised by the state or the pensioner, then issued a decision. The decision could be appealed to the National Pension Court in Berlin, whose president was also president of the National Insurance Office.[8] Most of the court's staff had been recruited from the National Insurance Office. The actual administrator of the court was Wilhelm Rabeling, a career civil servant.

The network of local social service agencies provided war victims with such services as job training, help in finding a job, and assistance in getting an apartment and in caring for children. Throughout the war, these tasks had been the responsibility of local and regional governments, and this arrangement was formalized in early 1919 by the "Ordinance concerning Social Services for Disabled Veterans and Survivors."[9]

II

The National Pension Law of 1920 was the last in a series of measures hastily adopted in 1919 and 1920 designed to alleviate the desperate conditions of the war victims. At a cabinet meeting in April 1919, the War Minister General Reinhardt argued:

I am firmly convinced that care for disabled veterans is entirely inadequate. Among the many discontents today, the discontent of the disabled veterans with their pensions is the most justified and the most seriously to be considered. The financial situation has not, up to now, permitted the Finance Ministry to satisfy my repeated requests for improvements in disabled veterans' care. Through price increases, the loss of value of the currency and the vigorous, and fully justified, agitation of the disabled veterans, conditions are now at such a point that any further delay in improvements threatens the entire public order.[10]

Most of the measures adopted were essentially stop-gaps; they were designed to increase benefits under the old laws to keep pace with inflation and to encourage re-employment of veterans.[11]

Two ordinances, however, were especially important. On 9 January 1919, the government issued the "Ordinance concerning Employment of the Severely Disabled." The measure decreed that "all public and private factories, bureaus and agencies are required to employ one severely disabled [veteran] for every 100 persons employed."[12] This measure, and subsequent amendments,[13] included provisions protecting the severely disabled veteran from losing his job, and a later amendment required that employers with 25 to 50 employees had to hire one disabled veteran, and another disabled veteran had to be hired for every 50 additional employees.

The other important ordinance was that concerning "Social Services for Disabled Veterans and Survivors," mentioned above. Issued on 8 February 1919, it represented in a sense a radical departure in war victims' care. During the war, the national government had tried to avoid the war victims issue. Though it did distribute 10 million marks to the states for social services between 1914 and 1918, it adamantly maintained that social services for war victims were a local responsibility.[14] The February 1919 ordinance changed this position totally; according to its first section: "The Reich . . . assumes responsibility for social services for disabled veterans and survivors," in cooperation with the individual states and private associations. Section 5 required individual states to establish War Victims Offices, which would administer social services. The official commentary accompanying the ordinance stated:

> In addition to the legislatively determined pensions, there are also social services for disabled veterans and survivors. The aim of these social services is, through job-counseling, -training and -placement, to return disabled veterans and survivors to productive work and to keep them in their social position. . . . The overwhelming majority of the states, all parties in the Reichstag, agencies concerned with war victims' care, as well as the associations of war victims, have always unanimously agreed that social services for war victims were a national matter.[15]

The ordinance also included a major concession to the war victims' organizations. Throughout the war, civil servants had refused to bargain with the war victims' groups; now the National Committee for War Victims' Care was attached to the newly formed Labor Office (later called the Labor Ministry), and representatives of the war victims were included in the committee. The committee was to function as a kind of pension parliament; delegates representing war victims, state social services offices, the Labor Ministry, labor, management, and private charities were to meet, when called by the Labor Minister, to discuss pension affairs. And each state social service office was required to set up an advisory council.

But although important concessions were made, this flurry of decrees had a major flaw. How everything would actually work and who would pay the different costs was left to be worked out sometime in the future. A half-century later, Anton Kirschensteiner recalled the confused conditions surrounding the adoption of the February ordinance; his comments reflect the general atmosphere in which the Republic's pension system was born.

It was early February 1919. We were preparing to leave [Berlin] for Weimar, where the National Assembly was to meet. After the leading officials had departed, it turned out that the draft of the Ordinance had disappeared; it later turned up . . . in the baggage belonging to the Labor Office.

. . . Secretary Bauer [of the Labor Office] invited us to meet in the *Schloss* on the evening of 7 February. I was amazed that the *Schloss* had no electricity. There was only a wire stretched across the ceiling, from which a single light bulb dimly glowed. . . . Friedrich Ebert, the future President, came into the room. After introductions, he sat down with us and we reported to him. He very quickly understood our proposals. In the middle of the conversation, he rose and went through the darkened room, looking for something. We silently watched him. He walked up to a French fireplace and flicked his cigar. In the dark, he hadn't seen the ashtray on the table, and he didn't want to dirty the fine room. . . . After Ebert's departure, the discussion quickly ended. . . . Geheimrat Kühnemann and I figured out the exact wording of the Ordinance on the way home in the train dining car on the back of a menu.[16]

Once he was back in Berlin, Kirschensteiner and his associates in the Labor Ministry began drafting the definitive pension law. Within a few months, a draft was circulating among the affected ministries, and the impatient war victims were assured that a pension law was on the way. Finally, in the spring of 1920, the draft was ready for presentation to the National Assembly.[17]

The first reading of the bill took place on April 19, 1920, and the second and the final readings on April 28. During the session on the 28th, Hermann Müller reported for the committee which had examined the bill that "no changes were suggested." Labor Minister Alexander Schlicke, present for the vote, "spoke of the great sacrifices the war had demanded, as well as the gratitude owed, and then discussed the details of the law. The heart of the law consisted of the pension provisions. Though the provisions might not satisfy all the hopes of the disabled veterans, the sufferings they endured were the result of the lost war, and were endured as well by the entire nation." Delegate Richard Meier "stressed that all Parties were united in their support of the law, so that the victims of the war could at last receive that to which they were entitled." With that, the National Pension Law was unanimously adopted.[18]

The law consisted of 103 articles. Unlike the labyrinthine National Insurance Law, the pension law was originally written so that even nonspecialists could interpret it. It was intended to be simple, clear, and concise, though it did not stay that way for long. To explain how the system was to work, the government published a pamphlet entitled "Disabled Veterans! Survivors! What Is the Nation Doing for You?".[19] The first step was up to the war victims themselves; pensions were not awarded, they had to be applied for. The soldier or widow had to go to the local pension office and fill out the necessary applications.

Then came the decision most crucial to the veteran: the determination as to whether the alleged health problem was service-related. Probability was enough, the new law said, and the old distinction between combat and non-combat injuries was dropped.[20] Still, even proving probability could be a complex affair. The decision was up to the doctor working for the pension office. If it was affirmative, the next step was determining the percentage of disability. As in the National Insurance Law, disability was based on a drop in earning capacity. Military rank ceased to play a role in determining disability pensions.[21] It was up to a doctor to consider a man's education, social position, prewar occupation, and other relevant factors, and to decide what percent the man's earning capacity had been reduced. Disability was measured from 20 percent to 100 percent in units of 10 percent. A 15 percent disability, for example, was raised to 20 percent, while a 14 percent disability was lowered to 10 percent.[22]

Fixing the percentage of disability was a difficult task for doctors, and war victims found their decisions frustrating. What did a doctor know about carpentering, running a lathe, or working on a farm? How could a doctor say that a disability was 40 percent and not 45 percent? Yet such a difference was of crucial importance. A man with a 40 percent disability was considered "lightly disabled," while a 45 percent disability would be raised to 50 percent and a man with that high a disability was considered "severely disabled" and, thus, eligible for a number of special allowances. In determining the percent of disability, doctors frequently disagreed with each other, and war victims began to suspect that a great deal of guesswork was involved.

Doctors then passed on the percentage of disability to the civil servants who used it to calculate the pension, which was determined in two basic steps.

Step one: A specific "base pension" was pegged to the percentage of disability. For example, a man with a 20 percent disability received 480 marks per year. In addition, men with a 50 percent or higher disability received a "severe disability allowance." Finally, according to provisions of the "equalization allowance," men who had had especially responsible positions before the war, or who would have had such positions had they not been injured, were entitled to a 25 to 50 percent increase in their pension. The base pension, severe disability allowance, and equalization allowance were combined; together they were labeled the "full pension."[23]

Step two: The "full pension" could be supplemented by a number of other allowances. People living in expensive parts of the country were authorized a "location allowance."[24] Because of the chronic inflation, everyone was entitled to a "cost of living allowance."[25] Men who needed special medical treatment at home could get a "care allowance."[26] If a disabled man were unemployed, he could be granted a "transition allowance,"[27] which would provide a minimum income to supplement his pension while he was looking for work. Wives did not get an allowance, but children did; every legitimate child under 18 years of age raised the full pension by 10 percent.[28] If a man died, his heirs could receive a "death allowance"[29] to cover burial expenses, as well as a "death benefit,"[30] which was the equivalent of three months pension.

A number of other benefits were available. Medical care and associated costs were paid by the government. Prostheses and other necessary equipment were provided. There were provisions to offset payments for job-training. Men who were more than 50 percent disabled could receive preference in civil service hiring.[31] Blind veterans were entitled to a seeing-eye dog.[32]

To calculate a widow's pension, civil servants assumed that the husband had been 100 percent disabled. His full pension would be calculated and the widow would be entitled to 30 percent of that amount. A woman over 50 years of age, or who was herself disabled, or who had children to support could receive 50 percent of the deceased husband's pension.

Each orphan was entitled to a pension. Again, the civil servants would assume that the father had been 100 percent disabled. Each orphan whose mother was alive received 15 percent of his or her deceased father's hypo-

Begging war invalid in the streets of Berlin. (Photo: Bundesarchiv Koblenz, Federal Republic of Germany)

thetical pension. Children with neither father nor mother living received 25 percent.

There were many other allowances. Women whose husbands had been disabled but whose deaths were not service-related could receive a small, temporary allowance in case of need. Parents who had been dependent on their deceased sons might also be eligible for a permanent pension or a temporary allowance.[33]

The National Pension Law guaranteed that the national government would reimburse both local governments for social services and the Insurance System for medical care provided.[34] The procedures for paying part of the pension as a single lump sum, which had been developed during the war, were retained.[35]

All these calculations were repeated millions of times after May 1920, for the adoption of the law meant that all applications, including those previously approved, had to be calculated according to the new provisions.

This herculean task was the first step in implementing the system, and it produced cries of outrage from the war victims. The reasons for their outrage are discussed in the next chapters.

George Grosz, "These war invalids are getting to be a positive pest!" (Estate of George Grosz, Princeton, N.J.)

CHAPTER 10

Building Up and Tearing Down the Pension System, 1920–1923

STORM WINDS!—*Reichsbund* headline, 1923

Eighteen months after the end of the Great War, Germany's pension program was finally in place. The National Pension Law explained the program's aims, and thousands of civil servants struggled to put the law into effect. More than five million war victims and their families had anxiously waited for the law, but soon after the pension system was launched, it lay in shambles.

The collapse of the system had much to do with the tumultuous times. In April 1920, Wolfgang Kapp attempted his putsch, and the following month, workers in the Ruhr staged a leftist rebellion. By the summer of 1920, Kapp and his allies were in exile or in hiding and left-wing radicals had been driven underground. The Republic had survived.

Right-wing terrorism continued, however, and in 1923, political violence erupted again. In October of that year, Communists launched an uprising in Hamburg, and troops were rushed to Dresden to suppress a legally elected Communist-Social Democratic state government in Saxony. In November, amid rumors of military plots, General Ludendorff and Adolf Hitler attempted their putsch in Munich, but the Republic still survived.

All this political turmoil reflected, and engendered, economic disorder. Though wartime inflation had eased a bit after 1920 and production and employment figures were tolerable, the French invasion of the Ruhr in January 1923 triggered a chain of events that culminated in hyper-inflation.

It was against this backdrop that the drama between the civil servants and war victims unfolded. The pension system collapsed because it was not designed for the load heaped on it, and because it was not strong enough to endure the political and economic storms of the early 1920s.

This chapter will describe that collapse and the war victims' efforts to understand and control what was happening to them.

I

The two pillars of the pension system were the pension offices and the pension courts. Whether a widow or veteran could receive medical care or social services depended on the decisions of the offices and courts, and between 1920 and 1923, both were in a state of confusion.

Because pensions approved before the National Pension Law had to be re-examined as well as new ones determined, the 300-odd local offices were swamped with applications. By the summer and fall of 1920, there was chaos in the pension offices. In February 1921, a Reichstag member and Social Democrat wrote in *Vorwärts:*

> Whoever has followed the creation of the National Pension Law and has contact with war victims knows that their fully justified complaints are not only directed against the law itself. Above all, complaints are directed against the delays in the implementation of the law. The majority of war victims still do not know what their pensions will be . . . Virtually scandalous conditions reign in the pension offices, conditions under which the war victims suffer. The work of these offices (or more accurately, the non-work) deserves the sharpest criticism. There can be no doubt that some of the civil servants haven't the least interest in the rapid implementation of the law, because they want to hold on to their jobs as long as possible. The work force in the pension offices, made up of civil servants from the most diverse branches of the government, is more heterogeneous than in any other part of the bureaucracy. Everyone knows that there is constant friction between these various civil servants, and that does not contribute to an efficient implementation of the law either . . .[1]

An article in the *Zentralblatt,* the newspaper of the nationalist Zentralverband, echoed this criticism.

> Complaints about the disastrous failure of the pension machinery grow every day . . . It is simply intolerable that conditions in the pension offices and courts are so bureaucratic that they drive the war victims mad. About the idea of a "simplification of procedures," not to mention the idea of "socially-conscious behavior" nothing more can be heard. And so yet again: Mr. Labor Minister, "quosque tandem"—how much longer?[2]

In April 1923, the Labor Ministry issued a report on pension applications. Between July 1921 and February 1923, pension officials processed more than 3,000,000 applications, an average of 169,814 pension applications per month. The most hectic period was early 1922; in March of that year, pension officials handled 211,825 applications. Fortunately, the report concluded, the workload was at last declining.[3]

Meanwhile, the workload in the pension courts was increasing. It was possible to argue with the doctors and civil servants in the pension offices, but if no agreement could be reached, the complaint was taken to the pension courts. By 1922 the courts were inundated with complaints.

The National Pension Court, when it opened for business in November 1919, consisted of three judicial panels. The following table outlines the court's workload.[4]

	Appeals	*Decisions*	*Backlog at year-end*
1919	750	61	689
1920	8486	3065 1	6110
1921	17,196	7778	15,528
1922	36,134	13,950	37,712
1923	33,134	28,072	43,186

The consequence was interminable delay. The court's size was expanded rapidly; in July 1921, the number of judicial panels increased to 12, and in September 1923, there were 32 panels, but the workload was out of control. Five years after the war's end, millions of war victims still did not know what their pensions would be. "Is it not a condition that cries to heaven," the *Reichsbund* complained bitterly, "that disabled comrades, and survivors struggling for their very existence, have to wait years before their pension applications are processed?"[5] A year later, the *Zentralblatt* reported:

The fact that the courts have been swamped with complaints against the decisions of the pension officials, is proof of the inadequacy of the National Pension Law . . . It is a regrettable situation, when war victims have to run to the courts in order to fight for their rights.[6]

Though appalled by the chaos, the civil servants struggling to manage the system were obsessed by the pension costs. They were concerned that the costs would devour what little national wealth there was.

Civil servants had never had any illusions about the cost of pensions. During the war, opposition to pension reform had been based primarily on the fear of incurring huge costs before the war was won;[7] after the war, officials worried about the cost of pensioning off the millions of men, widows, and orphans, and the worry grew as the economy became more fragile. From the beginning of the republic, finance ministers had made repeated demands to officials that costs be cut. For example, in September 1919, Finance Minister Erzberger wrote to all ministers:

> The grave financial condition of the nation demands that monies provided for the transition from the war- to a peace-time economy be managed with the greatest care, and with maximum saving. Further, the efforts at saving introduced in all areas . . . must be supported in every way.[8]

Expenditures, however, soared.

How much did pensions cost? No one knew. The number of persons eligible to receive pensions changed daily, and so did the value of the currency, especially in 1923. Still, some figures show, if not exact costs, at least orders of magnitude.

The best indicator of pension costs was the "General Pension Fund" item in the national budget. Though not all the costs of the pension system were included in this item—administrative costs, for instance, came under the Labor Ministry budget—and though not quite all the General Pension Fund money went to victims of the war, most of the money involved in the pension system was taken from this fund. The fund's size in the postwar years was as follows: 1919—1.3 billion marks; 1920—5.7 billion; 1921—8.1 billion; 1922—10.7 billion marks. What is striking about these figures is their size; in 1913, the entire national budget had been only about 3 billion marks.

What was the relative weight of pension costs in the total budget? After 1924, this was calculated precisely, as the next chapter will show, but for the years 1919 to 1923, calculating the impact of pension costs on the rest of the budget is very difficult. However, a rough idea can be obtained by considering the "ordinary, continuing expenses" portion of the budget. This section, composed of some seventeen items, included the regular yearly budgets of the various ministries, the financing of the national debt, funds re-distributed to the states, and monies for the General Pension Fund.

"Ordinary, continuing expenses" in millions of marks are shown below.

1919	12,121
1920	39,654
1921	45,578
1922	100,151

The General Pension Fund, as a percentage of these expenses, came to:

1919	10.7 percent
1920	14.3

1921	17.8
1922	10.6

These percentages are a bit misleading. Over half of the money in the budget went to the national debt and to transfer payments to the states and was thus never available to the ministries. Of the money available to the national government, the single largest percentage went to the General Pension Fund; the fund dwarfed the ministerial budgets. Certainly this is what attracted the attention of officials. Though finances during this period were confused, one point was clear: pensions to war victims cost a vast amount of money.[9]

By 1922, costs were literally frightening. The director of the local welfare office in Halberstadt, for example, wrote to the regional welfare office in Merseburg, in December 1922:

> In the months of October/December over 8 million marks were paid to war victims as cost-of-living allowances through the local finance office. The employee charged with disbursing funds paid out some 3,000 marks too much, as a subsequent audit demonstrated. Since he cannot obtain the 3,000 marks from the financial office, he has asked us to provide it.
>
> We do not have these funds available. Therefore, since it involves an experienced and trust-worthy employee, we request that you provide the required funds. Should this request be denied, we can assure you that no employee will agree to handle such vast sums of money.[10]

Somehow, a basic contradiction in government policy had to be relieved. Finance ministers demanded with ever increasing panic that costs be cut; pension costs, however, grew wildly. Finally, the government acted.

In November 1923, Finance Minister Hans Luther explained the financial requirements of the government to the Labor Minister. The basic problem, he began, was that the national government had assumed too many financial burdens, especially in the social welfare field. He continued:

> The goal must be a complete un-burdening of the national government. All that should, in my opinion, remain to the national government is legislation; the entire administration and execution of laws should be left up to regional and local governments. Participation of the national government in expenses is out of the question. The goal must equally be the reduction in size of the national bureaucracy. Above all, I have in mind reductions in social services for pensioners, disabled veterans and survivors, in family-aid programs and housing projects . . .[11]

The National Pension Law itself contained a number of provisions that were designed to reduce the pension burden. In the 1906/07 laws, for example, pensions were guaranteed to men with a 10 percent disability; in the 1920 law the minimum disability was 20 percent. The pension law also included income ceilings for pension recipients. The idea was that persons with high incomes would have their pensions reduced, though inflation made a mockery of the ceilings. By 1923, everyone received enormous, and worthless, incomes, yet under the income ceilings, pensioners could be cut from the roles. Most important, many of the law's allowances were discretionary. Civil servants could award them or not, on the basis of the applicant's "need." The cost-of-living allowance, for example, which originally every pensioner received, was changed and distributed only to those judged to be in "need." On top of all this, the state issued between 1922 and 1924 a series of new orders which drastically cut back the pension system.

One of the most serious blows was an amendment to the National Pension Law adopted in June 1923. The amendment eliminated from the pension rolls persons who were 20 percent disabled and raised the minimum to 30 percent. The *Reichsbund* estimated that the change eliminated some 489,000 veterans from the rolls.[12]

The Labor Ministry handled the amendment shrewdly. There just was not enough money for everyone, the ministry insisted. The lightly disabled should receive a small settlement and then be removed from the rolls. That way, the seriously disabled could receive a small increase while the overall budget could be reduced. In effect, the ministry was playing one group of veterans off against another, and in general, the tactic worked. The war victims organizations grudgingly agreed that, harsh as it was, the move was necessary.[13]

Within four months, war victims received another shock. In October 1923, the government issued a "Personnel Reduction Ordinance" designed to reduce government bureaucracy drastically. Though the measure was not directed against the war victims, they were affected by it. Disabled veterans were among the government employees dismissed. Both the *Reichsbund* and the *Zentralblatt* claimed that hundreds of severely disabled veterans were "thrown on to the street" because of the reductions.[14]

The reductions also sharply cut into the services available to war victims. Despite its immense case backlog, the National Pension Court staff was reduced by 13 percent, and nearly a quarter of the National Insurance Office staff was laid off.[15]

Two bills issued in February 1924 cut even more deeply into the pension machinery. One eliminated national financial support for local social services; henceforth, all social services for war victims would have to be funded by local governments.[16] This was a cruel blow for war victims. Regional and local governments seldom had the resources to provide the complex social services the war victims needed, and without funds from the national government, the local social services would be severely curtailed.

In addition, access to the National Pension Court was radically reduced. The staff at the court had urged throughout 1921 and 1922 that something be done to reduce the flood of appeals. The "Procedural Law" of February 1924 not only reduced the bases for appeal, but it also expanded the authority of the court to reject appeals without a hearing.[17]

By the end of 1923, then, many gains of the war victims' movement had been lost. The seven major organizations made a painful discovery. Despite their size and sophistication, despite the sympathy the government invariably expressed, despite all the talk about the "thanks of the Fatherland," the organizations were unable to protect their interests.[18]

II

As early as the summer of 1920, the war victims' groups had protested the inadequacies of the National Pension Law, and these protests were repeated throughout the following years. A February 1922 issue of the *Reichsbund,* for example, was devoted entirely to urgently needed amendments to the National Pension Law. The publication listed some 25 major changes needed in the law, all of which involved increased financial compensation and social services. The March issue continued the discussion and grouped the demands into three categories: increased pension rates; expanded social services; and improved medical care, including medical care for survivors.[19]

However, increased pension rates topped the list of priorities. The war victims insisted that the rates were ridiculously low. Arguments on the subject were extraordinarily convoluted. There was no "standard" pension, since the pensions and allowances were tied to the percentage of disability. Moreover, as pensions were adjusted for inflation, the rates varied rapidly. It is possible, however, to outline the financial conditions the war victims endured.

In February 1922, the Zentralverband submitted a statistical study to the Labor Ministry that tried to relate a number of separate variables.[20] Among other things, the study examined:

1. the monthly cost-of-living index published by the National Statistical Office, beginning in January 1921. This figure showed the minimum monthly income necessary to support a household with two adults

and three children. Costs of clothing and entertainment were not included in the index.

2. the pension of a 100 percent disabled veteran with three children, who received the standard (minimum) "equalization allowance."
3. the pension of a widow with three children.
4. the pension received by dependent parents.
5. the monthly income of the lowest ranking civil servant.

The resulting figures, in marks per month, are as follows:

	Minimum income index	100 percent disabled veteran	Widow's pension	Parents' pension	Civil servant's income
1920					
Apr.	–	750	551	174	975
June	–	750	551	174	975
Sept.	–	750	551	174	975
1921					
Jan.	900	814	596	188	1225
Apr.	875	814	596	188	1225
June	875	814	596	188	1225
Sept.	1100	934	681	218	1340
1922					
Jan.	1600	1034	716	288	1965

An obvious conclusion to be drawn from these figures is that even a 100 percent disabled veteran could scarcely live above the poverty level, and by January 1922, he dropped substantially below the minimum index. An ominous inference is that if 100 percent disabled veterans were this badly off, men with 90, 50, or 30 percent disabilities were in disastrous shape.

The widows' condition was catastrophic. A woman with three children to support presumably could survive with a smaller income than that needed by a five person household, but the gap between the widows' income and the poverty standard was still enormous. Parents were even worse off. Of course, they too could live on much less than a five-member family needed, but still, it is clear that their pension was too low to support them.

That the salary of the lowest paid civil servant was consistently *above* the minimum income level rankled greatly with war victims. The thought that even the lowliest bureaucrat in the pension office received more money than a 100-percent disabled hero of the Great War was infuriating.

Two ironies need to be pointed out here. When government officials considered the billions of marks devoted to pensions, they were horrified; when war victims considered the pittance they received, they were horrified too. Second, the pressure to increase pensions only placed the war victims on a treadmill. As inflation reduced the value of pensions, war victims demanded more expenditures, which only increased inflation, and in turn, reduced the value of the pension.[21]

It was not, however, only the provisions and rates provided by the National Pension Law but the entire process that infuriated the war victims. From the government's perspective, the system was rational and mathematical; the war victims saw it as arbitrary and capricious.

To begin with, there were all the papers to fill out, all the offices to visit, and all the lines to stand in. For example, a veteran would have to go to the local pension office, file an application, undergo a medical examination, and hope that his army records would turn up. If he needed medical care, he would have to go to the National Insurance System facilities, and they had their own forms to fill out. Help with a job, or re-education, came from the local social service agencies, and they had their own offices, forms, procedures, and lines. If there was a dispute, it had to be settled through a pension court, meaning more lines, more waiting, and more forms.

Some veterans tried to make light of all the paper work. An article called "Identification Papers" explained:

> There are a lot of them for disabled veterans, especially for us severely disabled veterans. In red and yellow and some have stripes; all sorts of different "papers" shine out of the vest pocket. One for the trains, one for the street-cars, one to show when you're waiting in the pension offices. And now, in the first days of January, O God, how often do you suddenly remember that you've forgotten to get your papers renewed.
>
> So you go to the social services office. In a line on the right, stand your comrades. Looks like a long wait.
>
> It might be a good idea to have "papers" which would help you get "papers" quickly. . . .[22]

But it was seldom funny. Dealing with the pension offices and courts was sometimes a harrowing experience. Commenting on procedures in the National Pension Court, the *Zentralblatt* asked angrily: "Does the triumph of justice really demand that the veteran or survivor stand at attention, and completely isolated, before the bar? Is it really necessary to use a tone of voice you usually hear in criminal proceedings, in order to suppress the fearful and unheard-of demands of the plaintiff?"[23]

The war victims took to the streets. In Regensburg in 1920, for example, troops and tanks had to be called in to break up a protest march by war victims.[24] They also expressed their anger through official channels. On November 14, 1921, delegates from all seven war victims' groups met with the President of the Republic. After introductions, delegate Schürmann, representing the Reichsbund, began: "The conditions of the war victims are catstrophic. The measures taken by the government are completely inadequate. . . . The unhappy financial condition of the nation is well known, but some sort of improvements must be introduced." A Frau Schaumberg, representing the Zentralverband, said: "We haven't come to beg, we've come to demand our rights! It's clear that the civil servants are far better thought of by the government. . . . We are worse off than the unemployed." President Ebert assured the delegation that the care of war victims was "close to his heart" and the problems were not the result of "malevolence" but of the general economic situation. The Labor Minister seconded the president's remarks. The war victims, however, were not impressed by the Labor Minister's comments. Said a delegate: "We've turned to the President, because we have lost all trust in the Labor Ministry; we no longer feel that our justified desires will be fulfilled by the ministry."[25] The meeting accomplished nothing. More conferences were arranged with Labor Ministry officials, war victims fumed and protested, but the steady decline in the pension system continued.

Why did the organizations, which in 1920 included more than one million women and men, prove so ineffective? One reason was that the movement, like that of the labor unions, suffered a drastic decline in membership during the years of astronomical inflation. In part, membership figures may have been misleading, as the groups themselves insisted. The figures were calculated according to dues paid, and as economic conditions deteriorated, fewer and fewer people were able to pay. In April 1918, the Reichsbund, for example, had 25,000 dues-paying members organized in 300 local chapters. In 1920, there were 651,000 members in 4,817 chapters and in 1922, 830,000 members in 7,000 chapters. In 1924, however, there were only 245,000 members in 4,075 chapters.[26] This decline in dues-paying members, even if it did not represent a loss of members' sympathies, did mean a precipitous drop in income.

Even as the groups declined, they came under subtle attack from the government. Though there was no evidence of a conspiracy by officials to discredit the groups, there was ample evidence that officials systematically reduced the ability of the war victims' organizations to defend their interests.

One method officials used was to reduce the war victims' greatest weapon, public sympathy. Again and again, officials stressed that the war victims had received their due and that further expenditures would place more burdens on already weary taxpapers. The pamphlet *Disabled Veterans! Survivors!* included the disclaimer:

Considering the monstrous financial burden placed on the entire nation, restraint had to be shown, so as not to place a completely unbearable burden on the nation . . . Therefore, many of the wishes of the war victims could not be met. They must and will recognize, however, that even the best will cannot make the impossible possible. They must and will recognize, that economically broken and only slowly recovering Germany, considering its other responsibilities, cannot give more than it now gives.[27]

Not surprisingly, this tactic drove a wedge between the war victims and the public, and slowly an image evolved of the pensioner as a shirker who lived at the public expense while everyone else had to scrimp and save. The war victims deeply resented this attitude. In 1921, the *Zentralblatt* complained that "the influence of the war victims and their organizations is being systematically reduced,"[28] and the following year, it accused the government of "stirring up hatred toward war victims."[29] In 1922, the *Reichsbund* told its readers: "The Labor Ministry has so influenced the social service agencies and the entire public opinion concerning war victims' care, that when the war victims' organizations present demands, they not only face serious difficulties with the government and the parliament, but they also face serious problems regarding public opinion."[30]

Elimination of the 1919 social service ordinance, which had required the states to set up separate offices to help war victims and, in effect, to treat them as special, particularly angered people. With the abrogation of this ordinance in 1924, the war victims were included among all the other welfare cases. This meant not only a sharp decline in social services available to them, but also that now they were simply one of the many "social problems." In Prussia's Rhine Province, for example, there had been a separate office for war victims, but after February 1924, they were cared for by an agency that also served "the needy, the insane, idiots, epileptics, the blind, and cripples."[31] War victims protested against this merger (which in many places had begun as early as 1922) but to no avail.[32]

Simultaneously, institutions designed to integrate representatives of the war victims into decision-making procedures lost their influence. The most conspicuous example of this was with the National Committee, which was attached to the Labor Ministry. Major pension actions were supposed to be brought before the committee before the ministry made any decisions. But in fact, the committee was rarely consulted.[33]

The greatest handicap the war victims faced, however, was their continuing division, which enabled the state to play one group against another. In 1919, for example, the Reichsbund and the Zentralverband were hard pressed for cash and both requested short-term government loans; the government's public affairs office supported the loans as a way of strengthening these two groups against the Communist Internationaler Bund.[34]

In late 1920, an effort began to heal the seven-way fracture in the movement.[35] At its Erfurt convention in November 1920, the Einheitsverband called for unification of the war victims' movement. But three of the groups showed no interest in merging. The little Bund erblindeter Krieger jealously guarded its neutrality. The Kyffhäuser Bund and the Deutscher Offiziersbund considered themselves veterans' groups first, and neither had any desire to merge with Social Democrats or Communists.

Still, a union of the remaining four mass organizations could have produced a "million member" movement and after an immensely complex series of negotiations, a formal summit took place in Weimar on April 16, 1921, attended by delegates from the Zentralverband, the Reichsbund, the Einheitsverband, and the Internationaler Bund. The talks were a disaster. The Internationaler Bund representatives insisted that the war victims' movement be integrated into the broader class struggle; when everyone else rejected this idea, the Internationaler Bundlers stalked out. The delegates from the social democratic Reichsbund and the nationalist Zentralverband could find no common ground. Negotiations collapsed. The Einheitsverband, which had promoted the talks in the first place, for a while seemed interested in merging with the much larger Reichsbund, but in the end, the Einheitsverband backed out, and in April 1922, officially informed the Reichsbund that plans for unification had to be dropped. At this point, a furious guerrilla war broke out as all of the organizations involved raided each others' local chapters for members. Ironically, the Einheitsverband, which had tried to organize a grand coalition, was decimated. It eventually reorganized under the name *Reichsverband deutscher Kriegsbeschädigter und Kriegshinterbliebener* (Reichsverband of Disabled Veterans and Survivors).

Why were the war victims unable to unify? They all talked about overcoming division. On specific issues, all seven groups could usually achieve some sort of compromise. And all of the war victims were disappointed with the pension system. Why, then, the hostility among the groups?

Institutional egoism played a role. Once established, the leadership of each group was loath to surrender its position of authority and independence. In a unified movement there could only be one chief, not seven. Convincing the other six to surrender their positions was a hopeless task.

But the division had a more profound cause. The appeal to neutrality was bankrupt. The war victims' groups denounced partisanship; yet, they all had been partisan from the first. Nor could the war victims avoid the divisions within German society; they could not rise above the social and economic crises of the times. Above all, they could not evade the divisive effects of the event so central to their lives. In writing about the war, the Reichsbund literature proclaimed "Never again!" while the Zentralverband literature staunchly defended the nobility and self-sacrifice of the German soldiers. The war victims, like the rest of the German people, had lost their common language. They could shout at each other, but not speak with each other.

Disabled veterans at a rally to protest pension reductions, Berlin Sportpalast, 1931.
(Photo: Ullstein, Berlin.)

CHAPTER 11

The War Victims' Movement and Weimar's Democratic Potential, 1924–1928

> The Reichsbund plays an important role in our political maturation and civic education of our people.
>
> —*Reichsbund*, October 1924

The middle years of the Weimar Republic, 1924–1928, attract far less attention than its feverish birth or violent end. Historians usually deny that Weimar was "doomed," and then proceed to outline in great detail all the reasons why it could not have survived anyway. Certainly this approach has history on its side; after all, the republic did collapse. Yet to see the republic exclusively from the perspective of 1933 is to miss the genuine democratic potential that it had earlier. This chapter will concentrate on some of the reasons for its collapse, and also on those factors that made democratic action possible during the republic. For all its sins, Germany did preserve a nervous sort of democracy between the world wars, and democracy was possible in part, because of the war victims. Their movement contributed in important ways to democratic debate and behavior in the republic.

The first part of this chapter outlines the major controversies about pensions between 1924 and 1927. The next sections concentrate on two war victims' demands: the extension of widows' benefits and the reform of the bureaucracy.

I

The issue in the pension debate between 1924 and 1927 was simple: successive governments were convinced that the system was unmanageable and had to be radically reduced, while the war victims' organizations believed that the system was inadequate and had to be vastly expanded.

The republic's Labor and Finance ministers frequently pointed to a wealth of statistics that "demonstrated" the extent to which the system was out of control. The officials claimed, for example, that the number of people on the rolls had increased, as the following figures show:[1]

Persons receiving permanent assistance	*1924*	*1926*	*1928*
disabled veterans (including men still on active duty)	771,353	792,143	820,211
widows	359,950	361,024	359,560
fatherless children	962,486	849,087	731,781
parentless children	65,486	62,070	56,623
parents (single)	131,187	141,064	148,230
parents (couples)	62,734	67,230	73,852
Persons receiving temporary assistance			
widows	6845	9987	12,441
fatherless children	3268	6337	8590
parentless children	169	396	537
parents (single)	—	6631	16,375
parents (couples)	—	10,354	22,772

But officials ignored the reason for the increase. The 1920 National Pension Law had eliminated men with disabilities of 10 percent, and the 1923 amendment had eliminated those with disabilities of 20 percent. Thus, between 1920 and 1923, nearly 800,000 disabled veterans were removed from the rolls.[2] Later, when the Labor Ministry agreed to reconsider some 20 percent disabilities, a horde of veterans rushed back into the system. Meanwhile, the number of widows on the rolls remained steady, and the number of needy parents went up. Only the number of orphans declined; when orphans reached 18, except in the most unusual circumstances, they were dropped from the pension rolls.

Officials pointed to another statistic with alarm. Petitions to the National Pension Court continued to grow.[3]

	Appeals	*Decisions*	*Backlog pending at year-end*
1924	15,316	39,889	18,613
1925	21,845	23,144	17,314
1926	34,793	26,471	25,636
1927	45,573	34,094	37,115

The 1924 drop from the previous year, in which 33,546 appeals were received, was the result of restrictions on grounds of appeal, but war victims quickly circumvented this hurdle. There was only one thing to do, Anton Kirschensteiner wrote to the president of the National Pension Court in 1926: "The constant increase in the number of appeals, and the consequent overburdening of the National Pension Court . . . require that thorough measures be taken. In this situation, only an effective cut back in the grounds of appeal can be considered."[4]

Meanwhile, the case load in the pension offices was staggering. In 1927, some 1,629,000 cases were processed, of which 442,000 were new applications. In 1928, 1,663,000 cases were still being considered.[5]

One set of figures, above all others, appalled officials—the costs of pensions. After the financial reforms of 1920 and 1921, about half of the funds available to the national government were either transferred back to the states or committed to reparations mandated by the peace treaties. Of funds remaining to the government, at least 30 percent were tied up in pension costs, as shown:[6]

	Funds available to Reich	Pension cost	Pension cost as percent of funds available
1924	3.4 billion marks	1.06 billion marks	31.2 percent
1925	4.1	1.42	34.1
1926	5	1.48	29.6
1927	5.2	1.61	30.9
1928	6	1.81	30%

One finance minister, testifying before a Reichstag committee in 1926, claimed that 40 percent of the government's money went for pensions.[7]

According to government officials, all these figures pointed to the need for cutting back the pension system. The war victims, however, had a different set of figures. In 1924, pensions were readjusted to conform to the new currency. Within months of the readjustment, pensioners claimed that the new rates were worse than the rates in 1914, which had been set by the 1906/07 laws. The *Zentralblatt,* the journal of the Zentralverband, published a table comparing pension rates under the old and the new law.[8]

Base Pension (in marks, monthly)

Disability	1906/07	May 1924 (without equalization allowance)
10 percent	19.50	—
20	24	—
30	28.50	4.10
40	33	5.50
50	37.50	8.20
60	42	10.25
70	46.51	13
80	51	16.40
90	55.50	20.50
100	60	27.30

The journal concluded:

So: the restrictions put through by the government succeeded. Of the original 1 1/2 million disabled veterans almost half have disappeared from the rolls . . . But still the government wasn't satisfied. Even after these restrictions, costs were still too high, and so the government cut back the pension rates themselves. If you compare the . . . rates of 1906 with the . . . 1924 rates, it's clear that the old rates . . . were significantly higher. The government, however, reduced rates at the very time it raised railroad ticket prices because, it said, the cost of living today is 50 percent higher than in 1914.

The seven war victims' groups believed that a third amendment to the National Pension Law was essential, not only to raise rates, but to expand the entire program. The Labor Ministry agreed that a third amendment was necessary, but for precisely the opposite reasons.

In the spring of 1925, under pressure from the war victims' lobbyists, the Reichstag began hearings on reform of the National Pension Law. The hearings plodded on until May 26, when they were brought up short by Finance Minister von Schlieben. His testimony was curt: the most that could be spent for improvements in the pension system was 220 million marks, a sum far below the one billion marks the war victims were demanding. The Reichstag could divide this amount any way it wanted, the minister said, but that was all the money available.

This put the hearing committee in a difficult position. Unable to agree on an amendment, it asked the Labor Ministry to come up with an amendment by mid-June.

The war victims' groups were not opposed to this procedure. They assumed that the Labor Minister would call the National Committee into session to debate the amendment. But, to their surprise, the committee was not called, nor was the draft amendment circulated among the war victims' groups for their opinion. When the text of the amendment leaked out, however, the war victims were furious.

On June 23, the groups jointly presented a counter-proposal to the Reichstag, and two weeks later delegates from the groups met with the committee. Yet, on July 21 the Reichstag passed the Labor Ministry's version virtually unchanged.[9]

The third amendment was not all bad, from the pensioners' perspective. There were rate increases for the especially needy, such as the severely disabled and dependent parents. However, most of the demands of the organizations had been denied.[10] The reason given by the Labor Ministry was: "Now as before, the financial situation of the nation, and especially the situation anticipated for the coming year, makes it necessary to restrict all avoidable expenditures."[11]

During the next two years, two more amendments were added to the National Pension Law. Their passage paralleled the events of 1925. The groups demanded improvements; the Labor Ministry urged restrictions;

the Reichstag passed the Labor Ministry's amendment, and the war victims protested.[12] Again and again, the war victims groups insisted that the Labor Ministry was their intractable foe. According to Paul Riemer, the keynote speaker at the Reichsverband's 1926 convention, "We had to fight the sharpest battle with out constant enemy, the Labor Ministry."[13] Karl Tiedt, the leader of the Internationaler Bund, and briefly a Communist member of the Reichstag, was even more emphatic, according to Reichstag minutes.

> *Tiedt:* It's the same routine as in the years gone by. . . . The organizations prove in their reports that the assurances of the government about care for survivors are nothing but lies, nothing but a swindle! (*Right! from the communists. President's bell.*)
> *Vice President Graef:* Representative Tiedt! This type of speech is unparliamentary.
> *Tiedt:* Yes, considering what the war victims have had to endure from this Reichstag, it's pretty hard to be parliamentary.[14]

The Labor Ministry had enormous influence in shaping legislation between 1924 and 1927, while the war victims' groups had little, and the Reichstag had even less. The legislation was formed by the civil servants. This was the point Erich Rossmann, one of the leaders of the Reichsbund, tried to make during the 1925 debate: "We don't need any parliamentary resolutions anymore, everything can be done nicely, thank you, by the bureaucracy . . . The result is that disabled veterans, in many cases, instead of demanding their rights, simply look for crumbs which might fall from the table of the almighty bureaucracy."[15]

It was in large measure this hostility to the bureaucracy that drove the seven groups together. After the failure of the 1921/1922 unification talks, there was never any serious effort at merger, and friction continued. Yet, the groups were able to present a united front against the Labor Ministry, not only because they disliked the pension system, but also because they had developed a common attitude toward social policy. Social policy, they agreed, was not bound by abstract laws of economics, as the finance and labor ministers argued. Throughout the middle years of the republic, the war victims groups battled to politicize and demystify social policy, to show that such policy rested on conscious human choice.

Two events in 1926 demonstrated to the war victims that pensions were unquestionably political. In that year, the National Pension Court reached its decision on General Walter von Lüttwitz's pension. A leader of the abortive Kapp Putsch of 1920, the general had been accused of treason and had gone underground. After he and his co-conspirators were granted amnesty in 1925, he surfaced and demanded a pension from the republic he had tried to overthrow. The National Pension Court finally decided in November 1926 that, as a retired soldier, Lüttwitz was entitled to a pension. The liberal and left-wing press was outraged that the "putschist Lüttwitz" could get a fat pension, at the very time when millions of disabled veterans and widows were being told that there was no money for them.[16]

In the same month, an even bigger pension bomb-shell exploded. For years, conservatives in the Reichstag had demanded that the Finance Minister publish the names of the republic's top pensioners. Finally, in November 1926, the Finance Ministry issued its report and the nation was shocked. Of the 1,857 top pensioners, almost all were retired civil servants or soldiers from the old regime, and their pensions were enormous: 104 civil servants received yearly pensions averaging 16,692 marks; 1,599 retired generals received pensions averaging over 12,000 marks.[17] This was at a time when a widow with two children received less than 3,000 marks a year.[18]

Except for the two right-wing groups, the war victims' organizations were unanimous in arguing that these pensions proved that the government's constant appeal to "economic reality" was a lie; who received what was a question not of economics but of politics. After 1926, the political center and left joined with the groups in demanding that pensions for generals and civil servants be reduced to free up funds for war victims.[19]

The groups, especially the Reichsbund, deeply resented the Finance Minister's influence on the pension system. During the 1925 debate in the Reichstag, for example, Erich Rossmann agreed that costs were high, but the fact remained that millions of war victims had to be cared for. And yet, he added: "Among the war victims outside there is the bitter feeling: as long as we were out there, in the mud and slime, then they made us all sorts of promises; now, when we're at home, these promises simply are forgotten. Now the only thing that matters are the calculations of the Finance Minister."[20] When the idea arose in 1927 of transferring the entire pension system to the Finance Ministry, the Reichsbund was outraged. Their newspaper proclaimed: "We war victims oppose the handling of our affairs as purely "fiscal" matters. We demand from pension officials a social sensitivity."[21]

The Reichsbund insisted that an adequate pension policy was inextricably bound up with a democratic political order. Together with the Internationaler Bund, the group took an uncompromising stand against war and militarism,[22] and its leadership was keenly aware that their organization, the largest war victims' group, had mobilized hundreds of thousands of women and men and had involved them in political action: "The Reichsbund plays an important role in the political maturation and civic education of our people."[23] Five years later, the Reichsbund insisted on the same point: "We take the opportunity once again, to make clear that we are an organization which stands firmly on the basis of democratic institutions."[24]

Peace, democracy, and social policy were all bound together, according to the Reichsbund. Pensions were not simply a technical, economic issue; they were, above all, a political issue. This argument served to make millions of war victims aware that it was not fate or economics but human, political choice that determined their lives. Thus, the politicization of the pension technology contributed to the development of democratic values.

Though democracy failed, some democratic elements did exist during the republic, to no small extent a result of action of the mass war victims' groups. The politicization of social policy was only one area in which the movement contributed to democratic values; another was in the political role of women.

II

During the Republic the condition of survivors, particularly war widows, was grim.[25] In 1930, Dr. Karl Nau published a detailed examination of the conditions of survivors in Darmstadt; his findings provide a glimpse into their lives. (The study was undertaken in 1928 and 1929, at the request of Darmstadt's welfare and youth office.)[26] Nau studied 556 widows, 768 fatherless orphans, and 65 parentless orphans. Almost half the women, 49.1 percent, were widows of blue-collar wokers, 13.4 percent were widows of white-collar employees, 17.9 percent were widows of self-employed men, and 19.6 percent were widows of civil servants.[27] About 30 percent of the widows were employed, and of that figure, only 17.3 percent had fulltime jobs—in most cases as cleaning women, house-keepers, or white-collar workers. Seventy percent had no outside employment, and their entire income came from their pensions, which were extraordinarily meager.[28] The highest pension that a widow of a skilled worker with two children could receive, for example, was about 1,848 marks a year. Even if she supplemented this with a part-time job, it was unlikely that she would have an income exceeding 3,000 marks a year, which was well below the poverty line.[29]

Nau calculated the income the deceased husbands would have earned and compared it to the widows' incomes. The results: 60 percent of the widows had incomes at least 10 percent lower than what their husbands would have earned, and nearly half of these women had incomes 20 percent or lower than their husbands' hypothetical incomes. About 25 percent of the women had incomes equivalent to what their husbands could have earned; 15 percent had higher incomes.[30] It was not the poor who suffered the greatest decline in income; they did not have much income to lose.[31] The wives of professionals experienced the greatest drop; in this group, some 78 percent had incomes that were only half of what their husbands would have earned.[32]

All this meant a mass decline in social position. Nau estimated that some 45 percent of the widows in Darmstadt had dropped into a lower social position following the death of their husbands. In any case, he concluded, "the fact is that an income based solely on the pension is, even in the best of circumstances, scarcely sufficient. . . . As for an existence-minimum, that only can be attained when the pension is supplemented by some other income. In fact, this occurs in many cases. Where, however, the pension is not supplemented, hardship unquestionably occurs."[33]

War widows, of course, had been saying this since 1914, and the war victims' movement increasingly focused on the needs of the widows. In the early days of the movement, however, women were not always welcome in the organizations. It was not until 1920, for example, that the Reichsbund accepted women as full members. After 1920, widows' issues became increasingly important to the entire movement.

One of the earliest issues involved women as lay judges on the pension courts. The movement demanded that, at least in cases involving survivors, women be allowed to serve as lay judges, and eventually, legislation was passed to this effect. But health care for widows was the most important issue.[34] In demanding that medical care be extended to widows, the movement was accepting the fact that widows were victims of the war and deserved the same benefits as disabled veterans.[35] For financial reasons, the Labor Ministry rejected the extension of medical benefits to survivors; nevertheless, the movement never abandoned the demand.

In the larger war victims' groups, the Internationaler Bund, the Reichsbund, the Reichsverband and the Zentralverband, women were accepted as equal members. They served on the executive committees, were part of delegations that debated with government officials, and were active in organizational affairs.

This alliance between veterans and widows was a unique element in the life of the Republic. Through the war victims' movement, women learned to take charge of their own lives, to participate in public affairs, and, together with their male allies, to confront the pension bureaucracy.[36]

III

The pension system was trapped in a maze of bureaucratic red tape. Bureaucrats themselves complained endlessly about this. For example, in September 1924, a representative of the Association of County Governments in Thüringen wrote to the Interior Ministry:

The work involved with the supplemental pensions is without question a major burden for the local social services offices. In the Weimar area, for example, there are some 2,200 people who receive the supplemental pension. That comes to 30,000 marks which must be distributed in the smallest sums every month. Requesting funds from the government, the constantly changing ways of calculating the pension, the precise calculations of payments, the careful watching of recipients to insure that they really are in need, the resolution of complaints, and lately the issuance of advance payments, all this requires two to three employees do nothing at all but handle the supplemental pension. . . .

By the fifth of every month, the funds distributed in the preceding month have to be reported. By the fifth of each quarter, the total number of recipients of the supplemental pension . . . must be reported. This particular report includes no fewer than 22 columns. By the fifth of each month, funds required for the next month have to be requested.[37]

While the officials complained about the inefficiency of the pension machinery, the war victims criticized its dehumanizing effects. A basic demand of the victims was that they be treated like "subjects" and not "objects," a theme as old as the movement itself.[38] How the pension machinery ground down human values is graphically depicted in a 1928 newspaper article. It is titled "Before the Pension Court," and it was written by a veteran's representative:

Königin-Augusta-Strasse 26. A colossal building of grey sandstone, with pillars and decorated facade. The hearing rooms begin just after you step through the giant doors. The long corridors are quiet and empty. Like a grave. A couple of guards go softly back and forth. Now and again, a bell trills loudly in the stillness. That means—consultations have ended, and that the parties, if they are present, can enter the room to hear the decision.

In this quiet building, the war still lives in its most frightful creations.

Hundreds and thousands of files contain the suffering of the victims of the mass murder, who, ten years later, are still demanding their thanks from the nation. One cannot really imagine the enormous pain which is stapled and filed in doctors' reports, in pension requests.

Nothing in this peaceful and official building suggests that behind almost every door it is a question of human fate, of life and death, of the naked existence of physically ruined people, that behind every door is a bitter struggle. Every half hour the bell rings, every half hour someone's fate is decided.

Room number 40. Fifteen cases to be heard. Disabled veterans from Berlin, Breslau, Koblenz, their hopes placed in this highest court. In the room, behind a barrier, sit four older men around a horseshoe-shaped desk. Before the chairman is a barricade of lawbooks, over which he can scarcely see. . . .

A representative from one of the organizations is speaking for a disabled veteran from Waldenburg. . . . Medical reports are read aloud. As always, they are against the veteran. In scientific, complicated, and incomprehensible language, the complaints of the patient are rejected. . . .

The position of the doctors in most cases simply can't be understood. They are on the side of the state. They are paid by the state. In reality, this is the cause of the pension arguments, since, in the end, what matters here is not human feeling, but the letter of the law. And the paragraphs of the law which are applied to the war victims are just as bungled, ambiguous, manipulable and dependent on judges' caprice as are all our laws.

One lay judge reads the medical report aloud. The judge next to him yawns, closes his eyes, opens them wearily: how many cases like this has he heard? No reason to get excited. A question of poison gas, a wagon axel rammed the man in the stomach . . . stomach pains? Ah—but the man already had bad teeth in 1913! The man has been taking stomach tablets for ten years, but they don't relieve the pain. Vomiting. . . .

Finally, my case. . . . I say: I don't know anything about the letter of the law. I know the man and his illness. He won't live much longer. It's frightful, the way he shivers, the way other people avoid him, the way his own children are kept from him. I say: all the paragraphs are crazy if the state doesn't give everything in such a case that the law says it can give. . . .

Consultations last ten minutes. Again the bell. Judgment: the court declares the man entitled to a "care allowance."

Finally, After 11 months. And how long will he enjoy his "care allowance?"

In the room, the next case is ready. The medical files are opened. The four judges look coldly and dully at the law books.

They are conducting the last mopping-up operation of the mass murder. After 10 years. You can't see the long rows of graves, which have already done their work.[39]

The system failed not only to show human sympathy but even to exhibit rationality. It seemed utterly arbitrary and capricious. For example, the case of Otto Götsch: In November 1915, he fell into a trench filled with icy water and afterward became almost totally blind. He applied for a pension. Ten years later, the National Pension Court ruled that Götsch had been blind before he was drafted, and that anyway, he would have gone blind someday. Therefore, no pension. Medical testimony supported the court's decision, but the veterans' press found the decision preposterous.[40]

There were scores of cases like this. Wilhelm Schmidt had lost a leg during the war. Since he could not handle an umbrella and his crutches at the same time, he bought a raincoat and asked the court to be reimbursed for its cost. For over a year, his case rested somewhere in the pension judiciary. "Legless" men were entitled to extensive benefits, but, the judges asked, did legless include those who still had one leg? The judges decided against Schmidt.[41] Paul Lauer, who had lost a foot in the war, asked the local pension office to compensate him for a special pedal for his bicycle. The cost was 20 marks. The office refused. Fourteen months later, the National Pension Court determined that Lauer was entitled to compensation.[42]

Franz Reimann was not as fortunate. In July 1916, he was declared 100 percent disabled, and in December 1916 and July 1921, doctors reconfirmed the opinion. In June 1924, however, another doctor decided that Reimann's problem was hereditary in nature, not service-related, and that therefore the pension should be canceled. Could doctors change a man's status like this? In January 1926 the National Pension Court said yes. A veteran could be removed from the pension rolls if his medical diagnosis changed. Reimann, meanwhile, had consulted another doctor, who argued that Reimann's condition was service-related, but the court was not convinced. Reimann was removed from the rolls.[43]

The war victims repeatedly charged that the bureaucracy itself was out of control and that laws were so convoluted that they were impossible to understand. Paul Riemer insisted in his speech at the Reichsverband's 1926 convention: "We suffer from a wealth of laws that we no longer can master. It is absolutely essential to demand of the lawmakers that they create laws that are simple, that they make laws people can understand."[44]

Officials certainly were not oblivious to this problem. Buried in the files of the National Pension Court is an article, that had been clipped from a Berlin newspaper and circulated among the judges. It was entitled "Legislative Necessity," and it said in part:

> Out of the massive chaos of all the new laws, which our parliament, with no good reason produces, even the technical expert can't make any sense. Meanwhile, the layman has long since given up and folded his hands on his lap. All the conscientiousness, all the intelligence, all the good will of our judges make no difference when confronted with this huge mass of legislation. Bad decisions are inevitable, considering the confusion of most of the laws. And yet, if the judge follows the letter of the law exactly, the decisions will be absolutely insane. . . . The laws divide everything up into the tinest details, as if through this specialization, every problem, every special class and group can be taken care of. The result is that the unity of the law has long since disappeared, and every session of the parliament only makes the situation more hopeless . . .[45]

A number of comments were scribbled on the article. One judge wrote: "read with interest." Dr. Rabeling wrote: "to the files." Although they were aware of the incomprehensibility of the laws, officials were unwilling or unable to do anything about it.

There was for the republic a grave danger here. Conservative groups, such as the Zentralverband, and the communist Internationaler Bund, had always been skeptical, if not hostile, toward the republic. The bureaucracy was for them only a manifestation of its insensitivity and incompetence. For groups such as the Reichsbund, it was extremely difficult to attack the pension bureaucracy, and yet to defend the republic. By 1928, their dilemma had become acute.

Poster: "National Socialist—or the sacrifices were in vain." (Photo: Langewies-che-Brandt, Munich)

CHAPTER 12

The End and the Beginning of the War Victims Problem, 1929–1939

GOVERNMENT ADMITS COLLAPSE OF SOCIAL INSURANCE—PENSIONS
AS OF 1 JUNE NOT YET SECURED—GOVERNMENT HELPLESS . . . this is
the frightful result of the black—red government of the past 14 years. The
end with terror is here.

—*Völkischer Beobachter*, May 29/30, 1932

German history does not flow, it lurches, often suddenly, sometimes violently. In its course, Golo Mann writes, "Disinterest in politics
gives way to hectic political activity, variety to complete uniformity; from
prostration, Germany rises to aggression, collapses again into chaos and
then with incredible speed recovers to a new and hectic prosperity."[1]
Certain years—1848, 1871, 1918, 1933, 1945—mark sharp, dramatic shifts in
German life. The history of the Weimar Republic conventionally ends in
1933, with good reason. Though the republic was never officially abolished, the National Socialist state was something new. The story of the
German victims of the Great War might well end in that year too; after
1933, their organizations disappeared, and the political aspects of the problem at long last receded.

Yet these apparent shifts of German history are misleading. Day followed day, month followed month, social and economic structures proved
amazingly impervious to change, the same people collected taxes and directed traffic. In particular, 1918 did not mean a radical break in German
life, and in some ways, neither did 1933. The war victims did not disappear,
the republic's institutions designed to care for them continued to function,
and in fact, the continuity between 1933 and 1939 is as striking as the
obvious change. The decisive difference in the war victims issue is much
more properly marked in 1939. After that date, the victims of the Great
War ceased to be a unique group. They were joined by a new generation of
war victims.

The first section of this chapter will concentrate on the war victims' experience in the last frantic years of the Republic, 1929 to 1933. The second section will examine their lives in the National Socialist state, which proclaimed that war victims were its "first citizens."

I

In the spring of 1929, the government ran out of pension money. The trouble started with the Labor Ministry's decision in December 1927 to reconsider men with 20 percent disabilities who had been excluded from the pension rolls. The result was a staggering increase in the number of disabled veterans receiving pensions; in 1926, there was 792,143 disabled veterans on the rolls, and by 1930, the number had jumped by over 13 percent, to 897,940.[2] The Labor Ministry had not programmed enough funds into the 1928/29 budget to cover all the new people, and the pension fund fell some 78 million marks short. The Finance Minister, Rudolf Hilferding, was furious. He insisted that Labor Minister Rudolf Wissell do something to bring the pension system under control. Above all, Hilferding demanded, access to the system had to be drastically curtailed.[3] When plans were made for the 1929/30 budget, the government was determined to cut pension costs.[4]

The government's financial problems went beyond pensions, however. By 1929, pressure for cuts in social programs was intense. Virtually all of German industry demanded that the budget be slashed,[5] and after the economic shocks of 1929 and 1930, the pressure to dismantle the welfare machinery was irresistible.

The sudden collapse of the German economy was dizzying. Every indicator of economic health plunged within a matter of a few months. If 1928's industrial production is set at 100, for example, industrial production for the following years was: 1929—100; 1930—87; 1931—70; 1932—58. Changes in per capita social product were: 1928: +1 percent; 1929: −5 percent; 1930: −4.2 percent; 1931: −12 percent; 1932: −5 percent. Worst of all were the unemployment figures. In 1928, about 6.3 percent of the labor force was unemployed; in 1929, unemployment was 8.5 percent; 1930, 14 percent; 1931, 21.9 percent; and 1932, 29.9 percent.[6]

The response of the government of Heinrich Brüning, which came to office in March 1930, was radical retrenchment. Brüning explained:

I will resist to the end any type of inflationary measures, whatever they might be. I will resist them not only because it is right, not only in order to protect the weak, but because I am convinced that a genuine balance in the German economy, whatever the bitter price might be, must be restored. I am convinced that any inflationary measure will, ultimately, disrupt this balance, and will simply cover over all the mistakes of the past.[7]

This effort to cut spending was seen by the war victims as a full-scale government assault. In the spring of 1930, Erich Rossmann warned his colleagues in the Reichsbund: "This much is sure, that socially reactionary forces have launched a total offensive against the pension system. In parliament, we are engaged at present in a kind of pension trench war."[8]

The "war" had escalated when Adam Stegerwald, the Labor Minister in the first Brüning cabinet, told parliamentary leaders that deep cuts were essential in public spending in general, and in war victims' care in particular:

> The labor minister briefly explained the possibility of a quick amendment to the disabled veterans' law. He explained that this amendment had already been planned by his predecessor, who had agreed that it was necessary. The purpose of the amendment was to cut the number of persons receiving pensions, especially considering that the number of pensioners had gone up by 64,000 in the preceding year. Quick action is essential, in order to prevent a similar increase this year.[9]

Every aspect of the pension system came under attack. The 1929/30 budget cut some 36 million marks from pensions, despite the increased number of disabled veterans on the rolls, and subsequent administrative action by the Labor Ministry restricted other benefits: lump-sum payments were reduced; new medical examinations were stepped up to eliminate frauds; and advance payments were denied.[10]

The most determined assault on the pension system began in 1930. Under the first emergency decree of July 26, 1930, compensation for indirect injury was denied and severe restrictions were imposed on new applications. The decrees of 1931 and 1932 were devastating.[11] Pension payments were no longer calculated from the date of application but from the date when the officials finally approved the application; educational benefits and benefits for widows, orphans, and parents were cut; and lump-sum payments were virtually eliminated. In 1931, the *Zentralblatt* reported some 22 major cuts in benefits since 1929.[12] The following year, the Bund erblindeter Krieger listed some 18 different measures that reduced blinded veterans' benefits,[13] and a Reichsbund pamphlet contained more than 24 major reductions and restrictions.[14]

The war victims publicly protested in every major city. In May 1931, the Reichsbund reported that more than a half-million war victims had surged into the streets to denounce the government's actions. In June 1932 police were called when a mob of disabled verterans tried to storm the Labor Ministry on Scharnhorststrasse in Berlin.[15] Delegations from the groups met unsuccessfully with Labor Ministry officials,[16] and at the sessions of the National Committee on War Victims' Care, representatives of the war victims denounced government policies.[17]

The war victims' press exploded with indignation. Between 1929 and 1933, newspapers and journals carried such headlines as "Intolerable Hardship," "Fight and Don't Give Up," "The Murderous Emergency Decree," "The Blow against the War Victims."[18] In an editorial, the *Zentralblatt* told the government: "We warn yet again, in this final hour, with all the earnestness and seriousness at our command, against the morally and politically questionable measures which have been taken against the war victims. May our warning receive the attention it deserves."[19] Letters were fired off to government officials. In a letter to President von Hindenburg, the Reichsbund leadership raised the specter of radicalization, saying: "From a political viewpoint too, we warn most seriously against these new attacks on pensions. Nothing is won for the public good, and much is lost if the great majority of the war victims, as a result of these governmental measures, are radicalized to the left or to the right."[20] In a letter to Chancellor Brüning on behalf of the survivors of reserve officers, a woman wrote pithily: "A government which would pass such decrees has already judged itself."[21]

The warnings and protests left the government unmoved.

Between 1928 and 1933, the budget for veterans' pensions was slashed by about one-third, and during this time, the Labor Ministry continued to decree administrative reductions.[22]

Why were the war victims unable to protect themselves? There were a number of reasons. During the economic crisis, public support had been translated into suspicion, jealousy, and hostility. Since 1920 the government had warned taxpayers that the war victims' groups were too grasping. Industrialists, who urged social cutbacks, argued that the pension system was filled with frauds. The unemployed eyed pensioners unsympathetically, for they at least had some income. Some social service officials considered care for war victims more of a burden than a responsibility. The welfare office in Stralsund complained to the Union of Administrators in 1930 that cuts in war victims' benefits would shift the burden of care from the national government to the already hard-pressed local welfare offices.[23] Employers complained about the trouble caused by having to hire disabled veterans.[24] One manager wrote that healthy workers were often jealous of the pensions received by the severely disabled.[25]

Newspaper articles claimed that the pension system was rife with frauds, shirkers, and phonies. According to the *Berliner Tageblatt:* "It certainly appears that granting pensions to conscious or unconscious frauds overburdens the pension system. . . . A corrupting pension-neurosis threatens to infect the body politic."[26] An editorial of February 22, 1930, in Berlin's *Vossische Zeitung,* which claimed that scores of fradulent disabled veterans could be purged from the system, sparked angry replies by the war victims' organizations.[27] The Reichsbund, in November 1930, angrily denounced the wave of accusations of pension cheating that suddenly seemed to fill the press.[28]

The strangest attack on the war victims came from a book by Ernst Mann, *Moral der Kraft,* which had been written shortly after the war and had a modest revival after 1930. With bizarre logic, Mann claimed the disabled were consuming the resources of the healthy and, therefore, should voluntarily commit suicide. He urged disabled veterans in particular to perform this "last heroic deed." The war victims' press, of course, repudiated the book.[29] Commented the *Reichsverband:*

> Again and again it has been demonstrated, that those who are the most violent, are those who know the least about the war. Anyone who experienced the mass murder could never justify killing people, no matter how stupid he might be! "Destroy the weak and the sick!" Mass murder will solve impoverished Germany's problems about as much as slaughtering the innocents solved Israel's monarchy question.[30]

But at least one local politician seemed to take Mann seriously. The Reichsbund quoted a Nazi member of the Baden state legislature as saying: "It's just not right to spend millions of marks on the cripples, the diseased and the incurable, when hundreds of thousands of the healthy blow their brains out because of the economic crisis."[31]

At the same time, key institutions were in disarray. By 1932, the Reichstag lacked any ability to affect policy. Decisions in the National Pension Court were overwhelmingly (70–80 percent) against the war victims.[32] The court was ultimately controlled by the Labor Ministry, and the National Committee had no influence on the Labor Minister. And at the local level, the advisory councils, which included war victims and were designed to advise welfare officials, had ceased to function.[33]

Moreover, the victims of the Great War were getting older. The *Zentralblatt* reported in 1930 that the average disabled veteran was 50 years old.[34] The radicals of 1918 and 1919 now had jobs and families to consider. And a new generation had come of age, which had its own cares and did not see the needs of the war victims as crucial. The *Zentralblatt* commented mournfully:

In every meeting of disabled veterans, one sees more and more grey hair. . . .
We have no younger generation in our organization, to whom we could
transfer our duties—unless, of course, another war produces new legions of
cripples and sick, something we pray to God will not happen. . . . The new
generation will not have much time for the old man or woman, even if they are
disabled veterans or survivors. New generations will have their own worries,
and our calls for our rights will echo without response.[35]

But the major reason for the inability of the war victims to control their fate
was political. By 1931 the movement was divided among itself and incapable
of concerted action. All the protestations of neutrality, of being "above
politics," could not disguise the profound ideological differences among
the seven major groups. While the effort to politicize social policy (discussed in the last chapter) contributed to Weimar democracy, it also killed
the war victims' movement. Politics were more powerful in dividing the
movement than pension concerns were in uniting it.

The Internationaler Bund had been tied to the Communist Party since
1919, although Karl Tiedt, the Bund's founder, was far more a radical
democrat than a Leninist, and it was only after 1926, when he was ousted as
the Bund's leader, that the Bund became a disciplined extension of the
party.[36] Hugo Gräf, Tiedt's successor, was also a disabled veteran.[37] He
had long been active in the Internationaler Bund and in the Communist
Party. Under his leadership, the Bund followed the party line. With equal
vehemence it denounced Nazis and Social Democrats. According to one of
the Bund's 1932 pamphlets:

The National Socialists consider the pensioners to be unnecessary ballast, and
demand from them nothing less than voluntary suicide. . . . The red United
Front includes millions of workers, and white-collar employees, pensioners,
artisans and shopkeepers, all of whom suffer the greatest need. On the other
side, are the agents of capitalism, supported by the social democratic leaders,
who intend to continue the exploitation of the working masses.[38]

The Reichsbund, founded by Social Democrats, fully endorsed the
Republic. The government's policies put the Reichsbund in an awkward
position, however, for those policies were opposed by the majority of war
victims. The Reichsbund's chairman, Christoph Pfänder, warned the government of the discontent it was provoking: "It cannot be a matter of
indifference to you, if the great mass of the war victims are radicalized to the
left or to the right."[39]

Nevertheless, the Reichsbund defended the Republic and attacked the
Nazis both in print[40] and in public rallies. In July 1932, Pfänder, protected
by bodyguards from the social democratic Reichsbanner, addressed a

Reichsbund rally in Munich's Bürgerbräukeller. A Munich paper reported his speech:

"Uniforms are more important to the Nazis than the needs of the poor devils among the people. The people are only tools to the Nazis, to be used to get political power." To great approval, the speaker concluded by calling on the war victims not to allow themselves to be misused. They must not allow themselves to be deluded by the promises of a so-called "Third Reich"; instead, they must elect republicans, who have the courage and will to give the republic a social content.[41]

A 1932 pamphlet stated the Reichsbund's position:

The promoters of the Third Reich have betrayed the war victims! . . . The National Socialists intend to place war victims back under military domination!

We must decide: whether the German people will rule itself, by means of the democratic-republican constitution—or—whether rule by emergency decree will go on, leading to the scandal of a dictatorship. . . . From our Front experience we have learned that it is our mission to struggle for understanding among all nations, and at home, to struggle for a just social policy and an equal distribution of social burdens. . . . \

We in the Reichsbund declare that we support the democratic-republican constitution, and that we, as veterans and survivors, have the duty to insure that the republic has a clear social content.[42]

While the Internationaler Bund supported the Communists and the Reichsbund struggled to defend the republic, the other five groups had shifted sharply to the right. The Deutscher Offiziersbund and the Kyffhäuser Bund were veterans' groups first, and had always been anti-socialist and enthusiastically patriotic. Both had been sceptical of the Republic from the first. The Zentralverband also had been nationalist and anti-socialist since its beginnings in 1919. Moreover, the type of social policy its leader, Otto Thiel, advocated paralleled the position of the radical right.[43] Thus, in the Republic's crisis, it was no surprise that the Zentralverband looked to the right to find protection for war victims.

What was surprising was the attitude of the Reichsverband, which was ideologically to the right of the Reichsbund, but to the left of the Zentralverband. Periodically, the Reichsverband had hinted at merger with the Reichsbund, and it always supported the Republic. Yet, when *Vorwärts* asked an unnamed official of the Reichsverband to take a position regarding the Republic in 1931, the response was cautious: ". . . well, that is a delicate area of high politics. The Verband is not against the republic. But, many veterans feel that the old form of the state was better than the form today.''[44]

The National Socialists enthusiastically wooed the war victims, who were several million strong, possessed an extensive organizational apparatus, and were disgusted with the Republic's pension system—all of which made them an extremely attractive constituency to the Nazis. In November 1930, the Nazis created a special party section to concentrate on war victims; its leader was a Bavarian, Hanns Oberlindober. A junior officer during the war, Oberlindober was severely wounded in 1918. He attempted a career as a merchant in Munich, but was unsuccessful; in 1922, he drifted into the young National Socialist party and became a loyal party activist. In 1930, he organized the Nazi campaign to woo the war victims.[45]

Nazi literature promised a sweeping reform of the pension machinery, and pledged to honor war victims as the "first citizens of the state." Adolf Hitler, Nazi pamphlets pointed out, was himself a wounded veteran. He was the "unknown soldier" who had come back to life to lead the front generation in its recreation of the German nation. The literature appealed to the front experience as a unifying force. The National Socialists embodied the spirit of the front, the literature proclaimed; it was not a party, but a popular movement, dedicated to the values born in the trenches. Only the National Socialists, therefore, could understand the needs and desires of disabled veterans and survivors. The National Socialist Party, a 1930 editorial in the *Völkischer Beobachter,* the party newspaper, explained,

> has always stood for a just and extensive program of care for the victims of the war. It is a matter of honor, to care for the Front soldiers, who gave their blood for Germany, and who suffered physically and economically because of their self-sacrifice. May all the war victims stand united, prepared to struggle, in the ranks of our movement. You can be sure, war comrades, that only in a Third Reich which is based on the ideals for which you fought and bled, will your future be secure.[46]

By the summer of 1932, in the depth of the Republic's crisis, the war victims' movement was as paralyzed as the rest of the nation. While the Internationaler Bund supported the Communists and the Reichsbund supported the Republic, the other five groups merged into the Nazi movement. In July 1932, the Zentralverband and the Reichsverband held a joint convention in Bremen. Leaders of both groups attacked the republic's pension policies, and insisted that unity within the movement was essential. Therefore, the leaders concluded, the Reichsverband and the Zentralverband would merge into a single organization, which would be named the *Reichsverband deutscher Kriegsopfer.*

One of the delegates to the Bremen convention was Hanns Oberlindober, and after 1932, contacts between the newly created Reichsverband and the rapidly growing Nazi party became frequent. In September 1932, the *Völkischer Beobachter* featured an article by the Reichsverband's chairman, Dietrich Lehmann, who urged war victims to unify in a single, neutral, yet patriotic group. He regretted that "some" groups (meaning the Internationaler Bund and the Reichsbund) were still politically "partisan." The newly created Reichsverband, he concluded, would work diligently for all the war victims, and would avoid political partisanship.[47]

After January 30, 1933, when Hitler became chancellor, the Reichsverband rushed to forge some formal link with the triumphant Nazi party. Events in the first months of 1933 moved at blinding speed. In March, the Reichsverband joined with the Deutscher Offiziersbund, the Kyffhäuser Bund, and the Bund erblindeter Krieger in a temporary alliance called the *National Kampfgemeinschaft deutscher Kriegsopferverbände*. Representatives of this new alliance met with Oberlindober in Munich throughout March. In April, the Reichsverband, speaking on behalf of its coalition partners, issued a press release:

> Following the example of our honored Field Marshal von Hindenburg, and that of the people's chancellor, and disabled Front comrade, Adolf Hitler, who has taken up the task of rebuilding the German nation, the German, national war victims associations have decided to form a single national organization.[48]

The new group was called the National Socialist Reichsverband. Its leader was Hanns Oberlindober.

On April 14, 1933, Good Friday, the creation of the NS Reichsverband was announced during a memorial service for the war dead, which was broadcast over national radio.[49] Three months later, there was a final restructuring, as German war victims were "coordinated" into a single organization named *Nationalsozialistische Kriegsopferversorgung* (NSKOV), National Socialist War Victims Care. During ceremonies in Berlin's Herrenhaus, Oberlindober, the NSKOV's chairman, stated that finally German war victims were united, and concluded, "National Socialist War Victims' Care stands, its ranks closed, behind the unknown soldier of the World War, Adolf Hitler."[50]

It was relatively easy to unite the movement in July 1933, because the remaining two war victims' groups were dead by then. The Internationaler Bund was dispatched quickly. The German Communist Party was the National Socialist's first target, and the Bund was part of the Communist Party. In April 1933, Berlin police raided the Bund's headquarters, the Bund was abolished, and its leadership arrested or driven into exile.[51]

The death of the Reichsbund was more protracted. The organization campaigned vigorously against the Nazis. After Hitler's appointment, it bitterly observed: "now they are in power again, the opponents of the parliamentary system, the enemies of a free, popular government, the people opposed to the welfare state, the authoritarians."[52]

After the March 1933 elections, the Reichsbund announced that it would accept the people's choice, and concluded sadly, "to our Fatherland, and to our people, for whom we made the greatest sacrifices during the war, we will always remain faithful."[53]

The Reichsbund came under open attack in April 1933. Several local branches were taken over by National Socialists and the police. The leadership called an emergency meeting in Berlin, and there were talks with Oberlindober. Were there other alternatives? Could the Reichsbund have called on the widows and disabled veterans to resist the new regime openly? Unfortunately, there is no record of alternatives considered. All that remains is the *Reichsbund*'s final issue, which, in an article entitled "Farewell," explained:

> The survival of the Reichsbund is no longer possible. To date, 29 April, the day of the meeting to consider dissolving the Bund, 8 local branches have been taken over by the authorities. The takeover of the Reichsbund altogether is imminent. . . . It comes down to the question of letting each individual member decide. It is also a question, of opening up room for the new order. Every new order demands its sacrifices.[54]

By the summer of 1933, then, it seemed that the war victims' world had been revolutionized. But was it really?

II

In a sense, yes. The National Socialists promised a reform of the National Pension Law, and the amendment was adopted in July 1934. The amendment actually contained nothing radically new—pension rates were increased; a new "front-soldier allowance" was added; and some of the restrictions imposed during the Republic were eased. What was new was not the legislation, but the mood surrounding it.[55] The Nazis insisted that the war victims were the primary citizens of the state, and in a series of dramatic gestures, they honored the war victims as the Republic had never done. Veterans, widows, and parents received different colored badges, which entitled them to go to the head of the line in shops and enjoy the best seats in theaters. Children were taught to salute persons with the badges. In 1934, the twentieth anniversary of the Great War, all seriously disabled veterans received a free copy of *Mein Kampf*. Such occasions as the opening of old soldiers' homes were elaborate public events, with flags, banners, and parades.[56]

For war victims, these were not trivial gestures. After what they had been through in the Republic, all this attention and affection seemed proof of a positive change in public and official attitudes. Yet, nothing had really changed.

Not even the most dramatic actions of the new regime disrupted the bureaucratic routine that had been established during the Republic. When the National Pension Court was informed in April 1933 that the Internationaler Bund, an organization officials had worked with for over a decade, had been outlawed, the court officials' only worry was that this might disrupt cases involving members of the Bund.[57] When Jewish doctors were prohibited from treating war victims, the court expressed no surprise, let alone disagreement; its concern was how to identify Jewish doctors, and whether their exclusion would disrupt pending cases.[58] Even the most extraordinary documents failed to provoke the bureaucracy. In 1936, for example, a veteran named Richard Haberle wrote an intense, disjointed, letter to the National Pension Court. He was, he explained, a disabled veteran, and a stormtrooper. His physical condition had deteriorated badly; he was 100 percent disabled, he claimed, yet the court had refused to increase his pension. Government doctors, in fact, argued that he was insane. Haberle's rambling letter continued:

In 1933, I was imprisoned for 7 months; I won't go into the details of the crimes committed against me. In 1934, they threw me in prison for another 4 months, and in 1935 for another 7 months, always because I wouldn't stand for the things they did to me. Every request for an investigation was turned down. Later I was imprisoned for another 6 months. I ask, outraged, are the insane to be imprisoned in the Third Reich? Will the mentally ill be beaten until the flesh hangs from their bones? Will SS and SA men be allowed to murder a man, so he can't bring charges against them? Such attempted murders meant that in 6 weeks I was all but dead 13 times, such that my fellow prisoners had to call the medical personnel, etc. And what did I have to do when I had arisen from the dead? Yes. I had to pray to my murderers as if they were God. And so on. . . . And now the court says: it's an hereditary problem.

Prisoners had their heads held in toilet bowls until they almost drowned in human feces; prisoners were crucified on trees, bound with chains; 132 prisoners were shot down without cause, and so on and on, and just the sight of this

would destroy anyone already ill. Horrible. And the court says: it's hereditary. . . . I ask you again—where are my rights? Think over your answer—think
of your responsibility.

The court responded as it had since 1919: the decisions of the National
Pension Court were final; if the applicant had further legal trouble, he
should see an attorney.[59]

The bureaucratic structures were just as immovable. The 1936 procedures
in the pension system were no different from those of 1926, which infuriated
even supporters of the regime. A spokesperson for the survivors of reserve
officers wrote to Hanns Oberlindober.

And how are things really? The betrayal of the survivors of reserve officers,
committed by the Marxist regime, still has not been made good, despite all the
promises. . . .

We know that our leader, Adolf Hitler, has no knowledge of this, for he
would never stand for it. Therefore, we will do everything in our power to
break through the wall they have built around him, in order to explain our
needs to our leader.[60]

But though the bureaucracy was largely unchanged, the NSKOV was in
a sense something new. It did all the chores its predecessors had always
done: it helped war victims fill out forms, lodge complaints, and find jobs.
The NSKOV, however, was more than an interest group. It was an agency
of the state, designed to mobilize and discipline the war victims. A pamphlet
printed by Munich's NSKOV local demonstrates this role:

On Sunday, 12 November 1933, national elections will be held. We disabled
veterans and survivors naturally support fully the policies of the government.
As the "first citizens of the state" we are happily prepared to make our own the
will for peace of our Leader and comrade . . . Therefore, ALL MEMBERS WILL
MEET AT THEIR LOCAL HEADQUARTERS, and will march in unison to the
polling booths, with flags flying. For the members of Local XXVII it is a DUTY, to
take part in the peace demonstration of our local. NO ONE WILL BE EXCUSED![61]

After 1933, the war victims issue went into a steady decline. All the trends
the Republic's officials had hoped for, finally appeared after the end of the
Republic. The number of disabled veterans on the pension rolls, which had
increased so dramatically in the last years of the Republic, finally began a
slow decline. In 1930, 839,396 disabled veterans received pensions; in 1935,
the figure was 806,963; and in 1936, the number was 796,611.[62] Costs for
pensions plunged more sharply. Between 1928 and 1935, they dropped by

about 40 percent.[63] After two tumultuous decades, the war victims problem was finally under control. In a few years, an even more dreadful war victims problem would begin.

Otto Dix, "The Matchseller." (Photo: VEB Verlag der Kunst, Dresden)

CONCLUSION

Melancholia, Suicide, and Total Mobilization

> If in many of my productions terror has been the thesis, I maintain that terror is not of Germany but of the soul.
>
> —Edgar Allan Poe

On Sunday, July 30, 1930, the Reichsverband held its fifth annual convention in Berlin. Willibald Hanner, a disabled veteran and school teacher from Plauen, in Saxony, delivered the opening address. He talked about the Great War.

It's an old custom in the Reichsverband . . . , before we get down to the order of business, to remember those who lost their young . . . lives, out there. We think too of those who died of their wounds after the war. In this simple memorial service, which is for us a matter of conscience, we want to think of three things. We want to say that we will never forget those who stood shoulder to shoulder with us out there, even if they are forgotten by others today. We want to say that we stand in the service of those the soldiers left behind, and that our task is constantly to remind the conscience of the public about the survivors. Above all, we want to say that this quiet moment of remembrance is a source of strength for us. When we are tired from the cares of everyday, we remember what we fought for, and what we created.

And then, before our mind's eye, appears again that most frightful of all wars, which so affected the external, and internal, fate of our people. Everyone here experienced it differently, but everyone sensed the demonic quality of the war. It was like some elemental catastrophe, I don't know how else to say it, which threw the entire planet into torment. . . .

We know and feel, that the war didn't only have external effects. It did not just change the map of the world, it changed the soul of human beings. We ourselves cannot entirely sense the enormous impact of the war on the human spirit, because we were part of it . . . we who have lived through this inferno can never be free from it.

It has affected all our lives. That is why we have gathered here. A gash goes through all our lives, and that gash is the war. With a brutal hand, it has torn our lives in two. What do we still remember about the years before the war? That time is like a fairy tale, so far away, and when we try to remember it, our thoughts confront a dark, insurmountable wall, and that wall is the war. It was at this point that our second life began. It was not just a continuation of the first. As for the time before the war and the time after, we can't just say good or bad, bad or good. It is more honest to say: they are different, that's all. Behind everything is the war. We will never be free of it. Our joys are different. Care, seriousness, need, pain, a deep sense of responsibility, we can never escape them, no matter how hard we try; they follow us like a shadow. And I know: we will carry all this with us to our graves. The war is our fate; it has torn our lives.[1]

Nowhere in his speech did Hanner talk about the heroic ideal which had been so pervasive in 1914. By 1930 another mood had overtaken the victims of the Great War—heroism's antithesis, melancholia. The escape from melancholia was the last task of the war victims, and for most the escape took one of two forms: suicide or total mobilization.

I

At the height of the Great War, in 1917, Sigmund Freud published a brief paper entitled "Trauer und Melancholie," "Mourning and Melancholia." He wrote about the response to personal loss. "Mourning," Freud wrote, "is the reaction to the loss of a beloved person, or some abstraction like Fatherland, freedom, or some ideal, which stands in place of the beloved person."[2] Although abnormal, Freud continued, mourning was a necessary and culturally accepted behavior; melancholia, on the other hand, was a chronic, pathological exaggeration of mourning. The melancholy person was unable to overcome the sense of loss: moreover, the melancholy individual engaged in bitter self-recrimination and experienced a profound decline in self-esteem.[3]

The symptoms of melancholy—unresolved sense of loss, sense of inferiority, and consequent passivity—characterize the lives of the war victims. Everyone in Germany had been touched by violent, sudden death during the Great War, but the war victims were sure that they, more than anyone else, had been immersed in death.[4] Widows and orphans had lost loved ones; disabled soldiers had, in a sense, "risen from the dead."[5] War victims described themselves as the "special representatives of the dead,"[6] as "translators," who communicated both with the living and the dead.[7] The newspapers of the war victims were filled with reflections on the two million dead,[8] and the same questions recurred: "Why did you have to die? Why are there so many widows, so many children with no fathers? Why did all this unhappiness have to happen?"[9]

Somehow, the living needed to reconcile themselves with the dead—a constant theme in the war victims' newspapers. A favorite quote was from Walther Flex, who was himself killed in action in 1918. A dead soldier speaks to a living friend:

> Mourning is a hard thing, friend. Do you want to turn us into ghosts, or do you want to welcome us home? There is no third alternative, for those whose hearts beat in the hand of God. Don't turn us into ghosts, welcome us home! We want to be admitted among you, without disrupting your laughter. Don't turn us into frightful shadows. . . . Welcome the dead home, you living, so we can live and work among you.[10]

There were private, personal ways to reconcile oneself with the dead. Every home, for example, had its little memorial shrine, a picture of husband, son, or father on the wall or mantel, draped in mourning at the proper times, and this private ritual helped resolve the sense of loss.[11] But some kind of public ritual was essential to overcome the pervading experience of death, and it is here that the German people failed.

Most German soldiers were buried in other countries, and bringing bodies back home was virtually impossible.[12] In 1919, a number of army officers and civil servants, led by a Dr. Koeth, organized the *Volksbund deutscher Kriegsgräberfürsorge,* to care for soldiers' cemeteries abroad.[13] Koeth hoped that care for the dead might contribute to a sense of unity among the living. He wrote in 1921: "We intend to be an association . . . in which everyone, without distinction, can be united in the memory of the fallen of our people."[14]

In this effort, the Volksbund championed the proclamation of a national Memorial Day. Most courtries had a Memorial Day, the Volksbund argued, and Germany should have one too. In 1927, President Seims of the Volksbund, explained to the Reichstag:

> A point must be found somewhere in the German people, where unity of our torn people can be achieved. . . . Such a point can never be found in politics, or in religion, or in economic or social or artistic relationships. Shouldn't it be possible to unite the German people in the memory of the two million . . . ? Then, the two million will no longer be dead; they will be alive in the strength of our nation. They will no longer be ghosts . . . but sources of blessing for our lives and future. . . . Germany must live![15]

The Volksbund urged that the fifth Sunday before Easter, Reminiscere

Sunday, be adopted as *Volkstrauertag,* Memorial Day, but from the beginning, the organization ran into controversy. Catholics remembered their dead on All Souls Day, November 2nd. Jews honored their dead on Yom Kippur. Protestants celebrated the last Sunday of the church year, Latare Sunday, as the day to remember the dead. For some Protestants and Catholics, there was also *Buss-und Bettag,* a day of repentance, usually celebrated on the Wednesday before Latare Sunday. In addition, Saxony opposed the idea of a spring memorial day, because Leipzig held its fair in the spring. The Bavarian government had the second Sunday of November as its memorial day. Other parts of the country honored the dead on August 1st, the anniversary of the war's outbreak, or on November 11th, the anniversary of the war's end. Nationalist groups refused to accept the "republican" memorial day, while republican groups, like the Reichsbund, argued that the notion of a memorial day was too nationalistic.[16]

The small mountain of reports about Volkstrauertag presents a constant picture of haggling and bickering.[17] In the same city, various groups would celebrate memorial days on different dates, producing both confusion and very hard feelings. The national government wanted nothing to do with such a delicate issue, and repeatedly, cabinets refused to proclaim a national memorial day.[18] It was not until 1934 that Germany finally had a memorial day. The National Socialist government called it *Heldengedenktag,* Heroes' Memorial Day.

It was just as difficult to build a national war memorial. Other countries had memorials, often created around an unknown soldier. In Germany, the effort to construct a memorial produced angry disagreement. Even erecting local monuments produced disputes.

The government hoped that a national war memorial might contribute to national unity. In August 1924, on the tenth anniversary of the war's outbreak, President Ebert called for public contributions to be used for a monument. He charged the Interior Minister with planning the project.[19] By November 1925, the ministry had received over seventy suggestions for memorials, all of them contradictory. The *Stahlhelm,* the nationalist veterans' group, wanted a memorial forest to be dedicated in Thüringen. Konrad Adenauer, the mayor of Cologne, urged that an unknown soldier be buried next to Cologne's great cathedral. There were plans for monuments in the Harz mountains, and for an "isle of the dead" in the Rhine.[20] The Prussian state government, with some asperity, pointed out that its state capital, Berlin, was also the nation's capital, and therefore, the monument should be built in that city. When the national government failed to take any action, the Prussian government in 1930 announced plans to transform the neo-classical Neue Wache on Unter den Linden, into a war memorial. Lacking a better idea, the government adopted the Neue

Wache as a national monument and it was dedicated on June 12, 1931.[21] However, instead of putting the dead to rest, the whole experience exacerbated the sense that the dead were still not at peace.

A scandal in the last years of the Republic added to the disquiet. Shortly after the war's end, the French government began reorganizing the cemeteries in northern France. Dead soldiers were buried everywhere—in farmers' fields, in school yards, in the main streets of shattered villages. The French government wanted to exhume the corpses and transport them to central military cemeteries, and private contractors were hired to perform the task. Scandal surrounded the project from the start. Stories circulated about bodies being heaped helter-skelter on carts and dumped, like refuse, in mass graves, and there were stories of corpses being robbed. Rumors also circulated about contractors being paid for bodies they never moved. The whole affair began to appear in the German press in 1929, and the Germans were horrified. Articles in the right-wing, centrist and left-wing press condemned this disruption of the dead as monstrous.[22]

The dead, however, had never been at rest, at least in the war victims' journals and the Republic's literature.[23] In a *Zentralblatt* article, God permits the dead soldiers to look down on their country,

> . . . and the hundreds of thousands saw . . . their fellow citizens fighting each other in wild hatred, they saw whores, and blackmarketeers, and starving children, and everywhere, they saw only suffering and need and selfishness and hatred and jealousy . . . they saw Germany . . . and the hundreds of thousands wept bitterly . . . they buried their faces in their hands . . . and one spoke for all, very quietly: "We died for you—what are you doing?"[24]

The living had to free themselves from the dead, had to put them to rest; yet, this effort would only rouse the dead. This is what Heinrich Lersch warned in "Epitaph:"[25]

> Wanderer, wait!
> I tell you, you who sleep tonight:
> If you do not ask about the dead. . . .
> If you do not give me your thoughts,
> but think instead of your own joys—
> Then I will arise and rush to you,
> and kiss you with my torn lips,
> and show you my bleeding wounds,
> and you will dream of me all the night . . .
> for I and all who lay here
> died for Germany . . .
> and Germany must remember us,

> must stand for us—
> otherwise, Germany will be destroyed!
> Wanderer, go!

The dead were not at rest; the sense of loss was not overcome. This was one symptom of melancholia. Another was a sense of inferiority, which was manifested in a more subtle way. The veterans were not overtly self-critical; they denied any guilt. Someone else was responsible for the war: the allies, the Kaiser, the capitalists, the Communists, the Jews. Rarely, if ever, did veterans reflect on the fact that they had invaded other people's countries and had killed other people.[26]

Disabled veterans did not think of themselves as being inferior. The vehemence, however, with which they denounced others for implying that disabled veterans and survivors were inferior, suggested an extreme sensitivity to the issue. War victims frequently complained of being treated as inferior and of being neglected. In 1919, for example, the Bavarian Disabled Veterans League wrote to the Labor Ministry in Berlin that civilians were being hired as civil servants, whereas: . . . "disabled veterans and survivors, because of their injuries and illness, are treated as inferior people, whom one can surrender to suffering and need."[27] In 1921, discussing the "psychology of war victims," the *Zentralblatt* spoke of "mistrust, anger . . . and deep pessimism. . . . No more do the society ladies dress up in their Red-Cross uniforms, and visit the hospitals. The very sight of the wounds of the war victims horrifies them. . . . Everywhere, those who, through no fault of their own surrendered their best years to the war, everywhere, they are neglected."[28] A few months earlier, a veteran had written that, in a sense, veterans looked back at the war with a certain nostalgia.

> The disabled veteran gladly remembers the fighting, for those were the days when we were still healthy, and in full possession of our powers. We were not yet crippled and sick . . . Back then too, we weren't alone . . . because they needed us. Today, it's all different. With the enemy bullet that hit us, our lives were broken. We were turned into half-men. The time of suffering, and neglect, began.[29]

The sense of inferiority is also reflected in literature. A character in Alfred Döblin's *Berlin Alexanderplatz,* for example, says:

> "I am a cripple, we gave our blood at the Front, and now they make us wait, anything is good enough for us. . . . Always trouble, always trouble," he kept shouting. "We're nothing better than coolies, our children can croak the way we croaked."[30]

It is no surprise, then, that the war victims were extremely touchy about the stories critical of the pension system that appeared often in the last years of the Republic.[31] Accusations of fraud were especially painful, because they implied that the war victims were parasites and beggars. From the middle of the war, disabled soldiers and survivors had, in fact, struggled to distinguish themselves from the hordes of beggars the war had created. Soon troops of beggars, masquerading as disabled veterans, were everywhere. Characters straight out of Brecht's *Dreigroschenoper* could be found on streets and in train stations all over Germany.[32] In the last months of the war, the government began a vigorous campaign to stamp out beggars, and the press was filled with stories about the "plague of beggars."[33]

War victims were indignant at being associated with these frauds. One member of the Reichsbund reported that on his arrival at the Essen railroad station he had been approached by a beggar who pretended to be a disabled veteran. The real disabled veteran reported the fraud to the railroad police, who carted the phoney away. But when the disabled veteran left the train station, he was assailed by "ladies of low reputation," the beggar's accomplices. Something must be done, the veteran insisted, to stamp out the criminals and thieves who besmirched the reputation of war victims.[34] One of the cruelest names the organizations could hurl at each other was "beggar."[35] Constantly, the war victims insisted that they did not want handouts, that they wanted their rights. As the refrain of a poem entitled "Cripple's Song" repeated, "I don't want your pity."[36]

The war victims did want pity, however. Appeals to pity appeared regularly in their publications. "What the war victims need," the *Zentralblatt*, wrote in 1921, " . . . is not only the hand of fatherly justice, but the soft hand of the mother. After all, they are really sick children, not so much because of the medical problems they have, but because of the terrible shock they have endured."[37] The same tone is present in letters written to officials. A widow, who had applied for, but been denied, a pension, wrote to the president of the National Pension Court in 1931: "O Mr. President, can't you put yourself in the place of a poor widow, chained to her bed, who has to live on 20 marks a month of poor-relief?"[38] This appeal to pity was part of a broader temptation the war victims faced: an overwhelming tendency toward surrender, passivity, and inaction.

In 1916, Michael von Faulhaber, the Catholic bishop of Speyer, warned of the dangers of passivity among war victims and disabled veterans in particular: "Those who have been touched by death must not be allowed to wander around with their peg-legs and music boxes as they did after previous wars. They must not be permitted to sit around in pubs, telling their war stories and drinking away their pensions. . . . Even the blind cannot be permitted to become drones. Self-pity is like being buried alive." Among disabled veterans he had seen, Faulhaber continued, there was "a lack of emotional vigor, a frightening paralysis of will, a perverse kind of homesickness, and an endless grubbing for pensions."

The bishop's comments were typical and not surprising, for virtually everything in the veterans' experience encouraged dependence and passivity.[39] The army, like all armies, rigidly reduced the scope of autonomous action. Remarque wrote in *All Quiet on the Western Front,*

> With our young, wide-awake eyes, we saw that the classical idea of "Fatherland" which our teachers held, here amounted to a surrender of the personality, a surrender which even the meanest servant would never be required to make. . . . We were trained for heroism like circus ponies.[40]

The army also encouraged infantilism. It was one of the chief characteristics of the front soldier. Like children, soldiers were totally subordinate to the will of their superiors, and took a childish delight in simple physical pleasures, like warmth and food.[41] The soldier-child was not an autonomous, responsible adult, but a passive and helpless waif.[42]

The living often felt themselves already dead, and this too contributed to the feeling of passivity and helplessness. This confusion between the living and the dead was one implication of "Ich hatt' einen Kameraden," probably the most popular soldier's song.[43]

> I once had a comrade,
> a better you'll never find . . .
> A bullet came flying,
> was it for me or for you?
> Torn from life and dying,
> he lies at my feet,
> As if a part of me,
> As if a part of me.

In addition, as this book has shown, the pension machinery tended to limit the independence of the pensioner. War victims were often treated impersonally—as merely objects. This was most evident in the pensioner's relationship with the government doctor.

> Even at the very beginning of the pension system, a psychological problem appears. The application of a disabled veteran has to be checked. The applicant is invited for a physical. He is alone with the overworked doctor. The doctor asks a couple of questions, silently pokes and feels him, and the appli-

cant has no idea what is happening. Then the applicant is simply released . . . and yet, the applicant has so much in his heart![44]

That the pension system encouraged passivity was an observation officials took very seriously. Psychologists even invented a name for the difficulty—"pension neurosis." The term was used to describe the pleading, helpless behavior people displayed in the effort to win a pension. Opponents of social welfare programs constantly warned of the dangers of "pension neurosis."[45] In the spring of 1929, when the Labor Ministry was preparing major reductions in the pension system, the ministry sponsored a national conference on the problem.[46]

Though war victims resented the accusation that they were suffering from pension neurosis, the temptation to appeal to pity was marked, especially during the Republic's final crisis. In 1932, the Reichsbund published a booklet entitled *Notruf der Kriegsopfer,* the War Victims' Cry for Help. The booklet listed all the devastating cuts the government had made in the pension system. Then, it presented picture after picture of disabled veterans exposing their terrible wounds; each picture was accompanied by a brief text, which detailed the veterans' impoverished lives. The booklet was not an assertion of autonomy, nor a demand for rights. It was a cry for pity.[47]

The inability to resolve the sense of loss, the feeling of inferiority, and the tendency toward passivity were fixed characteristics of the war victims' lives, and the cumulative effect was melancholia. And it was this melancholia that helps explain the war victims' behavior in 1933, when the organizations they had so slowly and painfully created were rapidly dismantled.

II

In "Mourning and Melancholia," Freud described a number of specific behaviors of the melancholy person. Such a person manifests two apparently contradictory behaviors: a tendency toward suicide, and an equally strong drive toward manic action. According to Freud, both serve the same purpose. Both are methods of punishing the self by destroying it. Both are a means of escaping the unending pain of melancholia.[48]

One of the most striking qualities of the first months of National Socialist rule was the ease with which the Nazis eliminated their opponents. This was particularly true regarding the war victims' movement. A police raid on its national headquarters was enough to silence the Internationaler Bund, and the threat of raids sufficed to drive the Reichsbund, which had vociferously opposed the Nazis, into suicide.

The case of the Reichsbund is especially interesting. In the last years of the Republic, when the pension system was under constant attack, the Reichsbund displayed a peculiar fascination with suicide. In February 1931, it accused the government of driving war victims to despair. Between January 1927 and December 1929, the *Reichsbund* reported, some 233 of its members had killed themselves. Whether this suicide rate was statistically significant did not interest the Reichsbund—they were sure that suicide had become a major war victims' problem. Increasingly, the organization argued, war victims were concluding that their only choice was self-destruction.[49]

Only a few months later, the *Reichsbund* reported more suicides. In the second quarter of 1931 alone, it told its readers, 49 more members had killed themselves.[50] In July 1931 too, the paper printed a letter allegedly written by a severely wounded veteran. "Dear comrades," the letter began:[51]

> I just want to tell you what is happening to me. I've gone through a lot. I was in the war, started by the money-grubbers. My hand was hurt, I was hit twice in the shoulder and once in the head. . . . I have a severe head injury, and suffered brain damage. My nerves were finished. In Merkstein, I ran a little restaurant. I worked from morning until night, and the only thing I have to show for it are debts. I asked the veterans' office to guarantee a mortgage. . . . I told them that if they couldn't help, my family and I simply couldn't live any longer. . . . The office I asked told me that they couldn't do anything. . . . I've had enough. I would have done this on the 20th, only I didn't have a gun, and I want my family's end to be quick and painless. We learned that in the war. I was always a good father and took care of my family; anyone in Streiffeld can tell you that. And it's just because I don't want my family to have to live in poverty that I'm taking them with me. Maybe my action will help other disabled veterans. . . . Long live the world revolution.

After sending the letter to a friend, the writer killed his wife, three children, and himself.

Why the *Reichsbund* editors chose to print such a story is not clear. It may have been another appeal for pity from the government. However, it reflected a growing mood of hopelessness that finally overwhelmed the Reichsbund. In May 1933, the organization committed suicide.

The other war victims fled, as Freud might have predicted, into manic action. They dissolved their organizations and rushed to subordinate themselves to National Socialism. Melancholia, Wolf Lepenies writes, is in part a reaction to a deep sense of disorder, a loss of control over the outer world.[52] It reflects the loss of confidence in the ability to conquer the world, the failure of heroic action. One escape from melancholia is suicide, another is total mobilization.

One wing of the war victims' movement eagerly embraced a total mobilization disguised as a resurrection of the heroic. Ironically, however, this surrender of the self to a totally ordered world is itself a kind of suicide. This is one of the qualities Karl Prümm identifies in the life of Ernst Jünger. Total mobilization was Jünger's solution to the "ennui" of civilian life. Total mobilization comprises the best of two worlds: constant, violent, frantic action, within the context of absolute, rigid control. But it requires a surrender to systematic sadomasochism. The individual can destroy the self in a masochistic sacrifice to the total order. At the same time, this total order permits, and even encourages, the discharge against others of long pent-up rage. Jünger, the eternal soldier, found a solution to melancholia not unlike that of some of the war victims—a headlong dash into total mobilization.[53]

III

Erich Kuttner, who had been seriously wounded at Verdun, had organized the Reichsbund, and had been the leading figure in the war victims' movement in its early years, fled Germany in 1933. He became active in the anti-Nazi resistance. When he was captured during the German invasion of Holland in 1940, he tried to commit suicide, but failed. The German police interned him in a concentration camp. In 1942, Kuttner was shot to death by agents of the regime that many war victims had enthusiastically welcomed.[54]

Kuttner is a representative figure. Neither he nor the German victims of the Great War found balm for their wounds. National Socialism was no solution; in the end, it only produced a second generation of war victims. Yet the grimness of the fate of the victims of the Great War should not obscure the significance of their experience.

Understanding the war victims' lives is critical to understanding the consequences of the Great War. The war brought radical change to Germany. Though institutions and attitudes remained essentially the same, the lives of the war victims were profoundly altered. And their movement provided a moment of democracy. It mobilized women and men in behalf of the weakest members of society, and the largest war victims' group, the Reichsbund, consistently defended democratic values.

The movement also focused attention on the problem of social welfare, a problem chronic to industrial society. The bureaucratization of benevolence, social protest, the clash between economic and social priorities— these issues so familiar to modern society emerge with arresting clarity in the history of the German war victims.

Conclusion

The Germans of that generation, like us all, longed for concord. The parallel and intersecting roads they took, organized benevolence and epic politics, proved to be dead ends, but not entirely for reasons historians usually cite.

Organized benevolence failed partly because it was torpedoed by Germany's governing elites in the early 1930s. Deep cuts in welfare radicalized millions of people, including the war victims, and this provided a priceless opportunity for reckless demagogues like the National Socialists. But German organized benevolence failed even when it was funded. It failed because it was technocratic, bureaucratic, and propelled by a pseudo-social science. This rationalized charity spoke in a language so jargon-filled, it functioned in a manner so ponderous, it was so abstract, that it created for its wards a mysterious, capricious, and inhuman world.

Epic politics was sinister precisely because it was so appealing. Millenarian hypernationalism harnessed all the virtues and dreams of the nation, and promised a world free of conflicts and enemies. All it would take was a single paroxysm of self-sacrificial violence. Germans wanted peace and social harmony, and so they rushed off to war. Epic politics was bad not because it was ugly, but because it was so beautiful.

The war victims seem almost contemporary. This is preeminently the century of the survivor; the survivor of Hiroshima, the survivor of Auschwitz. The victims of the Great War were the first generation of survivors. They are our ancestors. Their experience is our own.

Notes

Abbreviations

BA	Bundesarchiv, Koblenz
BayHSta	Bayerisches Hauptstaatsarchiv, Munich
HHStA	Hessisches Hauptstaatsarchiv, Wiesbaden
HStA (Stuttgart)	Hauptstaatsarchiv, Stuttgart
KBKH	*Die Kriegsbeschädigten- und Kriegshinterbliebenen- Fürsorge*
RAM	Reichsarbeitsministerium
RGBl	*Reichsgesetzblatt*
RVG	Reichsversorgungsgesetz
RVGer	Reichsversorgungsgericht
ZStA (Merseburg)	Zentrales Staatsarchiv, Merseburg
ZStA (Potsdam)	Zentrales Staatsarchiv, Potsdam

Prologue: *The Memory of Mass Violence*

1. Antoine Prost, *Les anciens combattants et la société française, 1914–1939* (Paris: Presses de la Fondation Nationale des Sciences Politiques, 1977); Paul Fussell, *The Great War and Modern Memory* (New York: Oxford University Press, 1975); Klaus Vondung, ed., *Kriegserlebnis* (Göttingen: Vandenhoeck und Ruprecht, 1980).

1. *The Return of the Red Baron*

1. Nigel Hamilton, *The Brothers Mann* (New Haven: Yale University Press, 1978), p. 185.
2. Sigmund Freud, "Thoughts on War and Death," *The Standard Edition of the Complete Psychological Works* (London: Hogarth, 1957), XIV:292.
3. Philippe Ariès, *The Hour of Our Death* (New York: Knopf, 1981).
4. Thomas Mann, *Betrachtungen eines Unpolitischen* (Frankfurt/Main: S. Fischer, 1956), p. 1.

5. Georg Heym, "Krieg," in Kurt Pinthus, ed., *Menschheitsdämmerung* (Berlin: Rowohlt, 1920), p. 39.

6. *Taschen-Kommersbuch* (Cahr: Moritz Schauenburg, w.d.), p. 13; also, Winfried Elbers, "Das Soldatenlied als publizistische Erscheinung" (Diss., Munster, 1963).

7. Wolfgang Foerster, ed., *Wir Kämpfer im Weltkrieg* (Berlin: Deutsche Betriebsstelle amtlicher Publikationen, 1929), p. 2.

8. Werner Sombart, *Händler und Helden* (Munich: Duncker and Humblot, 1915), p. 64.

9. See Joseph Campbell, *The Hero with 1000 Faces* (Princeton: Princeton University Press, 1972); Mircea Eliade, *The Myth of the Eternal Return* (Princeton: Princeton University Press, 1974).

10. Campbell, *The Hero*, p. 30.

11. See Heinz Schlaffer, *Der Bürger als Held* (Frankfurt/Main: Suhrkamp, 1976). For a related discussion, see also Mark Girouard, *The Return to Camelot* (New Haven: Yale University Press, 1981).

12. Otto Rank, *Der Mythus von der Geburt des Helden* (Leipzig: F. Deuticke, 1909); C. G. Jung, *Symbole der Wandlung* (Freiburg: Walter, 1973); also, Richard Wagner, "Heldentum und Christentum," in *Sämtliche Schriften und Dichtungen* (Leipzig: C. F. W. Siegel, 1912), pp. 275–285; Lerke von Saalfeld, "Die ideologische Funktion des Niebelungenliedes in der preussisch-deutschen Geschichte" (Diss., Berlin, 1977).

13. Wolfgang Golther, *Deutsche Heldensage* (Dresden: L. Ehlermann, 1894), p. 1.

14. See Gertrud Oel-Willenborg, *Von deutschen Helden: Eine Inhaltsanalyse der Karl-May-Romane* (Cologne: Beltz Monograph, 1967).

15. Alfred Biese, ed., *Poesie des Krieges* (Berlin: Grote, 1916), p. 21.

16. Ernst Johann, ed., *Innenansicht eines Krieges* (Munich: Deutscher Taschenbuch, 1973), p. 24.

17. Walter Flex, *Gesammelte Werke,* (Munich: Beck, 1925), I:134–135. For a biographical sketch of Flex, see Robert Wohl, *The Generation of 1914* (Cambridge: Harvard University Press, 1979).

18. Heinrich Lersch, "Soldaten Abschied," in *Das dichterische Werk* (Berlin: Deutsche Verlags-Anstalt, 1934), p. 275.

19. Leo Sternberg, "Heldenblut," in Biese, *Poesie des Krieges,* pp. 93–94.

20. Lersch, "Erinnerung," in Julius Bab, ed., *Der deutsche Krieg im deutschen Gedicht* (Berlin: Morwe, 1919), II:313.

21. For example, Philipp Witkop, ed., *Kriegsbriefe gefallener Studenten* (Munich: Georg Müller, 1928), pp. 13, 26, 105; Letter from Fritz Simon to the Zionist Organization of Germany, Dec. 25, 1914, Cornell University Archives, 385 M— Letters of Fritz Simon; *Kriegsbriefe gefallener Juden,* ed. Bundes Verteidigungsministerium (Stuttgart: Seewald, 1961), p. 104.

22. Otto Braun, *Aus nachgelassenen Schriften eines Frühvollendeten,* ed. Julie Vogelstein (Berlin: Hermann Klemm, 1924), p. 183.

23. "Flieger Richtofen gefallen," *Vorwärts,* Apr. 24, 1918.

24. Manfred, Freiherr von Richtofen, *Der rote Kampfflieger* (edited and intro-

duced by Bolko, Freiherr von Richtofen) (Berlin: Im Deutschen Verlag, 1933), p. 239.

25. Witkop, *Kriegsbriefe*, pp. 255–256.

26. Letters of Fritz Simon, 385 M, Cornell University Archives, Ithaca, New York.

27. Leonard Frank, *Der Mensch ist gut* (Zurich: Max Rascher, 1918), p. 26.

28. Franz Marc, *Briefe aus dem Felde* (Berlin: Rembrandt, 1941), p. 88.

29. See Hans-Ulrich Wehler, *Das deutsche Kaiserreich, 1871–1918* (Göttingen: Vandenhoeck & Ruprecht, 1977), especially pp. 131–140. The generational conflict particularly absorbed prewar and postwar expressionists. See Walter Sokel, *The Writer in Extremis* (Stanford: Stanford University Press, 1959); Peter Gay, *Weimar Culture* (New York: Harper & Row, 1968).

30. Karlheinz Dederke, *Reich und Republik Deutschland, 1917–1933* (Stuttgart: Ernst Klett, 1969), p. 6.

31. Sombart, *Händler und Helden*, p. 63.

32. Letter from Bavarian War Minister to all Ministries and Deputy Commanding Generals, Sept. 12, 1917, "Bericht über Volksstimmung und Volksernährung," BayHStA (II) MF 56837.

33. Alice Salomon, *Von Kriegsnot und -hilfe und der Jugend Zukunft* (Berlin: Truebner, 1916), pp. iii–iv.

34. See especially Jürgen Kocka, *Klassengesellschaft im Krieg* (Göttingen: Vandenhoeck & Ruprecht, 1978).

35. See Theodor Schieder, *Das deutsche Kaiserreich von 1871 als Nationalstaat* (Cologne: Westdeutscher Verlag, 1961).

36. Letter from the Prussian Minister President to all Ministries, July 7, 1924, ZStA (Merseburg) Rep 191/Abt II/4368.

37. Letter from Reich Interior Minister Jarres to all State Governments, July 11, 1924, ZStA (Merseburg) Rep 191/Abt II/4368.

38. "Die Toten-Ehrung auf dem Königsplatz," *Berliner Montagspost*, Aug. 4, 1924, pp. 1–2, ZStA (Merseburg), Rep 191/Abt II/4368.

39. For accounts of the funeral see despatches from Wolffs Telegraphisches Büro, Nov. 17–20, 1925, BA R43I/710; "Zur Überführung des berühmten . . . Kampffliegers Manfred Freiherr von Richtofen nach Deutschland . . . ," *Illustrierte Zeitung*, Nov. 26, 1925, p. 817.

40. Von Richtofen, *Der rote Kampfflieger*, p. 260.

41. "Manfred von Richtofens Heimkehr," *Deutscher Offiziersbund*, Nov. 25, 1925, p. 1097.

2. The Aesthetics of Violent Death

1. Boris Urlanis, *Bilanz der Kriege: Die Menschenverluste Europas vom 17. Jahrhundert bis zur Gegenwart* (Berlin: VEB Deutscher Verlag der Wissenschaften, 1965), p. 349.

2. See, for example, "Zahlen—Die Toten des Weltkrieges," *Volkswille*, No. 277, Nov. 25, 1928, BA ZSg 103/1568.

3. Paul Monaco, *Cinema and Society* (New York: Elsevier, 1976), pp. 95ff.

4. Urlanis, *Bilanz*, p. 354.

5. Kurt Tucholsky wrote about these unhappy lists in his essay "Die Flecke," in *Politische Texte* (Hamburg: Rowohlt, 1971), p. 67.

6. Reichswehrministerium, *Sanitätsbericht über das deutsche Heer im Weltkriege, 1914/1918* (Berlin: E. S. Mittler, 1934), II:1.

7. *Sanitätsbericht*, II:6 (Table 1).

8. *Ibid.*, II:2.

9. Urlanis, *Bilanz*, p. 146.

10. Otto von Schjerning, ed., *Handbuch der ärztlichen Erfahrungen im Weltkriege, 1914–1918*, I, Chirurgie/Erster Teil (Leipzig: J. A. Barth, 1922), p. xvii.

11. *Sanitätsbericht*, III:62–64.

12. *Ibid.*, II:1.

13. *Ibid.*, III:14.

14. *Ibid.*, II:2.

15. *Ibid.*

16. Rudolf Meerwarth et al., *Die Einwirkung des Krieges auf Bevölkerungsbewegung und Lebenshaltung in Deutschland* (Berlin: Deutsche Verlags-Anstalt, 1932), pp. 62–63.

17. *Bund erblindeter Krieger: Entwicklung, Bedeutung und seine Stellung zur Rentenversorgung und Fürsorge* (Berlin: Bund erblindeter Krieger, 1926), BA R116/331.

18. Luise Frankenstein, "Die soziale Kriegsbeschädigtenfürsorge während des Krieges" (Diss., Universität Greifswald, 1920); Karl Nau, *Die wirtschaftliche und soziale Lage von Kriegshinterbliebenen* (Leipzig: Lühe, 1930).

19. Ulrich Dunker, *Der Reichsbund jüdischer Frontsoldaten* (Düsseldorf: Droste, 1977), pp. 72–76.

20. Constantin von Altrock, *Vom Sterben des deutschen Offizierkorps* (Berlin: E. S. Mittler, 1921), pp. 53ff.

21. Major Rohrbeck, *Taktik* (Berlin: E. S. Mittler, 1919), p. 37.

22. Urlanis, *Bilanz*, pp. 272, 298.

23. *Ibid.*, p. 159.

24. *Sanitätsbericht*, III:70–72.

25. John Keegan, *The Face of Battle* (New York: Vintage, 1977), p. 234.

26. Ernst Jünger, *Der Kampf als inneres Erlebnis* (Berlin: E. S. Mittler, 1922), p. 15.

27. There is no comprehensive history of German "Front-literature." There are, though, a number of valuable specialized studies. For example: Charles Genno and Heinz Wetzel, eds., *The First World War in German Narrative Prose* (Toronto: University of Toronto Press, 1980); Michael Gollbach, *Wiederkehr des Krieges* (Kronberg/Taunus: Scriptor, 1978); Herbert Cysarz, *Zur Geistesgeschichte des Weltkrieges* (Halle: Max Niemeyer, 1931); Julien Hervier, *Deux individus contre l'histoire: Drieu la Rochelle, Ernst Jünger.* (Paris: Klincksieck, 1978); Helmut Kaiser, *Mythos, Rausch und Reaktion: Der Weg Gottfried Benns und Ernst Jüngers* (Berlin: Aufbau, 1962); Karl Prümm, *Die Literatur des soldatischen Nationalismus der 20er*

Jahre (*1918–1933*) (Kronberg/Taunus: Scriptor, 1974); Walter Falk, *Der kollektive Traum vom Krieg* (Heidelberg: Carl Winter, 1977); Hans-Joachim Bernhard, "Der Weltkrieg 1914–1918 im Werk Ernst Jüngers, Erich Maria Remarques und Arnold Zweigs" (Diss., Universität Rostock, 1958).

28. Werner Beumelburg, *Die Gruppe Bosemüller* (Oldenburg: Gerhard Stalling, 1930), pp. 36–37.

29. August Stramm, *Dein Lächeln weint* (Wiesbaden: Limes, 1956), p. 77.

30. Jünger, *Der Kampf als inneres Erlebnis*, pp. 15–16.

31. See Fussell, *The Great War*, pp. 196–197; Karl Heinz Bohrer, *Die Ästhetik des Schrecken* (Munich: Carl Hanser, 1978); Wolfgang Kayser, *The Grotesque* (Bloomington: Indiana University Press, 1963).

32. See Prümm, *Die Literatur*, pp. 440ff.

33. Ernst Toller, *Eine Jugend in Deutschland* (Hamburg: Rowohlt, 1963), p. 78.

34. Erich Maria Remarque, *Im Westen nichts Neues* (Frankfurt/Main: Ullstein, 1979), p. 162.

35. Robert Jay Lifton, *Death in Life* (New York: Simon and Schuster, 1967), pp. 480–481.

3. *Wounds, Disease, and Insanity: The Soldiers' War*

1. "Aus Gross-Berlin—Verwundete im Theater," *Vorwärts*, Dec. 7, 1914.

2. See Dr. Fritz Brüning, "Die Kampfmittel im Weltkriege und ihr Wirkung auf den Körper," in Schjerning, *Handbuch*, I/pt. 1, pp. 3–26.

3. Medical Department, United States Army, *Wound Ballistics* (Washington, D.C.: Government Printing Office, 1962).

4. See, for example, "Die Dum-Dum Geschosse," *Vorwärts*, Sept. 9, 1914.

5. Remarque, *Im Westen*, p. 147.

6. Letter from Dr. Schlange, Chief Surgeon, X Army Corps, to War Ministry, Oct. 10, 1914, BA R86/2400.

7. *Sanitätsbericht*, III:75.

8. Wilhelm Hoffmann, *Mein Weg zum Gluck* (Munich: Lehmanns, 1931), p. 37.

9. Marc, *Briefe*, pp. 74–75, 81.

10. A. M. Frey, *Die Pflasterkästen: Ein Feldsanitätsroman* (Berlin: G. Kiepenheuer, 1929), p. 102.

11. *Ibid.*, p. 259.

12. Otto von Schjerning (Chief Army Medical Corps), *Die Tätigkeit und die Erfolge der deutschen Feldärzte im Weltkriege* (Leipzig: J. A. Barth, 1920), p. 16.

13. For a picture of the war from a corpsman's perspective, see Frey, *Die Pflasterkästen*.

14. Beumelburg, *Die Gruppe Bosemüller*, pp. 234–235.

15. Germany was divided into twenty-five corps areas. When the war broke out, the corps went to the Front, and a Deputy Commanding General stayed behind to administer the corps area at home. Often these generals were retired officers recalled to active duty. During the war their powers were extensive. See especially Wilhelm Deist, *Militär und Innenpolitik im Weltkrieg* (Düsseldorf: Droste, 1970).

16. "Aus Gross-Berlin—Am Bahnhof," *Vorwärts,* Nov. 21, 1914.

17. Bab, *Der deutsche Krieg,* I:130. Dr. "Owlglass" was the pseudonym of Hans Erich Blaich, a poet, and a doctor who worked with the psychiatrist Dr. Kraepelin.

18. "Merkblatt für Einarmige," BayHStA (Kriegsarchiv) MKr 12677. See also David Katz, *Zur Psychologie des Amputierten und seiner Prosthese,* supplement 25 to *Zeitschrift für angewandte Psychologie.*(Leipzig: J. A. Barth, 1921).

19. See Hoffmann, *Mein Weg.* Also: *Bund erblindeter Krieger: Entwicklung, Bedeutung und seine Stellung zur Rentenversorgung und Fürsorge* (Berlin: Bund erblindeter Krieger, 1926), BA R116/331.

20. Reichsarbeitsministerium, *Deutschlands Kriegsbeschädigte, Kriegshinterbliebene und sonstige Versongungsberechtigte* (Berlin: Reichsarbeitsministerium, 1924).

21. Frankenstein, *Die soziale Kriegsbeschädigtenfürsorge,* p. 117 (Appendix 6).

22. Andreas Latzko, *Men in War* (New York: Boni and Liveright, 1918), p. 233.

23. Paul Alverdes, *Die Pfeiferstube* (Potsdam: Rütten & Loening, 1941), pp. 46–47.

24. Erich Maria Remarque, *Der Weg zurück* (Frankfurt/Main: Ullstein, 1977), pp. 24–25, 120.

4. The Medical Solution to the War Victims Problem

1. *Verfass. Preuss. Landesversammlung.* 30. Sitzung, 4. Juni 1919. Förmliche Anfrage der Abgeordneten Dr. Beyer (Westpreussen) und Genossen über Fürsorge für die aus dem Kriegsdienst hervorgegangenen Geisteskranken und Nervenleidenden, ZStA (Potsdam) 39.01/9338.

2. For an introduction to the history of medicine in Germany, see: Walter Artelt and Walter Rügg, eds., *Der Arzt und der Kranke in der Gesellschaft des 19. Jahrhunderts* (Stuttgart: Ferdinand Enke, 1967); Walter Artelt et al., *Städte-, Wohnungs-, und Kleidungshygiene des 19. Jahrhunderts in Deutschland* (Stuttgart: Ferdinand Enke, 1969); Paul Diepgen, "Politik und Zeitgeist in der deutschen Medizin des 19. Jahrhunderts," *Historisches Jahrbuch,* 55, 2/3 (1935), 439–452; Alfons Fischer, *Geschichte des deutschen Gesundheitswesens* (Hildesheim: Georg Olms, 1965); Hans-Heinz Eulner, *Die Entwicklung der medizinischen Spezialfächer an den Universitäten des deutschen Sprachgebietes* (Stuttgart: Ferdinand Enke, 1970); Hans-Georg Güse and Norbert Schmacke, *Psychiatrie zwischen bürgerlicher Revolution und Faschismus* (Kronberg: Athenäum, 1976); Gunter Mann, ed., *Biologismus im 19. Jahrhundert* (Stuttgart: Ferdinand Enke, 1973); Gunter Mann et al., eds., *Medizin, Naturwissenschaft, Technik und das zweite Kaiserreich* (Göttingen: Vandenhoeck & Ruprecht, 1977).

3. See Erwin Ackerknecht, *Rudolf Virchow* (Madison: University of Wisconsin Press, 1953); Mann et al., *Medizin.*

4. G. Hohorst, J. Kocka, and G. A. Ritter, eds., *Sozialgeschichtliches Arbeitsbuch* (Munich: Beck, 1975), p. 66.

5. Christian Kliche, "Die Stellung der deutschen Militärarzte im ersten Weltkriege" (Diss., Free University of Berlin, 1968), p. 7.

6. Douglas McMurtrie, *The Evolution of National Systems of Vocational Reeducation for Disabled Soldiers and Sailors* (Washington: Government Printing Office, 1918), pp. 147–148.

7. For example, see McMurtrie, *Evolution,* p. 156; also the photos in the Rehse Sammlung, BayHStA.

8. For a discussion of this relationship in the years before the war, see Hannah Decker, *Freud in Germany: Revolution and Reaction in Science, 1893–1907* (New York: International Universities Press, 1977).

9. Sandor Ferenczi et al., *Psycho-Analysis and the War Neuroses* (London: International Psycho-Analytical Press, 1921), pp. 2–3.

10. "Anhaltspunkte für die militärische Beurteilung der Frage der Dienstbeschädigung oder Kriegsdienstbeschädigung bei den häufigen psychischen und nervösen Erkrankungen der Heeresangehörigen, auf Grund von Beratungen des Wissenschaftlichen Senats bei der Kaiser Wilhelms-Akademie," BA R116/317.

11. "Fachärztliches Gutachten von Dr. Bratz, betr. Landesbriefträger Wilhelm S., 6 Juni 1922," BA R116/4.

12. Oskar Maria Graf, *Wir sind Gefangene* (Munich: Deutscher Taschenbuch, 1981).

13. Toller, *Eine Jugend,* p. 70.

14. See Diepgen, "Politik und Zeitgeist," pp. 439–452.

15. For example: Hans Würtz, *Der Wille siegt* (Berlin: Hermann Kalkoff, 1916).

16. E. G. White, *In den Fussspuren des grossen Arztes* (Hamburg: Advent, n.d.), p. 115.

17. Letter from Bavarian War Minister to Medical Sections I, II, III Army Corps, April 15, 1915, BayHStA (Kriegsarchiv) MKr 12677.

18. Reichsausschuss für das ärztliche Fortbildungswesen, ed., *Gesundheitswesen und soziale Fürsorge im deutschen Reich* (Berlin: Reichsdruckerei, 1928), pp. 225ff.

19. See Susan Sontag, *Illness as Metaphor* (New York: Vintage, 1978).

20. Arnold Zweig, *Erziehung vor Verdun* (Frankfort/Main: Fischer, 1979), p. 18. For a discussion of front vermin, see A. E. Shipley, *The Minor Horrors of War* (London: John Murray, 1916).

21. Theodor Imme, *Die deutsche Soldatensprache der Gegenwart und ihr Humor* (Dortmund: F. W. Ruhfus, 1917), p. 95.

22. Schjerning, *Die Tätigkeit,* p. 17.

23. Pamphlet, "Ausschuss zur Beschaffung von Bade- und Desinfectionswagen für die Ost-Armee," ZStA (Merseburg) Rep 191/Abt II/3484.

24. Michael von Faulhaber, *Das hohe Lied der Kriegsfürsorge* (Berlin: Kameradschaft, 1916), p. 1.

25. Sigmund Freud, "Thoughts on War and Death," in *The Standard Edition of the Complete Psychological Works* (London: Hogarth, 1957), XIV:295.

26. "Protokol der Konferenz der Vertreter der Versicherten bei den Lan-

desversicherungsanstalten, 2 Aug. 1915," Referent Arbeitersekretär Wissell, ZStA (Potsdam) 39.01/6459.

27. Rudolf Wissel, "Zur Bekämpfung der Geschlechtskrankheiten," Oct. 24, 1916, BA N1 209, vol. 50—Rudolf Wissel.

28. Hermann Koetzle, *Das Sanitätswesen im Weltkrieg* (Stuttgart: Berger, 1924), p. 112.

29. See Chapter 3.

30. Dr. J. Jadassohn, "Geschlechtskrankheiten," in F. Bumm, ed., *Deutschlands Gesundheitsverhältnisse unter dem Einfluss des Weltkrieges,* I. Halbband (Berlin: Deutsche Verlags-Anstalt, 1928), pp. 257–258.

5. Widows and Orphans

1. Helene Hurwitz-Stranz, ed., *Kriegerwitwen gestalten ihr Schicksal* (Berlin: Carl Heymann, 1931), p. 22.

2. W. Rohrbeck, *Statistische Untersuchungen über die im Bereich des IV. Armeekorps wohnenden Witwen und Waisen,* ZStA (Potsdam) 39.01/8873.

3. *Ibid.*

4. Gerhard Bry, *Wages in Germany, 1871–1945* (Princeton: Princeton University Press, 1960), p. 84.

5. Rohrbeck, *Untersuchungen,* ZStA (Potsdam) 39.01/8873.

6. For an introduction to the history of women in Germany, see: Amy Hackett, "Feminism and Liberalism in Wilhelmine Germany, 1890–1918," in Bernice Carroll, ed., *Liberating Women's History* (Urbana: University of Illinois Press, 1976), pp. 127–137; Renate Bridenthal and Claudia Koonz, "Beyond 'Kinder, Küche, Kirche': Weimar Women in Politics and Work," in Carroll, *Women's History,* pp. 301–330; Richard J. Evans and W. R. Lee, eds., *The German Family* (Totowa, N.J.: Barnes and Noble, 1981); Helen Boak, "Women in Weimar Germany: The 'Frauenfrage' and the Female Vote," in Richard Bessel and E. J. Feuchtwanger, eds., *Social Change and Political Development in Weimar Germany* (Totowa, N.J.: Barnes and Noble, 1981), pp. 155–174; Tim Mason, "Women in Germany, 1925–1940," *History Workshop,* No. 1 (1976), pp. 74–113; Ursula von Gersdorff, *Frauen im Kriegsdienst, 1914–1945* (Stuttgart: Deutsche Verlags-Anstalt, 1969); Uta Ottmüller, *Die Dienstbotenfrage: Zur Sozialgeschichte der doppelten Ausnutzung von Dienstmädchen im deutschen Kaiserreich* (Munster: Verlag Frauenpolitik, 1978).

7. Richard Evans, *The Feminist Movement in Germany, 1894–1933* (Beverly Hills: Sage Publications, 1976), p. 23.

8. The movement was by no means homogeneous. See Jean Quataert, *Reluctant Feminists in German Social Democracy, 1885–1917* (Princeton: Princeton University Press, 1979); Evans, *The Feminist Movement;* Werner Thönnessen, *The Emancipation of Women* (New York: Urizen Books, 1976).

9. Hohorst, Kocka, and Ritter, *Sozialgeschichtliches Arbeitsbuch,* pp. 66–67.

10. Bry, *Wages,* p. 94.

11. Friedhelm Neidhart, *Die Familie in Deutschland* (Opladen: Leske, 1971), p. 53.

12. Hohorst, Kocka, and Ritter, *Sozialgeschichtliches Arbeitsbuch,* p. 26.

13. Hurwitz-Stranz, *Kriegerwitwen*, pp. 22–23.

14. Louis Guichard, *The Naval Blockade* (New York: Appleton, 1930), pp. 262–281.

15. Guichard, *Blockade*, pp. 262–281. Also: Marion Siney, *The Allied Blockade of Germany* (Ann Arbor: University of Michigan Press, 1957); Suda Lorena Bane and Ralph Lutz, eds., *The Blockade of Germany after the Armistice* (Stanford: Stanford University Press, 1942); *Denkschrift des Reichsgesundheitsamtes vom 16. Dez. 1916*, in *Ursachen und Folgen*, I:283–288; *Das Werk des Untersuchungsausschusses der Verfassunggebenden deutschen Nationalversammlung und des deutschen Reichstages*, IV, ed. Johannes Bell (Berlin: Deutsche Verlagsgesellschaft für Politik und Geschichte, 1927).

16. Evelyn Blücher, *An English Wife in Berlin* (New York: Dutton, 1920), p. 156.

17. Bumm, *Deutschlands Gesundheitsverhältnisse*, II. Halbband, pp. 36ff.

18. *Ibid.*, pp. 20–21.

19. Bry, *Wages*, p. 213.

20. Bumm, *Deutschlands Gesundheitsverhältnisse*, I. Halbband, pp. 56–58; also, *Denkschrift des Reichsgesundheitsamtes*, in *Ursachen und Folgen*, I:283–288.

21. Letter from the Bavarian Transportation Minister to all Postal Officials, Dec. 16, 1914, BayHStA (II) MInn 54032.

22. Hurwitz-Stranz, *Kriegerwitwen*, pp. 23–24.

23. Rohrbeck, *Untersuchungen*, ZStA (Potsdam) 39.01/8873.

24. *Hinterbliebenenfürsorge: Mitteilungen aus der Arbeit der Zentrale für private Fürsorge*, Aug. 1915, ZStA (Potsdam) 39.01/8868.

25. Rohrbeck, *Untersuchungen*, ZStA (Potsdam) 39.01/8873.

26. "Männer auf Lager für Frauen Gefallener," *Vorwärts*, Apr. 8, 1915.

27. Ludwig Preller, *Sozialpolitik in der Weimarer Republik* (Stuttgart: Franz Mittelback, 1949), p. 14.

28. Bry, *Wages*, p. 84.

29. P. Riedel, ed., *Ratgeber für die deutsche Kriegerfrau* (Berlin: C. A. Schwetschke, 1916), pp. 27–28. Also: *Hinterbliebenenfürsorge*, ZStA (Potsdam) 39.01/8868.

30. *Hinterbliebenenfürsorge*, ZStA (Potsdam) 39.01/8868.

31. Hurwitz-Stranz, *Kriegerwitwen*, pp. 37–38.

32. *Ibid.*, p. 27.

33. *Ibid.*, p. 31.

34. Bumm, *Deutschlands Gesundheitsverhältnisse*, I. Halbband, p. 115.

35. For a discussion of mortality by gender, see: Arthur Imhof, "Women, Family and Death. Excess Mortality of Women in Child-bearing Age in Four Communities in Nineteenth-Century Germany," in Evans and Lee, *The German Family*, pp. 148–175.

36. Bumm, *Deutschlands Gesundheitsverhältnisse*, I. Halbband, p. 122.

37. See, for example, *Die Nagelung von Kriegswahrzeichen*, ed. Nationalstiftung für die Hinterbliebenen der im Kriege Gefallenen, BayHStA (II) MK 19269.

38. See: Deutsche Hilfswerk für die Kriegs- und Zivilgefangenen, BA ZSg 1–E/44.

39. William Stern, ed., *Jugendliches Seelenleben und Krieg*, supplement 12 to

Zeitschrift für angewandte Psychologie und psychologische Sammelforschung (Leipzig: J. A. Barth, 1915), pp. 26–27.

40. Albert Speer, *Inside the Third Reich* (New York: Macmillan, 1970), p. 6.

41. Ernst Gläser, *Jahrgang 1902* (Bonn: Schaack, 1947), p. 276.

42. Stern, *Jugendliches Seelenleben*, p. 30.

43. Moritz Liepmann, *Krieg und Kriminalität in Deutschland* (Berlin: Deutsche Verlags-Anstalt, 1930), pp. 135–137.

44. *Ibid.*

45. Order of the Deputy Commanding General, XI Army Corps, I B No. 14072, Oct. 21, 1914, HHStA Abt 405/4239.

46. Letter from the Chairman of the County Assembly, Limburg, to the Provincial President in Wiesbaden, Dec. 30, 1915, HHStA Abt 405/4240.

47. Gertrud Moses, *Zum Problem der sozialen Familienverwahrlosung unter besonderer Berücksichtigung der Verhältnisse im Kriege* (Langensalza: Beyer, 1920), p. 41. Also: Sterling Fishman, *The Struggle for German Youth: The Search for Educational Reform in Imperial Germany* (New York: Revisionist Press, 1976); Peter Loewenberg, "The Psychohistorical Origins of the Nazi Cohort," *American Historical Review*, LVI (1971), 1457–1502.

6. *Political Prophylaxis: The German Welfare Tradition*

1. Victor Turner, *Dramas, Fields and Metaphors* (Ithaca: Cornell University Press, 1974), pp. 25ff.

2. Otto von Bismarck, *Werke in Auswahl* (Stuttgart: W. Kohlhammer, 1973), V:180–181.

3. For contemporary discussions of Sozialpolitik, see: Adolf Guenter, *Theorie der Sozialpolitik* (Berlin: W. de Gruyter, 1922); Ludwig Heyde, *Abriss der Sozialpolitik* (Leipzig: Quelle & Meyer, 1923); Hugo Schäffer, *Verwaltungsprobleme im Bereich des sozialen Versicherungswesens* (Stuttgart: Kohlhammer, 1930); W. Voss, *Sozialpolitik als Wissenschaft* (Jena: G. Fischer, 1925); Leopold von Wiese, *Einführung in die Sozialpolitik* (Leipzig: G. A. Gloeckner, 1921); E. v. Borsig, *Industrie und Sozialpolitik* (Berlin: F. Zillessen, 1924); Heinrich Brauns, *Wirtschaftskrisis und Sozialpolitik* (München Gladbach: Volksvereins-Verlag, 1924); Bruno Rauecker, *Sozialpolitik durch Produktionspolitik* (Duisburg: Echo, 1925).

4. See: Ludwig Bernhard, *Unerwünschte Folgen der deutschen Sozialpolitik* (Berlin: Springer, 1913): Price Collier, *Germany and the Germans* (New York: Scribner's, 1914), pp. 399ff; Albin Gladen, *Geschichte der Sozialpolitik in Deutschland* (Wiesbaden: Franz Steiner, 1974), pp. 58–70; Ullmann, "Industrielle Interessen."

5. Frederic Howe, *Socialized Germany* (New York: Scribner's, 1916), p. 161.

6. Emil van den Boom, "Die deutsche Arbeiterversicherung und ihre Kritiker," *Allgemeine Rundschau* (Munich), May 17, 1913, BA ZSg 124/577.

7. See Wehler, *Das deutsche Kaiserreich*, pp. 136–140. Also: Alexander Gerschenkron, *Bread and Democracy in Germany* (New York: Fertig, 1966); Hans-Jürgen Puhle, *Agrarische Interessenpolitik und preussische Konservatismus im wilhelminischen*

Reich, 1893–1914 (Bonn: Neue Gesellschaft, 1975); Robert Gellately, *The Politics of Economic Despair* (Beverly Hills: Sage, 1974); Schulamit Volkov, *The Rise of Popular Anti-Modernism in Germany: The Urban Master Artisans, 1873–1896* (Princeton: Princeton University Press, 1978).

8. *Gesetz betreffend die Krankenversicherung der Arbeiter,* vom 15. Juni 1883, *RGBl.* 1883/No. 4; *Unfallversicherungsgesetz,* vom 6. Juli 1884, *RGBl.* 1884/No. 19; *Gesetz betreffend die Invaliditäts- und Altersversicherung,* vom 22. Juni 1889, *RGBl.* 1889/No. 13; *Reichsversicherungsordnung,* vom 19. Juli 1911, *RGBl.* 1911/No. 42.

9. Gladen, *Sozialpolitik,* p. 65; Friedrich Syrup, *Hundert Jahre Staatliche Sozialpolitik, 1839–1939* (Stuttgart: W. Kohlhammer, 1957), pp. 119–121.

10. Niederschrift über die Abschiedsfeier für . . . Dr. Paul Kaufmann, Nov. 30, 1923, BA R116/2.

11. Bernhard, *Unerwünschte Folgen;* Collier, *Germany and the Germans,* pp. 399ff.

12. *Gesetz über die Pensionierung der Offiziere einschliesslich Sanitätsoffiziere des Reichsheers, der kaiserlichen Marine und der kaiserlichen Schutztruppen,* vom 31. Mai 1906, *RGBl.* 1906/No. 30; *Gesetz über die Versorgung der Personen der Unterklassen des Reichsheers, der kaiserlichen Marine und der kaiserlichen Schutztruppen,* vom 31. Mai 1906, *RGBl.* 1906/No. 30; *Militärhinterbliebenengesetz,* vom 17. Mai 1907, *RGBl.* 1907/No. 21.

13. Riedel, ed., *Ratgeber für die deutsche Kriegerfrau,* p. 16.

14. See, for example: Karl Erich Born, *Staat und Sozialpolitik seit Bismarcks Sturtz* (Wiesbaden: Steiner, 1957); Dieter Lindenlaub, *Richtungskämpfe im Verein für Sozialpolitik* (Wiesbaden: Steiner, 1967); James Sheehan, *The Career of Lujo Brentano* (Chicago: University of Chicago Press, 1966); Kenneth Barkin, *The Controversy over German Industrialization, 1890–1902* (Chicago: University of Chicago Press, 1970); Arthur Mitzman, *Sociology and Estrangement: Three Sociologists of Imperial Germany* (New York: Knopf, 1973); Wolfgang Mommsen, *Max Weber und die deutsche Politik* (Tübingen: J. C. B. Mohr, 1959); Werner Krause, *Werner Sombarts Weg vom Kathedersozialismus zum Faschismus* (Berlin: Rütten & Loening, 1962); Marie-Louise Plessen, *Die Wirksamkeit des Vereins für Sozialpolitik von 1872–1890* (Berlin: Duncker & Humbolt, 1975); Donald Rohr, *The Origins of Social Liberalism in Germany* (Chicago: University of Chicago Press, 1963).

15. McMurtrie, *Evolution,* p. 133.

16. Evans, *The Feminist Movement,* pp. 29ff; Quataert, *Reluctant Feminists.*

17. *21. Jahresbericht d. Berliner Frauenbunds über das Jahr 1915,* ZStA (Merseburg) Rep 191/Abt II/3679.

18. For a discussion of similar reform groups in the United States in the early nineteenth century, see Carroll Smith-Rosenberg, "Beauty, the Beast, and the Militant Women," in Nancy F. Cott and Elizabeth H. Pleck, eds., *A Heritage of Her Own* (New York: Simon and Schuster, 1979), pp. 197–221.

7. *The Administrative Solution to the War Victims Problem, 1914–1918*

1. Leonard Frank, *Der Mensch ist gut* (Zurich: Rascher, 1918), pp. 165ff.

2. *Sanitätsbericht*, III:19. In 1920, Dr. Schjerning had estimated that doctors had treated around 20 million cases (see Schjerning, *Die Tätigkeit*, p. 16). By 1934, the *Sanitätsbericht* estimated the number of cases treated at around 27 million. This is another example of the difficulty in obtaining precise medical statistics from the war.

3. Schjerning, *Die Tätigkeit*, p. 7.

4. Reichsarbeitsministerium, *Denkschrift über das Versorgungswesen*, No. 5725, Apr. 6, 1923, p. 10, BA R116/287.

5. The underlying idea of cultural hegemony is borrowed from Antonio Gramsci. For a discussion of the uneasy alliance within the German elite, see Geoff Eley, *Reshaping the German Right* (New Haven: Yale University Press, 1980).

6. Some of these groups included, for instance: *Deutscher Krieger-Hilfbund; von der Goltz Stiftung zur Unterstützung von Kriegsteilnehmern der türkischen Wehrmacht*, Landesarchiv, Koblenz Best 441/14901; *Verein für das Deutschtum im Ausland; Ostpreussenhilfe; Deutsche Hilfstätigkeit für Ostpreussen; Kriegsblindenstiftung; Deutscher Hilfsbund für kriegsverletzte Offiziere; Hilfe für kriegsgefangene Deutsche; Deutscher Verein für Sanitätsbunde*, HHStA Abt 405/6151: *Kaiserspende deutscher Frauen; Sammlungen für Lazarettzüge*, HHStA Abt 405/6094; *Deutsche Wohlfahrtsvereinigung zur Veranstaltung von Konzertabenden zum Besten der Witwen und Waisen gefallener Krieger*, HHStA Abt 405/6154.

7. Verzeichnis der Liebesgaben für die Truppen im Felde, Niederheimbach, 19.10.1914, Landesarchiv, Koblenz, Best 441/14900.

8. Letter from the Chairman of Höchst County to the Provincial President, Wiesbaden, Nov. 19, 1917, HHStA Abt 405/6359.

9. Letter from District Commander Landau to the Deputy Commanding General, II Army Corps, Nov. 23, 1916, BayHStA (Kriegsarchiv) MKr 11606.

10. Blücher, *An English Wife*, p. 305. For more on swindlers and beggars, see "Blindenfürsorge und Schwindel," *Münchner Neueste Nachrichten*, May 28, 1916, BayHStA (II) MK 15793; "Kriegsbeschädigte als Hausierer und Bettler," Erlass No. 350/6.17 AZS 6, July 19, 1971, Preuss. Kriegsmin., ZStA (Potsdam) 39.01/8861; Dr. Preuss, "Grossstädtische Kriegsbeschädigtenfürsorge," *KBKH*, 1, No. 2/3 (July/Aug. 1916), p. 74; "Männer auf Lager für Frauen Gefallener," *Vorwärts*, Apr. 8, 1915; "Gegen den Bettelunfug," *Voss. Zeitung*, Nov. 21, 1919, ZStA (Potsdam) 61 61 Re1/2322.

11. For material on Donner, see: Letter from Police Director, Berlin, to the Commissioner for Wartime Social Service in Prussia, Apr. 29, 1919; Letter from Fritz Maercker to Police Director, Berlin, Oct. 4, 1919, ZStA (Merseburg) Rep 191/Abt II/3789.

12. Material on Jacober is contained in BayHStA (Kriegsarchiv) MKr 11607.

13. Letter from the Prussian War Minister to the Interior Office, Mar. 7, 1915, ZStA (Potsdam) 39.01/8868.

14. *Reichstag Verhandlungen*, XIII Legis., II Sess., 12. Sitzung, May 29, 1915, p. 158.

15. *Ibid.*, pp. 169–170.

16. See: "Massnahmen gegen die wirtschaftlichen Kriegsfolgen," *Vorwärts*,

Aug. 23, 1914; "Die Not preisgegebene Familien von Kriegsteilnehmern," *Vorwärts,* Sept. 2, 1914; "Mängel bei der Familien Unterstützung," *Vorwärts,* Nov. 27, 1914; "Kriegsrenten und Hinterbliebenenfürsorge," *Vorwärts,* Apr. 24, 1915; "Die Fürsorge für die Kriegsbeschädigten," *Vorwärts,* Apr. 25, 1915.

17. *KBKH,* 1, No. 1 (June 1916), 3.

18. "Erste Sitzung des Arbeitsausschusses für Hinterbliebenenfürsorge," June 5, 1915, ZStA (Potsdam) 39.01/8868.

19. See comments by Reichstag Delegate Giesberts in "Protokol der Konference der Vertreter der Versicherten bei den Landesversicherungsanstalten," Aug. 2, 1915, ZStA (Potsdam) 39.01/6459.

20. Letter from the Saxon Minister of the Interior, to the County Chairman, Sept. 25, 1915, ZStA (Potsdam) 39.01/6459.

21. Letter from General Commission of German Unions, signed G. Bauer, to Dr. Delbrück, Interior Office, Feb. 18, 1915, BayHStA (Kriegsarchiv) MKr 12677.

22. See: *Richtpunkte für die Errichtung eine Beratungsstelle für Kriegsbeschädigte in München,* n.d., BayHStA (Kriegsarchiv) MKr 12677; *Das erste Jahr der Nürnberger bürgerlichen Kriegsinvalidenfürsorge, Feb. 1915–Feb. 1916,* ed. Stadtmagistrat Nürnberg, BayHStA (II) MH 16138; *Kriegsinvalidenfürsorge in der Pfalz: Bericht des kreisausschusses für Kriegsinvalidenfürsorge in Speyer,* ed. Kreisausschuss (Speyer: Zechner, 1916); Luise Frankenstein, "Die soziale Kriegsbeschädigtenfürsorge während des Krieges" (Diss., Greifswald, 1920).

23. See: Niederschrift—Erste Sitzung des Landesbeirats für Kriegsinvalidenfürsorge, Apr. 28, 1915, BayHStA (Kriegsarchiv) MKr 12677.

24. See: "Richtlinien für Fürsorge in Preussen," issued jointly by the War Ministry, Interior Ministry, Commerce Ministry, and Agriculture Ministry, BayHStA (Kriegsarchiv) MKr 12677.

25. "Verzeichnis der Hauptfürsorgeorganisationen," in *KBKH,* 1, No. 4 (Sept. 1916), pp. 213–214.

26. Bericht über die Verhandlungen im Reichsamt des Innern vom 19 Feb. 1915, betreffend die Durchführung der Berufsfürsorge für invalide Krieger, BayHStA (Kriegsarchiv) MKr 12677.

27. See: Anton Kerschensteiner, "Die gesetzliche Regelung der Kriegsbeschädigten- und Kriegshinterbliebenen-Fürsorge," *KBKH,* 3, No. 5–6 (Nov.–Dec. 1918).

28. For a biographical sketch of Kirschensteiner, see *Wer ist's?,* 1935.

29. *KBKH,* 1, No. 1 (June 1916), 2.

30. For example: Rudolf Wissell, "Die Arbeitsgemeinschaften zugunsten der Kriegsbeschädigten," *KBKH,* 1, No. 5–6 (Oct.–Nov. 1916), pp. 274–291; Oberregierungsrat Seitz, "Die Arbeitstherapie im Dienste der Kriegs- und Arbeitsinvalidenfürsorge," *KBKH,* 1, No. 8 (Jan. 1917), pp. 467–486; Friedrich Neumann, "Die Arbeitsmöglichkeiten für Kriegsverletzte und Kriegskranke im deutschen Hausgewerbe," *KBKH,* 2, No. 1 (July 1917), pp. 14–35; Oberamtmann Meyer, "Kriegsblindenfürsorge und Industrie in Württemberg," *KBKH,* 2, No. 6 (Dec. 1917), pp. 273–293; Dr. R. Radike, "Arbeitsleistungen Schwerverletzter in Industrie und Handwerk," *KBKH,* 2, No. 5 (Nov. 1917), pp. 258–260; Dr. K. Gaebel,

"Heimarbeit für Schwerkriegsbeschädigte," *KBKH*, 2, No. 3 (Sept. 1917), pp. 171–176.

31. Dr. Franz Schweyer, "Zur Frage der Berücksichtigung des Familienstandes und des Arbeitseinkommens bei Bemessung der militärischen Versorgung der Kriegsinvaliden," *KBKH*, 1, No. 1 (June 1916), pp. 23–25.

32. Letter from Treasury Secretary, signed Graf v. Roedern, to Reich Chancellor, July 22, 1917, ZStA (Potsdam) 15.01/12859.

33. Bericht über die erste Kommissionssitzung vom 2. Aug. 1917 betreffend Änderungen der Militär-Versorgungsgesetze, ZStA (Potsdam) 15.01/12859.

34. Letter from War Minister to the Treasury Secretary, Dec. 7, 1917, ZStA (Potsdam) 15.01/12859.

35. Letter from Treasury Secretary, signed Graf v. Rödern, to the War Minister, Dec. 18, 1917, ZStA (Potsdam) 15.01/12859.

36. Letter from Interior Office to Reich Chancellor, Mar. 6, 1918, ZStA (Potsdam) 15.01/12859.

37. See Kommissarische Beratung, June 28, 1918, comments of Freiherr von Langermann, ZStA (Potsdam) 15.01/12859.

8. *The War Victims Rebel, 1916–1919*

1. Letter from Deputy War Minister von Wandel to the Interior Office, Mar. 2, 1916, BayHStA (II) MF 56837.

2. Bericht über Volksstimmung und Volksernährung, Aug. 1917, Bavarian War Ministry, BayHStA (II) MF 56837.

3. For a discussion of war and sexuality, see Magnus Hirschfeld, *The Sexual History of the War* (New York: Cadillac, 1944); Klaus Theweleit, *Männer Phantasien* (Hamburg: Rowohlt, 1980). For a general discussion of women and the war, see Gersdorff, *Frauen im Kriegsdienst;* Evans, *The Feminist Movement;* Quataert, *Reluctant Feminists.*

4. Gertrude Atherton, *The White Morning* (New York: Frederick A. Stokes, 1918), pp. 94–95.

5. Blücher, *An English Wife,* p. 136.

6. *Ibid.,* p. 90.

7. Letter from the Mayor, Frankfurt/Main, to the Provincial President in Wiesbaden, July 19, 1917, HHStA Abt 405/6358.

8. See Foerster, Regierungsrat im Reichsarbeitsministerium, "Deutschlands Kriegsbeschädigte und Kriegshinterbliebene," *Reichsarbeitsblatt,* May 1, 1926, pp. 424–428; "Die Zahl der versorgungsberechtigten Kriegsbeschädigten und Kriegshinterbliebenen Deutschlands im Mai 1931," *Reichsbund,* Aug. 20, 1931, p. 174.

9. Hurwitz-Stranz, *Kriegerwitwen,* p. 28; also pp. 25, 32, 41.

10. Martha Karnoss, "Organisation der Kriegerwitwen," *Reichsbund,* May 20, 1932, p. 106.

11. Friedrich Lehmann, *Wir von der Infanterie* (Munich: Lehmann, 1929), p. 130; also Beumelburg, *Die Gruppe Bosemüller,* pp. 220–222; Remarque, *Im Westen,* p. 35.

12. See especially Richard Stumpf, *War, Mutiny and Revolution in the German Navy* (New Brunswick, N.J.: Rutgers University Press, 1967); Daniel Horn, *The German Naval Mutinies of World War One* (New Brunswick, N.J.: Rutgers University Press, 1969).

13. Letter of Fritz Simon, Jan 24, 1918, 385 M, Cornell University Archives, Ithaca, New York; Remarque, *Im Westen,* p. 133; Beumelburg, *Die Gruppe Bosemüller,* pp. 82–83.

14. For examples of this literature, see Ludwig Renn, *Krieg* (Berlin: Aufbau, 1979); Adam Scharrer, *Vaterlandslose Gesellen* (Berlin: Aufbau, 1975); Arnold Zweig, *Erziehung vor Verdun* (Frankfort/Main: S. Fischer, 1979); Graf, *Wir sind Gefangene;* Kurt Tucholsky, "Militaria," in *Politische Texte* (Hamburg: Rowohlt, 1971); Edlef Köppen, *Heeresbericht* (Hamburg: Rowohlt, 1979). For a general discussion, see Hans Kaufmann et al., *Geschichte der deutschen Literatur, 1917–1945* (Berlin: Volk & Wissen, 1978), pp. 308–315.

15. Letter from the Bavarian Representative in Berlin, signed v. Strössenreuther, to Bavarian Interior Ministry, Jan. 28, 1915, BayHStA (II) MKr 11606.

16. Hans Bernstein, *Militärische Invalidenfürsorge bei den Ersatztruppen* (Berlin: Vossische Buchhandlung, 1917), pp. 49–50.

17. Theodor Brugsch, *Artz seit fünf Jahrzehnten* (Berlin: Rütten & Loening, 1958), p. 214.

18. Blücher, *An English Wife,* pp. 241–242.

19. Letter from Georg, Willy und Otto Klapproth, to Chancellor Scheidemann, Feb. 14, 1919, BA R43I/705.

20. See: Preller, *Sozialpolitik,* p. 164; Dietmar Petzina, *Die deutsche Wirtschaft in der Zwischenkriegszeit* (Wiesbaden: Steiner, 1977), p. 16; Manfred Nussbaum, *Wirtschaft und Staat in Deutschland während der Weimarer Republik* (Berlin: Akademie, 1978), p. 31.

21. Letter from the Archbishop of Munich to the Bavarian Interior Ministry, May 13, 1916; Letter from Protestant Synod of Bavaria to the Bavarian Interior Ministry, May 13, 1916, BayHStA (II) MK 19267.

22. "Für eine Reichsstelle der Kriegsfürsorge," *Reichsbund,* Oct. 11, 1918.

23. See: Letter from the Bavarian War Ministry, signed Kuhler, to Commanders, I, II, III Army Corps, Dec. 12, 1916, BayHStA (Kriegsarchiv) MKr 12680; Letter from the Prussian War Ministry, signed Marquand, to all Commands, Feb. 2, 1917, BayHStA (Kriegsarchiv) MKr 12681; Letter from Deputy Surgeon General, II Army Corps, signed Korbacher, to Chiefs, Army Hospitals, II Army Corps, Feb. 10, 1917, BayHStA (Kriegsarchiv) MKr 12681.

24. Letter from Bund erblindeter Krieger, signed Friedel, to the Inspector General, II Army Corps, Oct. 23, 1918, BayHStA (Kriegsarchiv) MKr 12685.

25. See: Letter from Bund deutscher Kriegsteilnehmer, signature illegible, to the Bavarian Economics Minister, Dec. 2, 1919, BayHStA (II) MH 16228; Protokoll der Sitzung des Reichsministeriums vom 9. Aug. 1919, BA R43I/706.

26. Auguste Supper, "Die deutsche Frauen und der Krieg," *Der Sammler,* Nov. 27, 1917, BA ZSg 124/548.

27. Letter from *Reichsbund,* signed R. Gaissmaier, to Bavarian State Legislature, Oct. 16, 1918, BayHStA (Kriegsarchiv) MKr 12683.

28. Toller, *Hinkemann.* See also Ernst Weiss, "Franta Zlin," in Marcel Reich-Ranicki, ed., *Gesichtete Zeit* (Munich: Deutscher Taschenbuch Verlag, 1981), pp. 32–52.

29. Letter from the Prussian War Ministry, signed v. Wrisberg, to Deputy Commanding Generals, -Geheim-, Aug. 22, 1918, HHStA Abt 405/2749.

30. Letter from County Legislature, Hof, signed Hoeb, to the Bavarian Interior Ministry, July 1, 1918, BayHStA (II) MInn 66284.

31. Letter from Bavarian Police Commissioner, signed Deckt, to Bavarian Interior Ministry, Aug. 15, 1918, BayHStA (II) MInn 66284.

32. Letter from the Bavarian Interior Ministry to the War Ministry, Aug. 18, 1918, BayHStA (II) MInn 66284.

33. Schreiben des kommandierenden Generals d. I. bay. A.K., Gen. d. Art. Hoehn, an den bay. Ministerpräsidenten . . . 29 Aug. 1919—streng vertraulich—in *Quellen zur Geschichte des Parlamentarismus und der politischen Parteien,* ed. E. Matthias and H. Meier-Welcher (Düsseldorf: Droste, 1977), II:207.

34. Alverdes, *Pfeiferstube,* p. 38; for a similar story, see Siegfried Berger, "Julius Ammann," in *Die tapferen Füsse* (Merseburg: Stollberg, 1947).

35. *Bund erblindeter Krieger: Entwicklung, Bedeutung und seine Stellung zur Rentenversorgung und Fürsorge,* 4. ordentlicher Bundestag, Bund erblindeter Krieger, 5.–7. März 1926, BA R116/331.

36. See comments of Carl Legien in "Die Kriegsbeschädigten in der Industrie," *Vorwärts,* Aug. 26, 1916; "Kriegsbeschädigte!" *Vorwärts,* Apr. 4, 1917; "Die Arbeiter- und Angestelltenverbände an die Kriegsbeschädigten," *Berliner Volkszeitung,* Apr. 4, 1917, ZStA (Potsdam) 61 Re1/2323.

37. Letter from the General Commission of German Unions, signed G. Bauer, to Interior Office, Feb. 18, 1915; Letter from Bavarian Industriellen-Verband, signed A. Kuhlo, to Bavarian Foreign Office, June 14, 1915, BayHStA (II) MH 16139. Also Bekanntmachung der Vereinigung der deutschen Arbeitsgeberverbände, n.d., BayHStA (II) MH 16141.

38. Reichskanzlei, Sitzungen des Reichsministeriums, 15 Dez. 1919, BA R43I/1352; "Die Spandauer Kriegsbeschädigten—Tumulte," *Voss. Zeitung,* Dec. 13, 1919, ZStA (Potsdam) 61 Re1/2325.

39. BA ZSg 103/1422—Kriegervereine. Also Klaus Saul, "Der 'Deutsche Kriegerbund': Zur innenpolitischen Funktion eines 'nationalen' Verbandes im kaiserlichen Deutschland," *Militärgeschichtliche Mitteilungen,* Feb. 1969.

40. James Diehl, "The Organisation of German Veterans, 1917–1919," *Archiv für Sozialgeschichte,* XI (1971), 141–184.

41. The literature on German veterans' groups is enormous. Some basic works are James Diehl, *Paramilitary Politics in Weimar Germany* (Bloomington: University of Indiana Press, 1977); Ulrich Dunker, *Der Reichsbund jüdischer Frontsoldaten, 1919–1938* (Düsseldorf: Droste, 1977); Volker Berghahn, *Der Stahlhelm: Bund der*

Frontsoldaten, 1918–1935 (Düsseldorf: Droste, 1966); Karl Rohe, *Das Reichsbanner Schwarz-Rot-Gold* (Düsseldorf: Droste, 1966); Kurt Schuster, *Der rote Frontkämpferbund, 1924–1929* (Düsseldorf: Droste, 1975).

42. "Neuordnung des Mannschaftsversorgungsgesetzes," *Vorwärts*, Dec. 11, 1918, in *Quellen zur Geschichte*, p. 311.

43. "Die Kriegsbeschädigtenvereinigungen," ed. Reichsausschuss der *KBKH*, No. 119 (May 1917)—streng vertraulich—ZStA (Merseburg) Rep 191/Abt II/3649.

44. *Ibid.*, Letter from Reichsausschuss der *KBKH*, signed v. Winterfeldt, to Schriftleitung, *Rhein. Westfl. Anzeiger, Essener Anzeiger*, May 26, 1917; Letter from Reichsausschuss der *KBKH*, signed v. Winterfeldt, to Verband wirtschaftlicher Vereinigungen Kriegsbeschädigter für das Deutsche Reich, May 31, 1917, ZStA (Merseburg) Rep 191/Abt II/3649.

45. "Die Kriegsbeschädigtenvereinigungen," ed. Reichsausschuss der *KBKH*, No. 119 (May 1917)—streng vertraulich—ZStA (Merseburg) Rep 191/Abt II/3649.

46. "Ein Verband der Kriegsbeschädigten," *Vorwärts*, Apr. 12, 1917.

47. Letter from the Essen Verband, signed Hans Adorf, to Commissioner for Wartime Social Services in Prussia, Nov. 6, 1917, ZStA (Merseburg) Rep 191/Abt II/3649.

48. Protokoll über die Sitzung d. Tätigkeitsausschusses für *KBKH*, Rheinprovinz, Jan. 3, 1918, Landesarchiv, Koblenz, Best 403/13169.

49. Die Kriegsbeschädigtenvereinigungen, Hrsg. v. Reichsausschuss der *KBKH*—streng vertraulich—May 1917; Letter from Prussian War Ministry to all Deputy Commanding Generals, Aug. 11, 1918, ZStA (Merseburg) Rep 191/Abt II/3649. Also: "Ein Ariasbrief," *Reichsbund*, Nov. 1, 1918.

50. "Der Essener Verband in Ablösung," *Reichsbund*, Oct. 18, 1918; "Der gelbe Essener Verband gesprengt," *Vorwärts*, Sept. 26, 1918. Also: "Ein Sieg der kriegsbeschädigten Essener Richtung," *Rheinisch-Westfälischen Zeitung*, Sept 23, 1918; Rundschreiben an sämtliche Ortsgruppen des Verbands wirtschaftlicher Vereinigungen Kriegsbeschädigter, signed H. König—vertraulich—n.d., ZStA (Merseburg) Rep 191/Abt II/3649.

51. Erich Kuttner, "Wie der Reichsbund entstand," *Reichsbund*, May 20, 1932, pp. 94–96.

52. Erich Kuttner, "Die Heimkehr," *Vorwärts*, Dec. 31, 1916; "Bedarf es besonderer Vereinigungen der Kriegsteilnehmer und Kriegsbeschädigten?" *Vorwärts*, Jan. 21, 1917; "Zur Reform des Mannschaftsversorgungsgesetzes," *Vorwärts*, Apr. 4, 1917; "Brauchen wir eine Organisation der Kriegsteilnehmer?" *Vorwärts*, Apr. 8, 1917.

53. See Erich Kuttner, "Warum wir Kriegsteilnehmer und Kriegsbeschädigten uns zusammengeschlossen haben," *Vorwärts*, May 27, 1917; *Dank oder Recht? Ein Wort an die Kriegsteilnehmer und Kriegsbeschädigten*, Schriften des Bundes der Kriegsteilnehmer und Kriegsbeschädigten, No. 1, ZStA (Merseburg) Rep 191/Abt II/3740.

54. *50 Jahre Reichsbund: 1917–1967*, ed. Bundes Vorstand, Reichsbund, May 1967.

55. There are no biographies of Kuttner or Tiedt. For biographical sketches, see *Ursachen und Folgen*, Namen und Personen Register, p. 71; *Wer ist's?*, 1928; Her-

mann Weber, *Die Wandlung des deutschen Kommunismus* (Frankfurt/Main: Europäische Verlagsanstalt, 1969), pp. 323–324. Rossmann did write an autobiography, but it is devoted entirely to his fight against National Socialism; he does not mention his involvement in the war victims' movement; see Erich Rossmann, *Ein Leben für Sozialismus und Demokratie* (Stuttgart: Rainer Wunderlich, 1947).

56. See: Kurt Koszyk, *Deutsche Pressepolitik im ersten Weltkrieg* (Düsseldorf: Droste, 1968).

57. Kuttner, "Wie der Reichsbund entstand"; Letter from the Interior Office, signed Wallraf, to the Prussian War Ministry, Sept. 28, 1917, ZStA (Potsdam) 39.01/8869.

58. "Der Schandtat der Vaterlandspartei," *Vorwärts*, Jan. 9, 1918; "Polizei gegen den Bund der Kriegsbeschädigten," *Voss. Zeitung*, Feb. 14, 1918—both in ZStA (Potsdam) 61 Re 1/2324. Also "Kriegsteilnehmer gegen Heimkrieger," *Vorwärts*, Jan. 8, 1918; "Das Oberkommando gegen den Bund der Kriegsbeschädigten," *Vorwärts*, Jan. 18, 1918.

59. For example: "Die Kriegsteilnehmer und Kriegsbeschädigten gegen die Vaterlandspartei," *Vorwärts*, Nov. 12, 1917; "Kriegsbeschädigte gegen Vaterlandspartei," *Vorwärts*, Jan. 7, 1918.

60. "Unsere Demonstration vor dem Kriegsministerium," *Reichsbund*, Dec. 27, 1918; "Der Erfolg unserer Demonstration," *Reichsbund*, Jan. 8, 1919.

61. Frank, *Der Mensch*, pp. 200–201.

62. Remarque, *Der Weg zurück*, pp. 148–149.

63. Margarete Cordemann, *Wie es wirklich gewesen ist* (Gladbach: Scriftenmission, 1963), p. 195.

64. Cuno Horkenbach, ed., *Das deutsche Reich von 1918 bis Heute* (Berlin: Verlag für Presse, Wirtschaft und Politik, 1930), p. 66.

65. Besprechung in der Reichskanzlei mit Vertretern der Kriegsbeschädigten am Freitag, den 25. April 1919, BA R 43I/705.

66. "Die Kriegsbeschädigten im neuen Deutschland," *Reichsbund*, Nov. 22, 1918.

67. "Die Zersplitterung der Kriegsteilnehmerbewegung," *Vorwärts*, June 28, 1918.

68. Franz Behrens, *Die Organisation der Heeresentlassenen* (Hagen: Rippel, 1918); Reichsbund, ed., *Die Kriegsbeschädigten-Organisationen in Deutschland* (Berlin: Selbstverlag d. Reichsbundes, n.d.).

69. "Bundesarbeit im Ausland," *Deutscher Offizier-Bund*, Apr. 1, 1922.

70. "Spaltung des Reichsbundes der Kriegsbeschädigten," *Vorwärts*, Feb. 21, 1919; "Eine Absplitterung vom Reichsbund," *Reichsbund*, Feb. 28, 1919.

71. Erich Rossmann, "Warum sind wir parteipolitisch neutral?" *Reichsbund*, Mar. 7, 1919.

72. Reichsbund, ed., *Die K.B. Organisationen*, pp. 15–16.

73. Vermerk, "Mitglieger der K.B. u. K.H. Vereinigungen," prepared by Abt III, RAM, in response to letter from Kyffhäuser Bund to RAM, Oct. 15, 1921, ZStA (Potsdam) 39.01/7540.

9. The National Pension Law of 1920

1. *Gesetz über die Versorgung der Militärpersonen und ihrer Hinterbliebenen bei Dienstbeschädigung (Reichsversorgungsgesetz)*, vom 12. Mai 1920, *RGBl.* 1920, No. 112, p. 989.

2. *Kriegsbeschädigte! Kriegshinterbliebene! Was leistet das Reich für Euch?* (Berlin: Reichszentrale für Heimatdienst, 1920).

3. *Akten der Reichskanzlei*, ed. Karl Erdmann and Wolfgang Mommsen, *Kabinett Scheidemann* (Boppard: Boldt, 1971), "Ausführungen des Reichsfinanzministers vor dem Reichskabinett über die finanzielle Leistungsfähigkeit des Reichs," Apr. 26, 1919, p. 236.

4. *Die deutsche Nationalversammlung*, IV, 33. Sitzung, Apr. 9, 1919, pp. 2214–2215.

5. For contemporary guides to the system, see, for example, Josef Nothaas, "Die Kriegsbeschädigtenfürsorge unter besonderer Berücksichtigung Bayerns" (Diss., Munich, 1921); Alfred Dick, "Die Kriegsbeschädigtenversorgung" (Diss., Frankfurt/Hair, 1930).

6. Verordnung des Reichskanzlers vom 5. Okt. 1919, *RGBl.* 1919, p. 1784.

7. *Kriegsbeschädigte! Kriegshinterbliebene!*

8. See: Verfassung der Militärversorgungsgerichte u. des Reichs- Militärversorgungsgerichts, vom 18. Feb. 1919, BA R116/293.

9. Verordnung über die soziale Kriegsbeschädigten- und Kriegshinterbliebenenfürsorge, vom 8. Feb. 1919, *RGBl.* 1919, No. 37, p. 187; "Die Durchführungsbestimmungen der Länder zur Verordnung vom 8. Feb. 1919," *50 Jahre Kriegsopfer- und Schwerbeschädigtenfürsorge*, ed. Arbeitsgemeinschaft der deutschen Hauptfürsorgestellen (Munich: Arbeitsgemeinschaft der deutschen Hauptfürsorgestellen, 1969), p. 45.

10. *Akten*, Kabinett Scheidemann, "Kabinettssitzung vom 16. April 1919," p. 178.

11. Pertinent legislation included: *Bekanntmachung betreffend Ausführungsbestimmungen zum Gesetz über Kapitalabfindung an Stelle von Kriegsversorgung (Kapitalabfindungsgesetz) und zum Gesetze zur Ergänzung des Kapitalabfindungsgesetzes,* vom 11. Jan. 1919, *RGBl.* 1919, No. 6, p. 23; *Verordnung, betreffend eine vorläufige Landarbeitsordnung,* vom 24. Jan. 1919, *RGBl.* 1919, No. 21, p. 111 (sec. 19); *Verordnung über die Errichtung von Arbeitskammern im Bergbau,* vom 8. Feb. 1919, *RGBl.* 1919, No. 42, p. 202 (sec. 2, no. 5); *Verordnung über die Einstellung von Arbeitern und Angestellten während der Zeit der wirtschaftlichen Demobilmachung,* vom 3. Sept. 1919, *RGBl.* 1919, No. 167, p. 1500 (sec. 13); *Grunderwerbsteuergesetz,* vom 12. Sept. 1919, *RGBl.* 1919, No. 179, p. 1617 (sec. 21).

12. *Verordnung über Beschäftigung Schwerbeschädigter,* vom 9. Jan. 1919, *RGBl.* 1919, No. 6, p. 28 (sec. 1).

13. The measure was altered on Feb. 1, 1919, *RGBl.* 1919, p. 132; Mar. 11, 1919, *RGBl.* 1919, p. 301; Apr. 10, 1919, *RGBl.* 1919, p. 389; June 14, 1919, *RGBl.* 1919, p. 581, Aug. 11, 1919, *RGBl.* 1919, p. 1382, and Sept. 24, 1919, *RGBl.* 1919, p. 1720.

14. See especially the remarks of Anton Kirschensteiner in *50 Jahre*, p. 33.

15. *Ibid.*

16. *Ibid.*

17. It would, of course, be of great interest to trace the precise evolution of the law as it circulated among the ministries. Available evidence does not, unfortunately, permit such a reconstruction.

18. *Die deutsche Nationalversammlung,* IX:376.

19. *Kriegsbeschädigte! Kriegshinterbliebene!*

20. RVG secs. 1–2.

21. RVG sec. 26.

22. RVG sec. 27.

23. RVG secs. 27–29.

24. RVG sec. 51.

25. RVG sec. 87.

26. RVG sec. 31.

27. RVG sec. 32.

28. RVG sec. 30.

29. RVG sec. 34.

30. RVG sec. 35.

31. RVG sec. 33.

32. RVG secs. 4–20.

33. RVG secs. 37–49.

34. RVG secs. 4–23.

35. RVG secs. 72–85.

10. *Building up and Tearing down the Pension System,*
1920–1923

1. Richard Meier, "Fürsorge für die Kriegsopfer," *Vorwärts,* Feb. 2, 1921.

2. "Quosque Tandem—Wie lange noch?" *Zentralblatt,* July 1, 1921.

3. "Denkschrift über das Versorgungswesen," RAM, Reichstag Druck No. 5725, Apr. 6, 1923.

4. Letter from RVGer, signed Dr. Rabeling, to the Labor Minister, Aug. 4, 1928, BA R116/299.

5. "Drohender Zusammenbruch des Reichsversorgungsgerichts," *Reichsbund,* June 1, 1921.

6. "Die Notlage der Kriegsopfer in der Plenarsitzung des Reichstages," *Zentralblatt,* June 1, 1922.

7. See Chapter 7.

8. Letter from Finance Minister Erzberger to the Cabinet, Sept. 29, 1919, BA R43I/866. See also: Letter from Finance Minister Erzberger to the Assistant to the Chancellor, Aug. 13, 1919, BA R43I/866.

9. *Reichshaushaltspläne für 1919, 1920, 1921, 1922,* BA RD 47/1.

10. Letter from the War Victims Care Office, Halberstadt, to Regional War Victims Office, Merseburg, Dec. 15, 1922. ZStA (Potsdam) 39.01/8890.

11. *Akten,* Kabinett Stresemann, II, No. 256, "Der Reichsfinanzminister (Dr. Luther) an den Reichsarbeitsminister," Nov. 21, 1923, p. 1157.

12. "Zur Neuwahl des Reichstages," *Reichsbund,* Apr. 1924.

13. "Die Verabschiedung der Novelle zum RVG," *Reichsbund,* June 27, 1923.

14. See "Gegen die Entrechtung," *Reichsbund,* Jan. 1924; "Zum Personalabbau," *Reichsbund,* Jan. 1924; "Unsere Protestkundgebungen," *Reichsbund,* Feb. 1924; "Ein neues Jahr—und neue Kämpfe," *Zentralblatt,* Jan. 1924; "Und der Reichstag?" *Zentralblatt,* Mar. 1924.

15. "Weitere Abbau der Versorgungsrechtsprechung," *Reichsbund,* Feb. 1924.

16. *Verordnung über die Fürsorgepflicht,* Feb. 13, 1924, *RGBl.* 1924, I:100.

17. *Verordnung über das Verfahren in Versorgungssachen,* Feb. 19, 1924, *RGBl.* 1924, I:59. Also "Geschäftslage des Reichsversorgungsgerichts, 1928," BA R116/296; Letter from President RVGer, signed Rabeling, to RAM, Apr. 4, 1922; Letter from RAM, signed Kerschensteiner, to President RVGer, Sept. 8, 1922, BA R116/294.

18. For a review of war victims' opinion at this time, see "Neue Enttäuschungen," *Zentralblatt,* Apr. 16, 1922; "Das Ringen um die Existenz," *Zentralblatt,* June 1, 1922; "Unerträgliche Zustände im Versorgungswesen," *Zentralblatt,* July 1, 1923; "Das Teuerungsgesetz: Eine weitgehende Rechtlosmachung der Kriegsopfer," *Reichsbund,* Aug. 1, 1922; "Die Not und unsere Abwehrmassnahmen," *Reichsbund,* Dec. 30, 1922; "An die Mitglieder des Reichsbundes," *Reichsbund,* Oct./Nov. 1923.

19. "Anträge zur Abänderung des Reichsversorgungsgesetzes," *Reichsbund,* Feb. 1, 1922, and Mar. 1, 1922. Also: "Zur Abänderung des RVGs," *Zentralblatt,* Feb. 1, 1922.

20. "Unsere Tabelle," *Zentralblatt,* Feb. 1, 1922.

21. See, for example: "Kriegsopfer und Teuerung," *Zentralblatt,* Sept. 1, 1921; "Das Steigen der Indexziffer," *Zentralblatt,* Mar. 1, 1922; "Die Lebensunterhaltskosten," *Zentralblatt,* May 16, 1922; "Die Forderung auf Ausgleich der Teuerung," *Reichsbund,* Jan. 15, 1922; "Teuerung und Rente," *Reichsbund,* May 1, 1922; "Die Not und unsere Abwehrmassnahmen," *Reichsbund,* Dec. 30, 1922. The most important discussion of government finance during this period is Peter-Christian Witt, "Finanzpolitik und sozialer Wandel in Krieg und Inflation, 1919–1924," in Hans Mommsen et al., eds., *Industrielles System und politische Entwicklung in der Weimarer Republik* (Düsseldorf: Droste, 1977), I:395–426.

22. "Ausweise," *Der Einheitsverband,* Jan. 15, 1922.

23. "Psychologische Streiflichten auf das Versorgungswesen," *Zentralblatt,* Apr. 16, 1921.

24. "Tanks gegen Kriegsbeschädigte," *Vorwärts,* Sept. 30, 1920.

25. "Niederschrift über den Empfang der Vertreter der Spitzenorganisationen der Kriegsopfer bei dem Herrn Reichspräsidenten am 14. Nov. 1921," ZStA (Potsdam) 06.01/180.

26. "Der Aufstieg des Reichsbundes," *Reichsbund,* May 20, 1932.

27. *Kriegsbeschädigte! Kriegshinterbliebene!*

28. "Der Versorgungsgerichte," *Zentralblatt*, July 16, 1921.

29. "5 Milliarden für den Kriegsopfer!" *Zentralblatt*, May 16, 1922.

30. "Die Forderung auf Ausgleich der Teuerung," *Reichsbund*, Jan. 15, 1922.

31. *Handbuch über den preussischen Staat*, ed. Preuss. Staatsmin. (Berlin, 1925), p. 826.

32. For example: "Die Teuerungsmassnahmen," *Zentralblatt*, June 16, 1922; "Reich und Fürsorgepflicht," *Reichsbund*, Mar. 1, 1924.

33. "Niederschrift über die Sitzung des Gesetzgebungausschusses der Reichsausschusses der K.B.- und K.H.-fürsorge, am 7. Juli 1920," BA R116/231; also, for example: "Die Reform des Reichsausschusses," *Zentralblatt*, Nov. 16, 1921; "Aus dem Reichsausschusses," *Reichsbund*, Mar. 1, 1922.

34. Letter from the Assistant to the Chancellor to the Public Information Office in the Chancellery (Reichszentrale für Heimatsdienst), Nov. 19, 1919, BA R43I/706.

35. The following narrative was re-created out of reports in the war victims' newspapers, especially "Rückblick und Ausblick," *Reichsbund*, Jan. 1, 1922; "Der Stand der Verschmelzungshandlungen," *Reichsbund*, Mar. 1, 1922; "Erfolgloses Ende der Einigungsverhandlungen," *Reichsbund*, May 1, 1922; "Zum Abbruch der Verschmelzungsverhandlungen," *Reichsbund*, July 1, 1922; "Rundschau," *Zentralblatt*, Apr. 16, 1921; "Weimar," *Zentralblatt*, May 1, 1921; "Der Stand der Einigungsverhandlungen," *Zentralblatt*, Oct. 1, 1921.

11. *The War Victims' Movement and Weimar's Democratic Potential, 1924–1928*

1. Reichsarbeitsministerium, *Deutschlands Kriegsbeschädigte, Kriegshinterbliebene und sonstige Versorgungsberechtigte* (Berlin, 1924); Reichsarbeitsministerium, *Die Ergebnisse der Zählung der Kriegsbeschädigten und Kriegshinterbliebenen* . . . (Berlin, 1926); "Denkschrift über die Ergebnisse der Zählung der Kriegsbeschädigten und Kriegshinterbliebenen vom Mai 1928," Reichsarbeitsministerium, ZStA (Potsdam) 01.01; Foerster, "Die Zahl der versorgungsberechtigten Kriegsbeschädigten und Kriegshinterbliebenen im Mai 1928," *Reichsarbeitsblatt* (Nichtamtlicher Teil), Aug. 25, 1928.

2. Foerster, "Deutschlands Kriegsbeschädigte und Kriegshinterbliebene," *Reichsarbeitsblatt*, June 24, 1926, pp. 424–428.

3. Letter from RVGer, signed Dr. Rabeling, to RAM, Aug. 4, 1928, BA R116/299.

4. Letter from RAM, signed Kirschensteiner, to President RVGer, Oct. 4, 1926, BA R116/296.

5. "Die Arbeit der Versorgungsbehörden," *Versorgung—Fürsorge. Organ des Verbandes der Kriegsbeschädigten und Kriegerhinterbliebenen des deutschen Reichskriegerbundes Kyffhäuser und seiner Landesgruppen*, Oct. 21, 1928.

6. See Reichsrat, *Vergleichende Übersicht der Reichsausgaben, 1927*, BA R43I/878; Reichsrat, *Ausgaben und Einnahmen von Reich, Ländern und Gemeinden, 1932*, BA R43I/882; Karlheinz Dederke, *Reich und Republik Deutschland, 1917–1933* (Stutt-

gart: Klett, 1978), pp. 276–277; Karl-Bernhard Netzband et al., *Währungs- und Finanzpolitik der Ära Luther, 1923–1925* (Tübingen: J. C. Mohr, 1964).

7. See Foerster, "Deutschlands Kriegsbeschädigte und Kriegshinterbliebene," *Reichsarbeitsblatt,* June 24, 1926, pp. 424–428; Reichstag, 98. Sitzung, July 21, 1925; Zweite und dritte Beratung der dritten Abänderung des *Reichsversorgungsgesetzes* . . . , comments of Erich Rossmann, BA R116/325.

8. "Dem neuen Reichstag zum Willkommengruss!" *Zentralblatt,* May 1, 1924.

9. "Der Werdegang der neuen Novelle," *Zentralblatt,* Aug. 1, 1925: *Organisations-Entwurf eines dritten Gesetzes zur Abänderung des Reichsversorgungsgesetzes und anderer Versorgungsgesetze,* June 23, 1925, BA R116/325.

10. "Was bringt die Novelle?" *Zentralblatt,* July 15, 1925.

11. *Begrundung zum Entwurf eines dritten Gesetzes zur Abänderung des Reichsversorgungsgesetzes* . . . , Reichsarbeitsministerium, n.d., BA R116/325.

12. See, for example: "Kriegsopfern und Reichstag," *Zentralblatt,* July 1, 1926; "Der Kampf der Regierung gegen die deutschen Kriegsopfer," *Zentralblatt,* Oct. 16, 1926; "Ein fünfte Novelle zum RVG—Schwere Enttäuschung für die Hinterbliebenen, Wieder nur Teilarbeit," *Reichsbund,* Nov. 1, 1927; "Weihnachtsenttäuschung," *Reichsbund,* Dec. 15, 1927.

13. *Reichsverband deutscher Kriegsbeschädigter und Kriegerhinterbliebener: Verbandstag, 18.–21. Juli 1926* (Berlin: Reichsverband, 1926).

14. Reichstag, 222. Sitzung, 1. Juli 1926. Zweite und dritte Beratung des vierten Gesetzes zur Abänderung des Reichsversorgungsgesetzes. . . . BA R116/325.

15. Reichstag, 98. Sitzung, 21. Juli 1925. Zweite und dritte Beratung der dritten Abänderung des Reichsversorgungsgesetzes. . . . BA R116/325.

16. In der Versorgungssache des Generals der Infanterie Walter Freiherr von Lüttwitz . . . gegen den Reichsfiskus . . . , 23. Nov. 1926. Reichsversorgungsgericht, BA R116/314; "Lüttwitz bezieht seine Pension," *Berliner Tageblatt,* Jan. 14, 1927, BA R116/254; "Dem Putscher die dankbare Republik," *Berliner Morgenpost,* Jan. 15, 1927, BA R116/254; "Die Pension des Putschgenerals Lüttwitz," *Vorwärts,* Jan. 15, 1927, BA R116/254.

17. *Denkschrift über die Pensionen und Wartegelder der Reichskanzler, Reichsministern und Staatssekretäre, sowie über die Pensionen der Generäle aller Grade,* Reichsfinanzministerium, Nov. 19, 1926, BA R116/321.

18. See below.

19. "Die Pension der Generäle," *Weser Zeitung,* Dec. 3, 1926, BA ZSg 103/1522; "Die 'nationalen' Fresser an der Futterkrippe der Republik," *Volkswille,* Dec. 4, 1926, BA ZSg 103/1522; "Die hohen Pensionäre der Republik," *Frankfurter Zeitung,* Dec. 2, 1926, BA ZSg 103/1522.

20. Reichstag, 98. Sitzung, 21. Juli 1925. Zweite und dritte Beratung der dritten Abänderung des *Reichsversorgungsgesetzes,* . . . . BA R116/325.

21. "Auflösung Versorgungs- und Hauptversorgungsämter?" *Volkswille,* Jan. 27, 1928, BA ZSg 103/1568.

22. "Nie wieder Krieg," *Reichsbund,* July 1924; "Warum sind wir Gegner des Krieges," *Reichsbund,* Aug. 1924; "Soldaten und Pazifismus," *Reichsbund,* Feb. 15, 1925; "Nie wieder Krieg," *Reichsbund,* Apr. 15, 1925; "An die Toten des Welt-

krieges," *Reichsbund,* Jan. 1, 1927; "Die Kunst gegen den Krieg," *Reichsbund,* May 10, 1930.

23. "Reichsbund und Staatsbürgertum," *Reichsbund,* Oct. 1924.

24. "Weiter Zersplitterung," *Reichsbund,* Aug. 25, 1929.

25. For a typical article, see "Der Daseinskampf der Kriegerwitwen," *Berliner Tageblatt,* July 16, 1921, ZStA (Potsdam) 61 Re1/2326.

26. Karl Nau, *Die wirtschaftliche und soziale Lage von Kriegshinterbliebenen* (Leipzig: Lühe, 1930).

27. *Ibid.,* p. 10.

28. *Ibid.,* p. 26.

29. *Ibid.,* p. 42.

30. *Ibid.,* p. 59.

31. *Ibid.,* p. 86.

32. *Ibid.,* p. 59.

33. *Ibid.,* pp. 100–101.

34. *Reichsverband deutscher Kriegsbeschädigter und Kriegerhinterbliebener: Verbandstag, 1926* (Berlin: Reichsverband, 1926).

35. See *Organisations-Entwurf,* 1925, BA R116/325.

36. Martha Karnoss, "Organisation der Kriegerwitwen," *Reichsbund,* May 20, 1932.

37. Letter from the Association of Thuringen County Governments, signed Röhing, to Thuringen Interior Ministry, Sept. 1, 1924, BA R116/1196.

38. See Erich Kuttner, "Warum wir Kriegsteilnehmer und Kriegsbeschädigten uns zusammengeschlossen haben," *Vorwärts,* May 27, 1917.

39. H. G., "Termin im Reichsversorgungsgericht," *Die Weit am Abend,* Dec. 26, 1928, ZStA (Potsdam) 61 Sta 1.

40. In der Versorgungssache des Arbeiters, ehemaligen Armierungssoldaten, Otto Götsch . . . RVGer, Aug. 28, 1925, BA R116/183; "Gerechtigkeit in Nöten," *Reichsverband,* Nov. 1925.

41. In der Versorgungssache des Kaufmanns, ehemaligen Sergeaten der Landwehr, Wilhelm Schmidt . . . RVGer, Mar. 28, 1925, BA R116/327.

42. In der Versorgungssache des Zimmermanns, ehemaligen Musketiers, Paul Lauer . . . RVGer, June 30, 1925, BA R116/303.

43. In der Versorgungssache des Kaufmanns, ehemaligen Unteroffiziers, Franz Reimann . . . RVGer, Jan. 14, 1926, BA R116/303.

44. *Reichsverband . . . Verbandstag, 1926.*

45. "Die Not der Gesetzgebung," *Berliner Blatt,* Feb. 21, 1928, BA R116/339.

The End and the Beginning of the War Victims Problem, 1929–1939

1. Golo Mann, *The History of Germany since 1789* (New York: Praeger, 1974), p. 4.

2. See Chapter 11.

3. Oberregierungsrat Foerster, "Die Zahl der versorgungsberechtigten Kriegsbeschädigten und Kriegshinterbliebenen im Mai 1933," RAM, *Bayerische Kriegszeitung,* Sept. 15, 1933, BayHStA Sammlung Rehse III/9–13.

4. See: "Der Zehn-Milliarden-Haushalt des Reiches," *Reichsbund,* Jan. 25, 1929; "Abstriche im Haushalt für Versorgung und Ruhegehalter?" *Reichsbund,* Apr. 25, 1929; "Kalter Abbau," *Reichsbund,* Sept. 25, 1929.

5. "251 Millionen RM jährlich Einsparungen bei der Kriegsopferversorgung gefordert," *Reichsbund,* Apr. 10, 1930; "Reichsfinanzen und Kriegsopfer," *Reichsbund,* Dec. 24, 1929.

6. Statistics are from Wolfgang Michalka and Gottfried Niedhart, eds., *Die ungeliebte Republik* (Munich: Deutscher Taschenbuch Verlag, 1980), pp. 403, 415.

7. Michalka and Niedhart, *Die ungeliebte Republik,* p. 307.

8. Erich Rossmann, "Die Entwicklung der parlamentarischen Lage für die Kriegsopfer seit dem Hamburger Bundestag," *Reichsbund,* May 25, 1930.

9. Niederschrift über eine Parteiführerbesprechung vom 8. Mai 1930, nachmittags 4:30 Uhr) im Reichskanzlerhaus, BA R43I/881.

10. "Die Versorgung der Kriegsbeschädigten und Kriegerhinterbliebenen im Reichshaushalt 1929"; "Anträge zur 6. Novelle," *Zentralblatt,* Apr. 1929; "Die Versorgungskatastrophe!" *Zentralblatt,* Nov. 1929.

11. *Verordnung des Reichspräsidenten zur Behebung finanzieller, wirtschaftlicher und sozialer Notstände,* July 26, 1930 (*RGBl.,* 1930, I:311); *Zweite Verordnung des Reichspräsidenten zur Sicherung von Wirtschaft und Finanzen,* June 5, 1931 (*RGBl.,* 1931, I:279); *Dritte Verordnung des Reichspräsidenten zur Sicherung von Wirtschaft und Finanzen, und zur Bekämpfung politischer Ausschreitungen,* Oct. 6, 1931 (*RGBl.,* 1931, I:537); *Vierte Verordnung des Reichspräsidenten zur Sicherung von Wirtschaft und Finanzen und zum Schutze des inneren Friedens,* Dec. 8, 1931 (*RGBl.,* 1931, I:273); *Verordnung des Reichspräsidenten über Massnahmen zur Erhaltung der Arbeitslosenhilfe und der Sozialversicherung sowie zur Erleichterung der Wohlfahrtslasten der Gemeinden,* June 14, 1932 (*RGBl.,* 1932, I:273). See also Preller, *Sozialpolitik,* pp. 396ff.; Nussbaum, *Wirtschaft und Staat,* sec. III; Karl Dietrich Bracher, *Die Auflösung der Weimarer Republik* (Düsseldorf: Droste, 1978), pt. 2.

12. "Was man den Kriegsopfern schon zumutete," *Zentralblatt,* Sept. 1931.

13. Letter from *Bund erblindeter Krieger* to the Assistant to the Chancellor, Oct. 20, 1932, BA R43I/709.

14. *Notruf der Kriegsopfer* (Berlin: Reichsbund, 1932).

15. "Dumpfer Groll," *Reichsbund,* Oct. 25, 1929; "Eindruchsvolle Kundgebungen gewaltiger Kriegsopfermassen," *Reichsbund,* May 10, 1931; "Demonstrationen vor dem Arbeitsministerium," *Berliner Tageblatt,* June 18, 1932, BayHStA Sammlung Rehse III/9–13.

16. "Empfang beim Reichsarbeitsminister," *Zentralblatt,* June 1930.

17. Niederschrift des Reichsausschusses vom 17. Juni 1930; 17. März 1931; 8. Sept. 1931; 4. Juli 1932. ZStA (Potsdam) 39.01/8899.

18. "Unterträgliche Härten," *Reichsbund,* June 10, 1931; "Kämpfen und nicht Zweifeln!" *Reichsbund,* June 20, 1931: "Die morderische Notverordnung," *Reichsbund,* July 20, 1931; Erich Rossmann, "Der Schlag gegen die Kriegsopfer," *Volkswille,* June 1, 1931, BA ZSg 103/1568.

19. "Wir warnen in letzter Stunde," *Zentralblatt,* Feb. 1931.

20. Letter from the Reichsbund, signed "Der Vorstand," to President von Hindenburg, Apr. 22, 1931, BA R43I/709.

21. Letter from Interessenvertretung der Kriegshinterbliebenen der Offiziere des Beurlaubtenstandes, signed Magdalen Schmelzer, to Dr. Brüning, Apr. 28, 1930, BA R43I/709.

22. *Statistisches Jahrbuch für das deutsche Reich* ed. Statistischen Reichsamt (Berlin, 1934), p. 416. See also Reichsrat, *Ausgaben und Einnahmen von Reich, Ländern und Gemeinden,* 1932, BA R43I/822; Reichsrat, *Vergleichende Übersicht der Reichs-Ausgaben, . . .* 1927, BA R43I/878; "Der Reichshaushalt 1930," *Reichsbund,* May 10, 1930.

23. Letter from Welfare Office, Stralsund, to Vorsitzenden der Ostdeutschen Dezernenten-Vereinigung, Mayor Pick, Stettin, June 6, 1930, BA R36/1190.

24. Letter from Bavarian Wholesalers Association, signed Josef Dorn, to Economic Ministry, June 15, 1927, BayHStA (II).

25. O. G. Schmidt, "Schwerbeschädigte und Arbeitgeber," *Zentralblatt,* Apr. 1929.

26. "Überspannte Forderungen?" *Reichsbund,* Oct. 10, 1929.

27. "Sparkonto: Kriegsopferversorgung," *Der Deutsche,* Mar. 5, 1930, BA ZSg 103/1568; "Sparkonto: Kriegsopferversorgung," *Zentralblatt,* Apr. 1930.

28. "Unverschämte Hetze gegen die Kriegsopfer," *Reichsbund,* Nov. 10, 1930.

29. "Die Moral der Kraft," *Zentralblatt,* Mar. 1931, "Kriegsbeschädigte hängt euch auf," *Reichsbund,* Feb. 10, 1931.

30. "Moral der Kraft," *Reichsverband,* special issue 1931, BA R116/207.

31. "Unerhörte Gefühlsroheit eines badischen Landtagsabgeordneten." *Reichsbund,* Apr. 25, 1930.

32. Ergebnis der Rechtsprechung des RVGers nach dem statistischen Jahresbericht für das Jahr 1927; Geschäftslage des RVGers, 1928, BA R116/298.

33. Letter from Prussian Mayors' Association to Mayor Halle, June 15, 1927, BA R36/1193.

34. "Der Leser hat das Wort," *Oldenburgische Landeszeitung,* June 28, 1930, BA ZSg 103/1568.

35. "Wann wir alt werden," *Zentralblatt,* Feb. 16, 1926.

36. For a brief biographical sketch of Tiedt, see Hermann Weber, *Die Wandlung des deutschen Kommunismus* (Frankfurt/Main: Europäische Verlagsanstalt, 1969), II:323–324.

37. Weber, *Die Wandlung,* II:141.

38. *Alle Kriegs- und Arbeitsopfer . . . wählen den Arbeiterkandidaten Ernst Thälmann,* n.d., BayHStA (V) F–209.

39. "Standpunkt der Kriegsopfer," *Münchner Zeitung,* Apr. 27, 1931. BA ZSg 103/1568.

40. "Feinde der Kriegsopfer," *Reichsbund,* Apr. 20, 1932, "Heraus zur Wahl!" *Reichsbund,* July 20, 1932.

41. "Massen-Protestkundgebung der münchner Kriegsopfer," *Münchner Post,* July 2/3, 1932, BayHStA Sammlung Rehse III/9–5.

42. "Kriegsopfer Aufgepasst!" July 31, 1932, BayHStA (V) F–192.

43. Otto Thiel, "Morgen wird gewählt—alter und neuer Mittelstand in der deutschen Politik," *Leipziger Neueste Nachrichten,* Sept. 13, 1930, ZStA (Potsdam) 61 Re 1/459.

44. "Missbrauchte Kriegsopfer," *Volkswille,* Jan. 22, 1931, BA ZSg 103/1568.

45. For a brief biography of Oberlindober, see *Wer ist's?,* 1935 (Leipzig: Degener, 1935): also, "Die Entwicklung der Kriegsopferversorgung bei der NSDAP," *Deutsche Kriegsopferversorgung,* Dec. 10, 1932.

46. "Entrechtung der deutschen Kriegsopfer," *Völkischer Beobachter,* Aug. 3–4, 1930. BA ZSg 103/1568; also, *Nationalsozialismus und Kriegsopfer,* n.d., BA R116/304; "Endgultiger Zusammenschluss der deutschen Kriegsopfer in der NSKOV," *Völkischer Beobachter,* July 13, 1933. BA R116/254.

47. "Zusammenschluss der Kriegsverletzten-Organizationen," *Völkischer Beobachter,* July 27, 1932, ZStA (Potsdam) 61 Sta 1/1148; "Zusammenschluss der Kriegsbeschädigten-Organisationen," *Hannoversche Landeszeitung,* July 27, 1932, BA ZSg 103/1568; "Ein Hort der deutschen Kriegsopfer," *Zentralblatt,* Sept. 1932; Dietrich Lehmann, "Zusammenschluss deutscher Kriegsopferverbände," *Völkischer Beobachter,* Sept. 9, 1932, BA ZSg 103/1568.

48. "Vereinheitlichung der Kriegsopferbewegung," *Berliner Börsen Zeitung,* Apr. 6, 1933, ZStA (Potsdam) 61 Sta 1/1150.

49. "Auf dem Wege zur Einheit!" *Zentralblatt,* May 1933.

50. "Endgültiger Zusammenschluss der deutschen Kriegsopfer in der NSKOV," *Völkischer Beobachter,* July 13, 1933, BA R116/254; Hanns Oberlindober, "Ein Jahr National-Sozialistische Kriegsopferversorgung," *Deutsche Kriegsopferversorgung,* May 1934, BayHStA Sammlung Rehse I/7–5.2.

51. Letter from the Police Commissioner, Berlin, to the National Insurance Office, Apr. 11, 1933, BA R116/311.

52. "Von Schleicher zu Hitler," *Reichsbund,* Feb. 20, 1933.

53. "Die Stimme der Kriegsbeschädigten," *Vossische Zeitung,* Mar. 16, 1933, ZStA (Potsdam) 61 Sta 1/1150.

54. "Zum Abschied," *Reichsbund,* May 1933.

55. "Die Verbesserung der Kriegsopferversorgung," *Völkischer Beobachter,* July 6, 1934, BA ZSg 124/563; Syrup, *Hundert Jahre,* pp. 525–536. The basic account of National Socialist social policy is Timothy Mason, ed., *Arbeiterklasse und Volksgemeinschaft* (Opladen: Westdeutscher Verlag, 1975).

56. "Die Kriegsopfer sind die ersten Bürger des Staates," *Berl. Börsen Zeitung,* Dec. 3, 1933, ZStA (Potsdam) 61 Sta 1/1150; Verordnung zur Durchführung der Verordnung des Reichspräsidenten über die Stiftung eines Ehrenkreuzes, July 13, 1934, BA R116/209.

57. Letter from the Police Director, Berlin, to National Insurance Office, Apr. 11, 1933, BA R116/311.

58. RVGer, Bersprechung vom 19. Dez. 1936, BA R116/259; Letter from RVGer to RAM, Sept. 10, 1937, BA R116/312.

59. Letter from Richard Haberle to President, RVGer, Oct. 14, 1936, BA R116/197.

60. Letter from Interessenvertretung der Kriegshinterbliebenen der Offiziere

des Beurlaubtenstandes, signed Magdalen Schmelzer, to Reichsführer Oberlindober, July 27, 1934, BA R43II/1285.

61. Nat.-Soz. Kriegsopferversorgung—Ortsgruppe XXVII, untitled, BayHStA
(V) F–33.

62. Vortrag über "Pflegezulage" von Regierungsrat Reinbach, Nov. 7, 1936, BA
R116/259.

63. *Statistisches Jahrbuch, 1934,* p. 416; *Statistisches Jahrbuch, 1936,* p. 446.

Conclusion: *Melancholia, Suicide, and Total Mobilization*

1. Reichsverband, *Verhandlungsbericht 5. ordentlicher Verbandstag, Juli 1930.*

2. Sigmund Freud, "Trauer und Melancholie," in *Das Ich und das Es* (Frank-
furt/Main: Fischer, 1978), p. 105.

3. Freud, "Trauer . . . ," p. 106.

4. See Wolf Lepenies, *Melancholie und Gesellschaft* (Frankfurt/Main: Suhr-
kamp, 1972); Alexander Mitscherlich and Margarete Mitscherlich, *Die Unfähigkeit
zu Trauern* (Munich: Piper, 1979); Robert Jay Lifton, *Death in Life* (New York:
Random House, 1967); Robert Jay Lifton, *The Broken Connection* (New York:
Simon and Schuster, 1979); Ernest Becker, *The Denial of Death* (New York: Free
Press, 1973).

5. "Unsere Toten sollen leben!" *Zentralblatt,* Nov. 1, 1927.

6. Letter from *Reichsverband,* signed Riemer, to Reichskanzler, July 13, 1926, BA
R43I/713.

7. "Wir grüssen die Toten," *Zentralblatt,* Nov. 1929.

8. For example: "Unseren Toten," *Reichsbund,* Nov. 15, 1919; "Das Fest der
Auferstehung," *Zentralblatt,* Apr. 1928; "Osterglocken," *Zentralblatt,* Apr. 1929;
"Das Vermächtnis unserer Toten," *Reichsbund,* Nov. 20, 1931.

9. "Unseren Toten," *Reichsbund,* Nov. 15, 1919.

10. Martha Harness, "Dem Gedenken der Toten," *Reichsbund,* Nov. 1924;
"Volkstrauertag," *Zentralblatt,* Mar. 1, 1927.

11. Martha Harness, "Dem Gedenken der Toten," *Reichsbund,* Nov. 1924; Ernst
Glaser, *Jahrgang 1902,* p. 289.

12. Letter from Interior Minister to State Governments, Nov. 8, 1921, BayHStA
(II) MK 19280; "Überführungen in die Heimat," *Kriegsgräberfürsorge,* Dec. 1921.

13. On the general question of cemeteries, see George Mosse, "Sol-
datenfriedhöfe und nationale Wiedergeburt: Der Gefallenenkult in Deutschland,"
in Vondung, *Kriegserlebnis,* pp. 241–261.

14. *Kriegsgräberfürsorge,* Jan./Feb. 1921.

15. Speech by President Siems, of the *Volksbund,* before the Reichstag, Mar. 13,
1927, BA R43I/711.

16. Letter from the Federal Representative in Munich, signed Haniel, to Chancellor, Mar. 5, 1926, BA R43I/711; "Volkstrauertag am 1. März 1925," *Reichsbund,*
Feb. 15, 1925.

17. Letter from Interior Ministry, signed Severing, to the Assistant to the Chancellor Nov. 29, 1920, BA R43I/711; Niederschrift über die Verhandlungen, betreffend Volkstrauertag, Feb. 17, 1922, Apr. 8, 1925, Dec. 11, 1925, Nov. 29, 1929, ZStA

(Merseburg) Rep 191/Abt II/3908–3909; Letter from the Prussian Interior Minister, signed Severing, to the Prussian Provincial Presidents, Jan. 5, 1932, BA R43I/712.

18. Kabinettsprotokolle, Sitzung am 22. Feb. 1921, BA R43I/1363: Auszug aus der Ministerbesprechung aus dem Protokoll vom 15. Dez. 1927, BA R43I/711.

19. "Ein Ehrenmal für die Gefallenen," *Berliner Tageblatt*, Aug. 3, 1924, BA R43I/713.

20. Letter from the *Stahlhelm, Bund der Frontsoldaten,* signed Seldte, to the Chancellor, July 20, 1925, BA R43I/713; Letter from Mayor Konrad Adenauer, Cologne, to Chancellor Luther, June 2, 1925, BA R43I/713; Interior Ministry, *Zusammenstellung der dem R. Min d. Inn. bekannt gewordenen Vorschläge zur Errichtung eines Nationaldenkmals für die Gefallenen im Weltkriege*, Nov. 1925, BA R43I/713; Dr. R. Klapheck, *Die Toteninsel im Rhein*, BA R43I/713; F. A. Lattmann, *Das Reichs-Ehrenmal und Goslar*, n.d., BA R43I/713; *Deutsches Bauwesen*, Sonderdruck, *Zur Frage des Reichsehrenmals*, June 1927, BA R43I/715.

21. *Die neue Wache als Gedächtnisstätte für die Gefallenen des Weltkrieges* (Berlin: Deutsche Kunstverlag, 1931), BA R43I/712.

22. "Geschäfte mit Kriegergräbern," *Deutsche Zeitung*, Mar. 1, 1929, "Der französische Kriegsgräberskandal," *Vossische Zeitung*, Dec. 24, 1929. "Der Kriegsgräberskandal," *Vorwärts*, Jan. 20, 1930, "Tote als Geschäft," *Der Deutsche*, Feb. 2, 1930—all in ZStA (Potsdam) 15.01/13029. Also, "Geldgierige Hyänen des Schlachtfeldes," *Reichsbund*, Feb. 10, 1930.

23. Bertolt Brecht, "Legende vom toten Soldaten," in *Hauspostille* (New York: Grove Press, 1966), p. 309; Hans Chlumberg, *Wunder um Verdun* (Berlin: S. Fischer, 1932); Walter Flex, *Das Weihnachts-Märchen des 50sten Regiments* (Munich: Beck, n.d.); Ernst Toller, *Die Wandlung*, in *Prosa–Briefe–Dramen–Gedichte* (Hamburg: Rowohlt, 1961), pp. 235–285; "Der Geisterzung," *Reichsbund*, Aug. 7, 1920.

24. H. Steinmann, "Die Vergessenen," *Zentralblatt*, Oct. 1, 1921.

25. Heinrich Lersch, "Grabschrift," in *Das dichterische Werk* (Berlin: Deutsche Verlags-Anstalt, 1934), p. 292.

26. A poem such as Lersch's "Verstossen," in which a soldier is tormented by the realization that he has killed other human beings, is an exception. See Heinrich Lersch, "Verstossen," in Fünter Heintz, ed., *Deutsche Arbeiterdichtung, 1910–1933* (Stuttgart: Reclam, 1974), pp. 88–89.

27. Letter from Bavarian Bund-Kriegsbeschädigte to RAM, Nov. 1919, ZStA (Potsdam) 39.01/7539.

28. "Zur Psychologie der deutschen Kriegsopfer," *Zentralblatt*, June 16, 1921.

29. Gotthold Schanz, "Was Kriegsbeschädigte denken," *Zentralblatt*, Feb. 16, 1921.

30. Alfred Döblin, *Berlin Alexanderplatz* (Munich: Deutscher Taschenbuch, 1978), p. 99.

31. See Chapter 12, above. Also see comments by Paul Reimer in Reichsverband, *Verhandlungsbericht. 5. ordentlicher Verbandstag, Juli 1930* (Berlin: Reichsverband, 1930), p. 35.

32. For example, see Blücher, *An English Wife*, pp. 241–242; George Grosz, *Ein kleines Ja und ein grosses Nein* (Hamburg: Rowohlt, 1955), p. 120.

33. Kriegsmin. Erlass 350/6. 17 AZS 6 v. 19. 7. 17, Dec. 19, 1917, ZStA (Potsdam) 39.01/8861; "Grossstädtische Kriegsbeschädigten-Fürsorge," *KBKH*, No. 2/3 (July/Aug. 1916), 74; "Gegen den Bettelunfug," *Vossische Zeitung*, Nov. 21, 1919, ZStA (Potsdam) 61 Re 1/2322; "Eine Massenepidemie geheilt," *Berliner Tageszeitung*, Dec. 21, 1919, ZStA (Potsdam) 61 Re 1/2322.

34. "Im Kampfe gegen die Strassenbettelei unter dem Deckmantel-'Kriegsbeschädigter,'" *Reichsbund*, July 19, 1919.

35. For instance, "Neues Bettelunternehmen des Zentralverbandes," *Reichsbund*, Apr. 1, 1922.

36. "Krüppel—Song," *Reichsbund*, Sept. 10, 1930.

37. "Psychologische Streiflichter auf das Versorgungswesen," *Zentralblatt*, Aug. 16, 1921.

38. Letter from Anna Schulz to President, RVGer, May 31, 1932, BA R116/196.

39. Michael von Faulhaber, *Das hohe Lied der Kriegsfürsorge* (Berlin: Kameradschaft, 1916), pp. 19–20.

40. Remarque, *Im Westen*, pp. 21–22.

41. Erwin Stransky, *Krieg und Geistesstörung* (Wiesbaden: Bergmann, 1918), p. 53.

42. Marc, *Briefe*, p. 7; Remarque, *Im Westen*, p. 12. Also see Remarque, *Im Westen*, pp. 19, 25, 91; Paul Alverdes, *Reinhold im Dienst* (Munich: Langen & Müller, 1936), pp. 20, 96, 98; Remarque, *Im Westen*, p. 96; Beumelburg, *Die Gruppe Bosemüller*, p. 189; Alverdes, *Pfeiferstube*, pp. 32, 81; Franz Seldte, *M.G.K.* (Leipzig: Koehler, 1929), p. 257; Lehmann, *Wir von der Infanterie*, p. 192.

43. "Der gute Kamerad," in *Taschen-Kommersbuch*, p. 153.

44. "Psychologische Streiflichter auf das Versorgungswesen," *Zentralblatt*, Aug. 16, 1921.

45. Max Isserling, *Über psychische und nervöse Erkrankungen bei Kreigsteilnehmern* (Würzburg: Kabitzsch, 1917), p. 249; Moses, *Zum Problem*, p. 34; Friedrich Pause, "Das Schicksal von Renten- und Kriegsneurotikern nach Erledigung ihrer Ansprüche," *Archiv für Psychiatrie und Nervenkrankheiten*, Sonderdruck, 1926, BA R116/326; P. Schröder, "Rentensucht und moralischer Schwachsinn," *Deutsche Medizinische Wochenschrift*, Sonderabdruck, 1926, BA R116/326.

46. "Das Ergebnis der im März 1929 im Reichsarbeitsministerium abgehaltenen Konferenz über die 'Unfall- (Kriegs-) Neurose," *Zentralblatt*, Apr. 1929, BA R116/326.

47. Reichsbund, *Notruf der Kriegsopfer* (Berlin: 1932).

48. Freud, "Trauer . . . " pp. 113–114.

49. "Am Leben verzweifelt," *Reichsbund*, Feb. 25, 1931.

50. "Die morderische Notverordnung," *Reichsbund*, July 20, 1931.

51. "Ein grausige Tat und ein erschütterndes Document," *Reichsbund*, July 5, 1931.

52. Lepenies, *Melancholie und Gesellschaft*, pp. 19–34.

53. Prümm, *Die Literatur*, II, ch. 8.

54. See Friedrich Stampfer, *Erfahrungen und Erkenntnisse* (Cologne: Verlag für Politik und Wirtschaft, 1957), p. 212.

Bibliography

Unpublished Sources

This book is based primarily on archival sources. Each archival item has its own code, the first part of which identifies the archive, the second part the holding. Thus "BA R 116/2," for example, means Bundesarchiv, Koblenz, item R 116/2, which happens to be a file from the Reichsversorgungsgericht, the National Pension Court.

Some of the more important archival holdings I consulted: (a) The Bayerisches Hauptstaatsarchiv, Munich, Abteilung II, has the records of the Bavarian Interior Ministry (MInn series), and the Bavarian Ministry for Religious and Educational Affairs (MK series); from Abteilung IV, the Kriegsarchiv, the War Ministry records concerning disabled veterans (MKr 12677, etc.); in Abteilung V, pamphlets from the several war victims' groups (F 192, F 194, F 195). (b) In the Bundesarchiv, Koblenz, the records of the Reichskanzlei (R 43I/ 705–720) and the Reichsversorgungsgericht, the National Pension Court (R 116), were particularly valuable. (c) In the Hauptstaatsarchiv, Stuttgart, the Labor Ministry records (E 361). Records from the Prussian provincial administrations were very useful in (d) the Hessisches Hauptstaatsarchiv, Wiesbaden (Abt 405), and in (e) the Landesarchiv, Koblenz (Best. 403 and Best. 404). Some personal files of pensioners have survived, and though in general they are not open, some are available to scholars. The (f) Landesarchiv, Speyer, maintains some of these personal records. Both (g) the Zentrales Staatsarchiv in Merseburg and the (h) Zentrales Staatsarchiv in Potsdam have invaluable records. In Merseburg, the records from the Prussian Commissioner for Wartime Social Service (Rep 191/Abt II) were very helpful. In Potsdam, are the records from the Reich Labor Ministry (39.01) and the Reich Interior Ministry (15.01).

A number of periodicals from the 1920s and 1930s were devoted to war victims' issues. The official publications of the Reich Labor Ministry (*Reichsarbeitsblatt*) and the Reich Insurance Office (*Reichsversorgungsblatt*) are important sources. More important are the newspapers of the various war victims' groups; the newspaper usually had the same name as the group. Thus, the Reichsbund published a newspaper for its members called *Reichsbund*. Some of these publications are available through archives; others can be obtained through university libraries.

Readers interested in a complete list of archival sources and periodicals should consult my doctoral dissertation, which bears the same title as this book (Cornell University, 1982).

Published Sources

Ahnert, Kurt. *Sprühende Heeressprache.* (Nuremberg: Burgverlag, 1917).

Akten der Reichskanzlei. Ed. Karl Erdmann and Wolfgang Mommsen. (Boppard: Boldt, 1971).

von Altrock, Constantin. *Vom Sterben des deutschen Offizierkorps.* (Berlin: E. S. Mittler, 1921).

Alverdes, Paul. *Die Pfeiferstube.* (Potsdam: Rütten & Loening, 1941).

——. *Reinhold im Dienst.* (Munich: Langen & Müller, 1936).

Angell, James. *The Recovery of Germany.* (New Haven: Yale University Press, 1929).

Atherton, Gertrude. *The White Morning.* (New York: Frederick A. Stokes, 1918).

Bab, Julius. *Die deutsche Kriegslyrik.* (Stettin: Norddeutscher Verlag, 1920).

——, ed. *Der deutsche Krieg im deutschen Gedicht.* (Berlin: Morwe, 1919).

Bächthold, Hanns. *Deutscher Soldatenbrauch und Soldatenglaube.* (Strassburg: Trübners Bibliothek, 1917).

Balck, W. *Entwicklung der Taktik im Weltkrieg.* (Berlin: R. Eisenschmidt, 1920).

Bauer, Joachim. "Hysterische Erkrankungen bei Kriegsteilnehmern." (Kiel: Diss., 1916).

Baumgärtner, G. A. *Deutsches Kriegsbuch: Erinnerungsgabe der Bayerischen Kriegsinvalidenfürsorge.* (Munich: Knorr & Herth, 1916).

Baumgarten, Otto, et al. *Geistige und sittliche Wirkung des Krieges in Deutschland.* (Stuttgart: Deutscher Verlag, 1927).

Bejach, Kurt. "Die sozialen Aufgaben des Arztes bei der Wiederertüchtigung schwerbeschädigter Handwerker und Industriearbeiter." (Königsberg: Diss., 1919).

Benn, Gottfried. *Frühe Prose und Reden.* (Wiesbaden: Limes, 1950).

Beradt, Martin. *Erdarbeiter.* (Berlin: Fischer, 1919).

Berger, Siegfried. *Die tapferen Füsse.* (Merseburg: Stollberg, 1947).

Bergmann, Karl. *Wie der Feldgraue spricht.* (Giessen: Alfred Töpelmann, 1916).

Bernhard, Ludwig. *Unerwünschte Folgen der deutschen Sozialpolitik.* (Berlin: Springer, 1913).

Bernstein, Hans. *Militärische Invalidenfürsorge bei den Ersatztruppen.* (Berlin: Vossische Buchhandlung, 1917).

Beumelburg, Werner. *Douaumont.* (Oldenburg: Gerhard Stalling, 1923).

——. *Die Gruppe Bosemüller.* (Oldenburg: Gerhard Stalling, 1930).

Biese, Alfred, ed. *Poesie des Krieges.* (Berlin: G. Grote, 1916).

Binding, Rudolf. *Aus dem Kriege.* (Frankfurt/Main: Rütten & Loening, 1929).

——. *Der Wingult.* (Potsdam: Rütten & Loening, 1941).

——. *Die Waffenbrüder.* Potsdam: Rütten & Loening, 1925).

——. *Unsterblichkeit.* Potsdam: Rütten & Loening, 1941).

Bloch, Marc. *Memoirs of War, 1914–15.* (Ithaca: Cornell University Press, 1980).

Bloem, W. *Weltbrand.* (Berlin: Reimar Hobbing, 1931).

Blücher, Princess Evelyn. *An English Wife in Berlin.* (New York: Dutton, 1920).

Blum, Paul. *Menschen im Zwinger.* (Leipzig: Otto Hillmann, 1930).

Böttcher, Walter. "Die Waisenpflege der Stadt Berlin." (Giessen: Diss., 1923).

Brandt, Heinrich. *Trommelfeuer.* (Hamburg: Fackelreiter, 1930).

Braun, Otto. *Aus nachgelassenen Schriften eines Frühvollendeten.* Ed. Julie Vogelstein. (Berlin: Hermann Klemm, 1924).

Braun, Reinhold. *Unseren Kriegsbeschädigten.* (Berlin: Stiftungsverlag, 1916).

Brauns, Heinrich. *Katholische Sozialpolitik im 20. Jahrhundert.* (Mainz: Matthias-Grünewald, 1976).

Brecht, Bertolt. *Hauspostille.* (New York: Grove, 1966).

Breyer, Erich. "Zusammenfassung der Entwichlung und Umbildung der deutschen Kriegsbeschädigten Versorgung." (Jena: Diss., 1922).

Bröger, Karl. *Der Held im Schatten.* (Jena: Eugen Diederichs, 1930).

Brugsch, Theodor. *Arzt seit fünf Jahrzehnten.* (Berlin: Rütten & Loening, 1958).

Bullitt, Ernesta Drinker. *An Uncensored Diary from the Central Empires.* (Garden City: Doubleday, Page, 1917).

Bumm, Franz, ed. *Deutschlands Gesundheitsverhältnisse unter dem Einfluss des Weltkrieges.* (Stuttgart: Deutscher Verlag, 1928).

Carossa, Hans. *Tagebuch im Kriege.* Leipzig: Insel, n.d.).

Chlumberg, Hans. *Wunder um Verdun.* (Berlin: Fischer, 1932).

Cordemann, Margarete. *Wie es wirklich gewesen ist.* (Gladback: Schriftenmission, 1963).

Cysarz, Herbert. *Zur Geistesgeschichte des Weltkrieges.* (Halle: Max Neimeyer, 1931).

Delbrück, Joachim, ed. *Der deutsche Krieg in Feldpostbriefen.* (Munich: Georg Müller, 1917).

Delcourt, René. *Empressions d'argot allemand et autrichien.* (Paris: Boccard, 1917).

Deutsches Rotes Kreuz. *Die organisatorischen Aufgaben des roten Kreuzes.* (Berlin: Deutsches Rotes Kreuz, 1925).

Devine, Edward. *Disabled Soldiers' and Sailors' Pensions and Training.* (New York: Oxford University Press, 1919).

Dick, Alfred. "Die Kriegsbeschädigtenversorgung." (Frankfurt/Main: Diss., 1930).

von Dickhuth-Harrach, G. *Im Felde Unbesiegt.* (Munich: J. F. Lehmann, 1933).

Dix, Kurt. *Der grosse Krieg als Erlebnis und Erfahrung.* (Gotha: F. A. Perthes, 1915).

Dix, Otto. *Der Krieg.* (Berlin: Karl Nierendorf, 1924).

Döblin, Alfred. *Berlin Alexanderplatz.* (Munich: Deutscher Taschenbuch, 1978).

——. *November 1918.* (Munich: Deutscher Taschenbuch, 1978).

Dörken, Oskar. "Ein Beitrag zu dem Kapitel: Traumatische Kriegs-Neurosen und Psychosen." (Kiel: Diss., 1916).

Dwinger, Edwin. *Die Armee hinter Stacheldraht.* (Jena: Eugen Diedrichs, 1929).

——. *Die letzten Reiter.* (Bergisch Gladbach: Gustav Lubbe, 1978).

Bibliography

von Faulhaber, Michael. *Das hohe lied der Kriegsfürsorge*. (Berlin: Kameradschaft, 1916).

Ferenczi, Sandor, et al. *Psycho-Analysis and the War Neuroses*. (London: International Psycho-Analytical Press, 1921).

Finkenrath, Kurt. "Ein Beitrag zur Kriegshysterie auf Grund von Feld- und Heimatbeobachtungen." (Marburg: Diss., 1920).

Flex, Walter. *Gesammelte Werke*. (Munich: Beck, 1925).

Foerster, Wolfgang, ed. *Wir Kämpfer im Weltkrieg*. (Berlin: Deutsche Betriebsstelle amtlicher Publikationen, 1929).

Franck, Harry. *Vagabonding through Changing Germany*. (New York: Grosset & Dunlap, 1920).

Frank, Leonard. *Der Mensch ist gut*. (Zurich: Max Rascher, 1918).

Frankenstein, Luise. "Die soziale Kriegsbeschädigtenfürsorge während des Krieges." (Griefswald: Diss., 1920).

Freidländer, Prof. Dr. *Nerven- und Geisteskrankheiten im Felde und im Lazarett*. (Wiesbaden: Bergmann, 1918).

——. *Medizin und Krieg*. (Wiesbaden: Bergmann, 1918).

Freud, Sigmund. *Das Ich und das Es*. (Frankfurt/Main: Fischer, 1978).

——. *The Standard Edition of the Complete Psychological Works*. (London: Hogarth, 1957).

Frey, A. M. *Die Pflasterkästen: Ein Feldsanitätsroman*. (Berlin: Gustav Kiepenheuer, 1929).

Friedrich, Wolfgang, ed. *Im Klassenkampf: Deutsche revolutionäre Lieder und Gedichte aus der zweiten Hälfte des 19. Jahrhunderts*. (Halle: VEB Verlag Sprache und Literatur, 1962).

Fuchs, Gustav. *Der deutsche Pazifismus im Weltkrieg*. (Stuttgart: Kohlhammer, 1928).

von Gall, Freiherr, ed. *Taschenkalender für das Heer, 1917*. (Berlin: Georg Bath, 1916).

Gärtner, A., ed. *Weyl's Handbuch der Hygiene*. (Leipzig: J. A. Barth, 1918).

Geiger, Anni. *Der Lebensweg eines Kriegs-und Fürsorgekindes*. (Stuttgart: D. Gundert, 1929).

von Gerhardt, Dr. *Aus dem Seelenleben des Blinden*. (Frankfurt/Main: Emil Münster, 1917).

Gläser, Ernst. *Jahrgang 1902*. (Bonn: Schaack, 1947).

Goering, Reinhard. *Seeschlacht*. (Stuttgart: Reclam, 1975).

Golther, Wolfgang. *Deutsche Heldensage*. (Dresden: L. Ehlermann, 1894).

Goth-Emmerich, Luise. *Rosen vom Felde der Ehre*. (Munich: Verlag vom Bayerischen Kriegsarchiv, 1926).

Gottlob, Friedrich. "Die Versorgungsansprüche der Kriegsbeschädigten." (Greifswald: Diss., 1918).

Graf, Oskar Maria. *Wir sind Gefangene*. (Munich: Deutscher Taschenbuch, 1981).

Grote, L. R., ed. *Die Medizin der Gegenwart in Selbstdarstellungen*. (Leipzig: Felix Meiner, 1923).

Gundermann, Wilhelm. "Kriegschirurgischer Bericht aus des giessener Klinik über die ersten 5 Monaten des Krieges." (Giessen: Diss., 1915).

Günther, Adolf. *Theorie der Sozialpolitik,* (Berlin: 1922).

Harrfeldt, Hans. "Paralyse und Kriegsbeschädigung." (Kiel: Diss., 1917).

Hase, A. *Beiträge zur Biologie der Kleiderlaus.* (Berlin: P. Parey, 1915).

———. "Weitere Beobachtungen über Läuseplage," *Zentralblatt für Bakteriologie,* 2 (1915).

Haugg, Hans. "Methodik und Systematik der Kriegsbeschädigten und Kriegerhinterbliebenen Statistik." (Erlangen: Diss., 1922).

Hauser, Victor. "Der Versorgungsanspruch der Kriegsbeschädigten und Kriegshinterbliebenen und der Zulässigkeit des Rechtswegs." (Erlangen: Diss., 1920).

Hein, Alfred. *Eine Kompagnie Soldaten in der Hölle von Verdun.* (Minden: Wilhelm Köhler, 1930).

Hellwig, Albert. *Weltkrieg und Aberglaube.* (Leipzig: Heims, 1916).

Henck, Ed., ed. *Briefe einer Heidelberger Burschenschaft, 1914–1918.* (Baden: Moriz Schauenburg, 1919).

Herz, Richard. "Die Rechtsstellung des Kriegsbeschädigten." (Erlangen: Diss., 1922).

Herzog, Rudolf. *Kameraden.* (Berlin: August Scherl, 1922).

Heyde, Ludwig. *Abriss der Sozialpolitik.* (Leipzig: Quelle & Meyer, 1923).

Heyder, Albrecht. "Uber die hyperalgetische Form der Kriegshysterie." (Jena: Diss., 1920).

Hezel, O. et al. *Die Kriegsbeschädigungen des Nervensystems.* (Wiesbaden: Bergmann, 1918).

Hiddemann, Ernst. "Statistische Beiträge zu Frage der Kriegsneurosen." (Bonn: Diss., 1921).

Hirschfeld, Magnus. *The Sexual History of the War.* (New York: Cadillac, 1944).

His, Wilhelm. *Die Front der Ärzte.* (Bielefeld: Delhagen & Klasing, 1931).

Hochstetter, Gustav. *Der Feldgraue Büchmann.* (Berlin: Lustige Blatter, 1916).

Höcker, Hauptmann d. L., ed. *Liller Kriegszeitung.* (Berlin: W. Vobach, 1915).

Höcker, Paul. *An der Spitze meiner Kompagnie.* (Berlin: Ullstein, 1915).

Hoffman, Helmut. *Mensch und Volk im Kriegserlebnis.* (Berlin: Germanische Studien, 1937).

Hoffmann, Robert. "Über die Behandlung der Kriegshysterie in den badischen Nervenlazaretten." (Heidelberg: Diss., 1920).

Hoffmann, W. *Die deutschen Ärzte im Weltkrieg.* (Berlin: E. S. Mittler, 1920).

Hofmann, Karl. "Psychopathische Zustände bei Kriegsteilnehmern der Marine." (Kiel: Diss., 1920).

Horkenbach, Cuno, ed. *Das deutsche Reich von 1918 bis Heute.* (Berlin: Verlag für Presse, Wirtschaft und Politik, 1930).

Horn, Paul. *Die deutsche Soldatensprache.* (Giessen: Richersche Verlagsbuchhandlung, 1899).

Howe, Frederic. *Socialized Germany.* (New York: Scribner, 1916).

Hurwitz-Stranz, Helene, ed. *Kriegerwitwen gestalten ihr Schicksal.* (Berlin: Carl Heymann, 1931).

Bibliography

Illustrierte Zeitung. 26 November 1925. "Zur Überführung des Berühmten, am 21. April 1918 in Frankreich abgeschossenen Kampffliegers Manfred Freiherr von Richtofen nach Deutschland: Die Beisetzungs-Feierlichkeiten am 19. und 20. November," p. 817.

Imme, Theodor. *Die deutsche Soldatensprache der Gegenwart und ihr Humor.* (Dortmund: Ruhfus, 1917).

Isserling, Max. *Über psychische und nervöse Erkrankungen bei Kriegsteilnehmern.* (Würzburg: Kabitzsch, 1917).

Jaramillo Infante, Carlos. "Über psychogene Hör- und Sprachstörungen bei Kriegsteilnehmern." (Bonn: Diss., 1917).

Johann, Ernst, ed. *Innenansicht eines Krieges: Deutsche Dokumente, 1914–1918.* (Munich: Deutscher Taschenbuch, 1973).

Johannsen, Ernst. *Brigadevermittlung.* (Stuttgart: Reclam, 1977).

——. *Fronterinnerungen eines Pferdes.* (Hamburg: Fackelreiter, 1929).

——. *Vier von der Infantrie.* (Hamburg: Fackelreiter, 1929).

Jünger, Ernst. *Der Kampf als inneres Erlebnis.* (Berlin: E. S. Mittler, 1922).

——. *In Stahlgewitter.* (Stuttgart: Ernst Klett, 1961).

——. *Das Wäldchen 125.* (Berlin: E. S. Mittler, 1935).

Kafka, Franz. *Diaries, 1914–1923.* (New York: Schocken Books, 1976).

Kals, Heinz. *Unser Fühlen und Erleben vor dem Feind.* (Berlin: Kohler, 1917).

Katz, David. "Zur Psychologie des Amputierten und seiner Prosthese." *Zeitschrift für angewandte Psychologie,* Supplement 25. (Leipzig: J. A. Barth, 1921).

Kempf, Rosa. *Die deutsche Frau nach der Volksberufs- und Betriebszählung von 1925.* (Mannheim: J. Bensheimer, 1930).

von Kietzell, Ernst. *Weltkrieg und Bevölkerung.* (Munich: J. F. Lehmann, 1940).

Kimmle, Prof. Dr. *Das deutsche Rote Kreuz im Weltkrieg.* (Berlin: Heinrich Grund, 1919).

Kirchner, Ernst. *Davoser Tagebuch.* (Cologne: M. DuMont, 1968).

Kisch, Bruno. *Wanderungen und Wandlungen.* (Cologne: Greven, 1966).

Koetzle, Hermann. *Das Sanitätswesen im Weltkrieg, 1914–1918.* (Stuttgart: Berger, 1924).

Kohlhaas, Max. *Lebenserinnerungen.* (Stuttgart: W. Kohlhammer, 1967).

Kolb, Eberhard, and Reinhard, Rürup, eds. *Der Zentralrat der deutschen sozialistischen Republik, 19.12.1918–8.4.1919.* (Leiden: E. J. Brill, 1968).

König, S. *Die Wundbehandlung Kriegsverletzter.* (Heidelberg: J. Hörning, 1917).

Köppen, Edlef. *Heeresbericht.* (Hamburg: Rowohlt, 1979).

Koszyk, Kurt. *Deutsche Pressepolitik im ersten Weltkrieg.* (Düsseldorf: Droste, 1968).

Kracauer, Siegfried. "Vom Erleben des Krieges." *Preussisches Jahrbuch,* 161/3 (1915), 410.

Krämer, Karl. "Zur Behandlung der Kriegsneurosen." (Giessen: Diss., 1921).

Kraus, Karl. *Die letzten Tage der Menschheit.* (Berlin: Volk & Welt, 1978).

Krause, P. *Erfahrungen und Leistungen auf dem Gebiete der inneren Medizin.* (Munster: Aschendorfs, 1929).

Kriegsbriefe gefallener deutscher Juden. Ed. Bundes Verteidigungsministerium. (Stuttgart: Seewald, 1961).

Kriegsinvalidenfürsorge in der Pfalz: Bericht des Kreisausschusses für Kriegsinvalidenfürsorge in Speyer. (Speyer: Zechner, 1916).

Kunoth, Hans. "Die erste Hilfe bei Kieferverletzungen im Kriege." (Kiel: Diss., 1920).

van Langenhove, Fernand. *Wie Legenden entstehen.* (Zurich: Orell Fussili, 1917).

Langer, Norbert. *Die deutsche Dichtung seit dem Weltkrieg.* (Karlsbad: Adam Kraft Verlag, n.d.).

Latzko, Andreas. *Men in War.* (New York: Boni & Liveright, 1918).

Lehmann, Friedrich. *Wir von der Infanterie.* (Munich: J. F. Lehmann, 1929).

Lehmann, Walter. "Krieg und Frömmigkeit," *Preussisches Jahrbuch,* 161/1 (1915), 1–26.

Lersch, Heinrich. *Gedichte.* (Düsseldorf: Eugen Diedrich, 1965).

Lewin, Kurt. "Kriegslandschaft," *Zeitschrift für angewandte Psychologie,* 1917, XII:440–447.

Loewenfeld, L. *Die Suggestion in ihrer Bedeutung für den Weltkrieg.* (Wiesbaden: Bergmann, 1918).

Lorenz, Heinrich. "Beiträge zur Lehre der Kriegsneurosen." (Kiel: Diss., 1920).

Ludendorff, Erich. *Meine Kriegserinnerungen.* (Berlin: E. S. Mittler, 1919).

Ludendorff, Erich, ed. *Urkunden der obersten Heeresleitung über ihre Tätigkeit, 1916–1918.* (Berlin: E. S. Mittler, 1920).

McMurtrie, Douglas. *The Disabled Soldier.* (New York: Macmillan, 1919).

——. *The Evolution of National Systems of Vocational Reeducation for Disabled Soldiers and Sailors.* (Washington: Government Printing Office, 1918).

Maier, Reinhold. *Feldpostbriefe aus dem ersten Weltkrieg.* (Stuttgart: W. Kohlhammer, 1966).

Mälzer, Hans. "Umfang und Probleme der inneren Kriegslasten im Haushalt des deutschen Reiches." (Leipzig: Diss., 1933).

Marc, Franz. *Briefe aus dem Feld.* (Berlin: Rembrandt, 1941).

Mausser, Otto. *Deutsche Soldatensprache.* (Strassburg: Trübners Bibliothek, 1917).

Mayer, Ernst. *Die Krisis des deutschen Ärztestandes.* (Berlin: Julius Springer, 1924).

Mayo, Katherine. *Soldiers, What Next!* (Boston: Houghton Mifflin, 1934).

Meier, John. *Im Schützengraben an der Aisne.* (Cologne: Schaffstein, 1915).

Meier, John. *Das deutsche Soldatenlied im Feld.* (Strassburg: Trübners, 1916).

Menke, Josef. *Ohne Waffe. Das Kriegserlebnis eines Priesters.* (Paderborn: Ferdinand Schöningh, 1930).

Messner, August. "Zur Psychologie des Krieges," *Preussisches Jahrbuch,* 159 (1915), 216–232.

Mewes, Bernhard. *Die erwerbstätige Jugend.* (Berlin: Walter de Gruyter, 1929).

Michael, Wilhelm. *Infantrist Perhobstler.* (Berlin: Rembrandt, 1931).

Michaëlis, Edgar. "Zur Kenntnis der psychischen Erkrankungen bei Kriegsteilnehmern. (Giessen: Diss., 1916).

Michaelis, Herbert, et al., eds. *Ursachen und Folgen. Vom deutschen Zusammenbruch*

1918 und 1945, bis zur staatlichen Neuordnung Deutschlands in der Gegenwart. (Berlin: Dokumente-Verlag Dr. Herbert Wendler, 1963).

Moses, Gertrud. *Zum Problem der sozialen Familienverwahrlosung unter besonderer Berücksichtigung der Verhältnisse im Kriege.* (Langensalza: Beyer, 1920).

Müller, J. *Zur Naturgeschichte der Kleiderlaus.* (Vienna: Hölder, 1915).

Nagy, L. "Ergebnis einer Umfrage über die Auffassung des Kindes vom Krieg," *Zeitschrift für angewandte Psychologie,* Supplement, 1917.

Nau, Karl. *Die wirtschaftliche und soziale Lage von Kriegshinterbliebenen.* (Leipzig: Lühe, 1930).

Neumann, E. "Psychologische Beobachtungen im Felde," *Neurologisches Zentralblatt,* 33/23, 1 Dec. 1914, pp. 1243–1245.

Nobbe, Uwe. *Ein Kriegsfreiwilliger.* (Potsdam: Ludwig Voggenreiter, 1930).

Nordmann, Ernst. "Die Kriegserfahrungen auf dem Gebiete der sympathischen Augenerkrankungen. (Rostock: Diss., 1921).

Nothaas, Josef. "Die Kriegsbeschädigtenfürsorge unter besondere Berücksichtigung Bayerns." (Munich: Diss., 1921).

Otto, Willi. "Der heutige Stand der Kriegsbeschädigtenfürsorge." (Würzburg: Diss., 1922).

Pannwitz, Hans. "Die Ansiedlung von Kriegsbeschädigten vom Standpunkt der Sozialhygiene." (Rostock: Diss., 1920).

Pfeilschifter, Georg. *Religion und Religionen im Weltkrieg.* (Freiburg: Herder, 1915).

Pfülf, Emil. *Die Panik im Kriege.* (Munich: Ärztlichen Rundschau, 1918).

Platz, Hermann. *Krieg und Seele.* (München-Gladbach: Volksverein, 1916).

Preussisches Kriegsministerium. *Leitfaden der Kriegshinterbliebenenfürsorge.* (Berlin: Carl Heymann, 1919).

Quellen zur Geschichte des Parlamentarismus und der politischen Parteien. Ed. Kommission für Geschichte des Parlamentarismus und der politischen Parteien, Erich Matthias und Hans Meier-Welcker. (Düsseldorf: Droste, 1970).

Rank, Otto. *Der Mythus von der Geburt des Helden.* (Leipzig: F. Deuticke, 1909).

Raucheisen, Franz. *Westfront.* (Regensburg: Im Selbstverlag des Verfassers, 1927).

Reich, Richard. *Taschenbuch der Sozialversicherung.* (Stuttgart: Wirtschaft & Verkehr, 1925).

Reichsarbeitsministerium. *Sammlung ärztlicher Gutachten aus der Reichsversorgung.* (Berlin: Hobbing, 1932).

Reichsausschuss für das ärztliche Fortbildungswesen. *Gesundheitswesen und soziale Fürsorge im deutschen Reich.* (Berlin: Reichsdruckerei, 1928).

Reichsbund der Kriegsbeschädigten. *Die Kriegsbeschädigten-Organisationen in Deutschland.* (Berlin: Reichsbund, 1919).

——. *Notruf der Kriegsopfer.* (Berlin: Reichsbund, 1932).

Reichstag. *Verhandlungsberichte.*

Reichswehrministerium. *Sanitätsbericht über das deutsche Heer im Weltkriege, 1914–1918.* (Berlin: E. S. Mittler, 1934).

Remarque, Erich Maria. *Drei Kameraden.* (Munich: Kurt Desch, 1952).

——. *Im Westen nichts Neues.* (Frankfurt/Main: Ullstein, 1979).

——. *Der Weg zurück.* (Frankfurt/Main: Ullstein, 1977).

Renn, Ludwig. *Krieg–Nachkrieg.* (Berlin: Aufbau, 1979).

von Richthofen, Manfred. *Der rote Kampfflieger.* Ed. and introduced by Bolko, Freiherr von Richthofen. (Berlin: Im Deutschen Verlag, 1933).

Riege, Rudolf. *Holzschnitte vom Leben und Tod im Kriege.* (Berlin: Fritz Heyder, 1931).

Rilke, Rainer Maria. *Wartime Letters of Rainer Maria Rilke.* (New York: Norton, 1968).

Riss, Peter. *Stahlbad Anno 17.* (Hamburg: Fackelreiter, 1931).

Rohrbeck, Major. *Taktik.* (Berlin: E. S. Mittler, 1919).

Rolfes, Ernst. "Der Geist von 1914," *Preussisches Jahrbuch,* 158 (1914), 377–391.

Rommel, Erwin. *Infanterie griefft an.* (Potsdam: Ludwig Voggenrieter, 1943).

Rossmann, Erich. *Ein Leben für Sozialismus und Demokratie.* (Stuttgart: Rainer Wunderlich, 1947).

Sachs, Margarete. "Erfahrungen über Kriegsneurosen aus der Material d. Mannheimer Kriegsbeschädigten Fürsorge." (Heidelberg: Diss., 1921).

Salomon, Alice. *Von Kriegsnot und -hilfe und der Jugend Zukunft.* (Berlin: Truebner, 1916).

von Salomon, Ernst. *Die Geächteten.* (Hamburg: Rowohlt, 1962).

Schäffer, Hugo. *Verwaltungsprobleme im Bereich des sozialen Versicherungswesens.* (Stuttgart: W. Kohlhammer, 1930).

Scharrer, Adam. *Vaterlandslose Gesellen.* (Berlin: Aufbau, 1975).

Schauwecker, Franz. *Aufbruch der Nation.* (Berlin: Frundsbergverlag, 1930).

Schede, Franz. *Rückblick und Ausblick: Erlebnisse und Betrachtungen eines Arztes.* (Stuttgart: Hans Günther, 1960).

von Schjerning, Otto, ed. *Handbuch der ärztlichen Erfahrungen im Weltkriege, 1914–1918.* (Leipzig: J. A. Barth, 1922).

——. *Die Tätigkeit und die Erfolge der deutschen Feldärzte im Weltkriege.* (Leipzig: J. A. Barth, 1920).

Schmidt, Margarete. "Über die Pathogenese der Kriegsneurosen auf Grund der Erfahrungen des letzten Kriegs." (Breslau: Diss., 1921).

Scholz, Ludwig. *Seelenleben des Soldaten an der Front.* (Tübingen: J. C. B. Mohr, 1920).

Schulte, Hubert. "Merkfähigkeitsprüfungen bei Kriegshusterikern." (Marburg: Diss., 1921).

Schupp, J. *Eines Frieburger Theologen Kriegstagbücher.* (Karlsruhe: Badenia, 1969).

Schweyer, Franz. *Deutsche Kriegsfürsorge.* (Berlin: Carl Heymann, 1918).

Selch, Otto. *Nach zehn Jahren.* (Berlin: Osteuropa, 1930).

Seldte, Franz. *M.G.K.* (Leipzig: Koehler, 1929).

Shipley, A. E. *The Minor Horrors of War.* (London: John Murray, 1916).

Simmel, Ernst. *Kriegs-Neurosen und 'Psychisches Trauma.'* (Munich: Otto Nemnich, 1918).

Sombart, Werner. *Händler und Helden.* (Munich: Duncker & Humblot, 1915).

Sommer, R. *Krieg und Seelenleben.* (Leipzig: Nemnich, 1916).

Stampfer, Friedrich. *Erfahrungen und Erkenntnisse.* (Cologne: Politik & Wirtschaft, 1957).

Statistisches Reichsamt. *Statistisches Jahrbuch für das deutsche Reich.*

Stein, Philipp. *Der Soldat im Stellungskrieg.* (Berlin: R. Eisenschmidt, 1918).

Steindorff, Ulrich. *Kriegstaschenbuch.* (Leipzig: B. G. Teubner, 1916).

Steinmetz, Rudolf. *Soziologie des Krieges.* (Leipzig: J. A. Barth, 1929).

Stekel, Wilhelm. *Unser Seelenleben im Kriege.* (Berlin: Salle, 1916).

Stellricht, Helmut. *Trotz Allem! Ein Buch der Front.* (Munich: J. F. Lehmann, 1930).

Stelzner, Helenfriederike. "Erschöpfungspsychose bei Kriegsteilnehmern mit besonderer Berücksichtigung der Dämerzustande," *Archiv für Psychiatrie,* 57 (1917), 796–836.

Stern, William, ed. *Beiträge zur Psychologie des Krieges. Zeitschrift für angewandte Psychologie,* Supplement 21. Leipzig: J. A. Barth, 1920.

——. *Jugendliches Seelenleben und Krieg. Zeitschrift für angewandte Psychologie,* Supplement 12. Leipzig: J. A. Barth, 1915.

Stern, William, and Otto Lipmann, eds. *Beiträge zur Psychologie des Krieges.* (Leipzig: J. A. Barth, 1920).

Stransky, Erwin. *Krieg und Geistesstörung.* (Wiesbaden: Bergmann, 1918).

Strehl, Karl. *"Die Kriegsblindenfürsorge."* (Marburg: Diss. 1921).

Stumpf, Richard. *War, Mutiny and Revolution in the German Navy.* (New Brunswick, N.J.: Rutgers University Press, 1967).

Sturm, Richard. "Über soziale Folgen von Kriegsneurosen." (Bonn: Diss., 1920).

Sulzbach, Herbert. *With the German Guns.* (London: Leo Cooper, 1973).

Taschen-Kommersbuch. (Cahr: Moritz Schauenburg, n.d.)

Tecklenburg, August. *Auf zu den Waffen!* (Göttingen; Vandenhoeck & Rupprecht, 1915).

Timpe, Georg. *Von Verwundeten und Toten.* (Warendorf: J. Schnell, 1915).

Toller, Ernst. *Eine Jugend in Deutschland.* (Hamburg: Rowohlt, 1963).

Toller, Ernst. *Hinkemann.* (Stuttgart: Reclam, 1977).

Toller, Ernst. *Feuer aus den Kesseln.* (Berlin: Gustav Kiepenheuer, 1930).

Toller, Ernst. *Prosa–Briefe–Dramen–Gedichte.* (Reinbeck bei Hamburg: Rowohlt, 1961).

Tucholsky, Kurt. *Deutschland, Deutschland über alles.* (Reinbeck bei Hamburg: Rowohlt, 1980).

——. *Politische Texte.* (Reinbeck bei Hamburg: Rowohlt, 1971).

Uhthoff, Kurt. "Über die Kriegsblinden Schlesiens." (Breslau: Diss., 1921).

von Unruh, Fritz. *Opfergang.* (Berlin: Erich Reiss, 1919).

Verband deutscher Kriegsbeschäigter und Kriegsteilnehmer, ed. *Die Organisation der Heeresentlassenen.* (Berlin: Otto Rippel, 1918).

Volkmann, Ernst, ed. *Deutsche Dichtung im Weltkrieg.* (Leipzig: Reclam, 1934).

Voss, W. *Sozialpolitik als Wissenschaft.* (Jena: G. Fischer, 1925).

von der Vring, Georg. *Soldat Suhren.* (Berlin: J. M. Spaeth, 1928).

Wagner, Richard. "Heldentum und Christentum," in *Sämtliche Schriften und Dichtungen.* X:pp. 275–285. (Leipzig: C. F. W. Siegel, 1912).

Wagner, Wilhelm. "Der Einfluss der Arbeitsbehandlung und ihrer Hilfmittel auf die Wiederherstellung Kriegsbeschädigter für ihren späteren Beruf, erläutert an zwei Fällen." (Berlin: Diss., 1917).

Wegeleben, Siegfried. *Das Felderlebnis.* (Berlin: Furche-Verlag, 1921).

Wehner, Josef. *Sieben vor Verdun.* (Munich: Albert Langen, 1936).

Weinberg, Josef. "Boden, Arbeit und Kapital bei der Ansiedlung Kriegsbeschädigter in der Landwirtschaft unt. bes. Berücks. d. bayer. Verhältnisse." (Erlangen: Diss., 1922).

Weiss, Ernst. "Franta Zlin," in *Gesichtete Zeit,* ed. Marcel Reich-Ranicki, (Munich: Deutscher Taschenbuch, 1981).

Werk des Untersuchungsausschusses der deutschen verfassungsgebenden Nationalversammlung und des deutschen Reichstages, 1919–1926. (Berlin: Deutsche Verlag für Politik und Geschichte, 1926).

Westmann, Stephen. *Surgeon with the Kaiser's Army.* (London: W. Kimber, 1968).

White, Ellen. *In den Fussspuren des grossen Arztes.* (Hamburg: Advent Verlag, n.d.).

von Wiese, Leopold. *Einführung in die Sozialpolitik.* (Leipzig: G. A. Gloeckner, 1921).

von Winterfeldt, Joachim. *Tagebuchblätter und Briefe.* (Munich: J. Schön, 1917).

Witkop, Philipp, ed. *Kriegsbriefe gefallener Studenten.* (Munich: Georg Müller, 1928).

Witkowski, Carl. *Reichsversicherungswesen und Kriegsfürsorge.* (Berlin: Kameradschaft, 1915).

Wölbling, Paul, ed. *Die Kriegsbeschädigten-Ansiedlung.* (Berlin: Carl Heymann, 1918).

Württembergs Heer im Weltkrieg. Ed. Das Amtliche Württembergische Kriegswerk. (Stuttgart: Berger, 1920).

Würtz, Hans. *Der Wille siegt.* (Berlin: Hermann Kalkoff, 1916).

Zehn Jahre Deutsche Geschichte. Ed. Reichskabinett. (Berlin: Otto Stollberg, 1928).

Zöberlein, Hans. *Der Glaube an Deutschland.* (Munich: Zentralverlag der NSDAP, 1941).

Zweig, Arnold. *The Case of Sergeant Grischa.* (New York: Viking, 1929).

——. *Erziehung vor Verdun.* (Frankfurt/Main: Fischer, 1979).

von Zwiedeneck-Südenhorst, Otto. *Sozialpolitik.* (Leipzig: J. A. Barth, 1911).

Secondary Sources

Abraham, David. "Constituting Hegemony: The Bourgeois Crisis of Weimar Germany," *Journal of Modern History.* 51 (1979), 417–433.

Ariès, Philippe. *The Hour of Our Death.* (New York: Knopf, 1981).

Arps, Ludwig. *Auf sicheren Pfeilen: Deutsche Versicherungswirschaft vor 1914.* (Göttingen: Vandenhoeck & Ruprecht, 1971).

Artelt, Walter, and Walter Rügg, eds. *Der Arzt und der Kranke in der Gesellschaft des 19. Jahrhunderts.* (Stuttgart: Ferdinand Enke, 1967).

Artelt, Walter, et al., eds. *Städte-, Wohnungs-, und Kleidungshygiene des 19. Jahrhunderts in Deutschland.* (Stuttgart: Ferdinand Enke, 1969).

Bibliography

Becker, Ernest. *The Denial of Death.* (New York: Free Press, 1973).

Berg, Jan, et al. *Sozialgeschichte der deutschen Literatur von 1918 bis zur Gegenwart.* (Frankfurt/Main: Fischer Taschenbuch, 1981).

Berghahn, Volker. *Der Stahlhelm: Bund der Frontsoldaten, 1918–1935.* (Düsseldorf: Droste, 1966).

Bernhard, Hans-Joachim. "Der Weltkrieg 1914–1918 im Werk Ernst Jüngers, Erich Maria Remarques und Arnold Zweigs, ein Beitrag zum Problem des Realismus in der deutschen Literatur des 20. Jahrhunderts. (Rostock: Diss., 1958).

Bessel, Richard, and E. J. Feuchtwanger, eds. *Social Change and Political Development in Weimar Germany.* (Totowa, N.J.: Barnes & Noble, 1981).

Best, Otto, ed. *Expressionismus und Dadaismus.* (Stuttgart: Reclam, 1978).

Böhme, Helmut. *Prolegomena zu einer Sozial- und Wirtschaftsgeschichte Deutschlands im 19. und 20. Jahrhundert.* (Frankfurt/Main: Suhrkamp, 1978).

Bohrer, Karl Heinz. *Die Ästhetik des Schreckens. Die pessimistische Romantik und Ernst Jüngers Frühwerk.* (Munich: Carl Hanser, 1978).

Böhret, Carl. *Aktionen gegen die 'kalte Sozialisierung,' 1926–1930.* (Berlin: Duncker & Humblot, 1966).

Born, Karl Erich. *Staat und Sozialpolitik seit Bismarcks Sturz.* (Wiesbaden: Steiner, 1957).

Born, Karl Erich. *Die deutsche Bankenkrise, 1931.* (Munich: R. Piper, 1967).

Bracher, Karl Dietrich. *Die Auflösung der Weimarer Republik.* (Düsseldorf: Droste, 1978).

Bruck, W. F. *Social and Economic History of Germany from William II to Hitler.* New York: Russell & Russell, 1962).

Bry, Gerhard. *Wages in Germany, 1871–1945.* (Princeton: Princeton University Press, 1960).

Büse, Hans-Georg, and Norbert Schmacke. *Psychiatrie zwischen bürgerlicher Revolution und Faschismus.* (Krongerg/Ts.: Athenäum, 1976).

Bütow, Thomas. *Der Konflikt zwischen Revolution und Pazifismus im Werk Ernst Tollers.* (Hamburg: Hartmut Lüdke, 1975).

Büttner, Peter. "*Freud und der erste Weltkrieg.*" (Heidelberg: Diss., 1975).

Carnegie Endowment for World Peace. *Economic and Social History of the World War, German Series.* (Stuttgart: Deutsche, 1927–1937).

Carroll, Berenice, ed. *Liberating Women's History.* (Urbana: University of Illinois Press, 1976).

Castellan, George. *L'allemagne de Weimar.* (Paris: Armand Colin, 1969).

Cru, Jean. *War Books.* (San Diego: San Diego University Press, 1976).

Decker, Hannah. *Freud in Germany: Revolution and Reaction in Science, 1893–1907.* (New York: International Universities Press, 1977).

Dederke, Karlheinz. *Reich und Republik Deutschland, 1917–1933.* (Stuttgart: Klett, 1978).

Deist, Wilhelm, ed. *Militär und Innenpolitik im Weltkrieg, 1914–1918.* (Düsseldorf: Droste, 1970).

Demeter, Karl. *The German Officer Corps.* (London: Weidenfeld & Nicholson, 1965).

Deutsche Akademie der Wissenschaften zu Berlin. Zentral Institut für Geschichte. Arbeitsgruppe Erster Weltkrieg. Leitung: Fritz Klein. *Deutschland im ersten Weltkrieg*. (Berlin: Akademie, 1970).

Diehl, James. "The Organization of German Veterans, 1917–1919," *Archiv für Sozialgeschichte*. 11 (1971), 141–184.

Diehl, James. *Paramilitary Politics in Weimar Germany*. (Bloomington: Indiana University Press, 1977).

Diepgen, Paul. "Politik und Zeitgeist in der deutschen Medizin des 19. Jahrhunderts," *Historisches Jahrbuch*. 55, no. 2/3 (1935), 439–452.

Domandi, Mario. "The Germany Youth Movement." (Ph.D. diss., Columbia University, 1960).

Donner, Wolf. *Die sozial- und staatspolitische Tätigkeit der Kreigsopferverbände*. (Berlin: Duncker & Humblot, 1960).

Doss, Kurt. *Reichsminister Adolf Köster, 1883–1930. Ein Leben für die Weimarer Republik*. (Düsseldorf: Droste, 1978).

Dunker, Ulrich. *Der Reichsbund jüdischer Frontsoldaten, 1919–1938*. (Düsseldorf: Droste, 1977).

Eichenlaub, Rene. *Ernst Toller et l'expressionisme politique*. (Paris: Honoré Champion, 1977).

Elbers, Winfried. "Das Soldatenlied als publizistische Erscheinung." (Münster: Diss., 1963).

Elze, Walter. *Das deutsche Heer von 1914*. (Osnabrück: Biblio, 1968).

Engelberg, Ernst. *Deutschland 1871–1897*. (Berlin: VEB Deutscher Verlag der Wissenschaft, 1979).

Engelsing, Rolf. *Sozial- und Wirtschaftsgeschichte Deutschlands*. (Göttingen: Vandenhoeck & Ruprecht, 1973).

Erdmann, Karl Dietrich. *Die Weimarer Republik*. (Munich: Deutscher Taschenbuch, 1980).

Eulner, Hans-Heinz. *Die Entwicklung der medizinischen Spezialfächer an den Universitäten des deutschen Sprachgebietes*. (Stuttgart: Ferdinand Enke, 1970).

Evans, Richard. *The Feminist Movement in Germany, 1894–1933*. (Beverly Hills: Sage, 1976).

Evans, Richard J., and W. R. Lee, eds. *The German Family*. (Totowa, N.J.: Barnes & Noble, 1981).

Eyck, Erich. *A History of the Weimar Republic*. (New York: Atheneum, 1970).

Falk, Walter. *Der kollektive Traum vom Krieg*. (Heidelberg: Carl Winter, 1977).

Faulenbach, Bernd, ed. *Geschichtswissenschaft in Deutschland*. (Munich: C. H. Beck, 1974).

Feldman, Gerald. "Les fondements politiques et sociaux de la mobilisation économique en Allemagne, 1914–1916," *Annales*, 24 (1969).

Feldman, Gerald. *Army, Industry and Labor in Germany, 1914–1918*. (Princeton: Princeton University Press, 1966).

Feldman, Gerald, and Homburg, Heidrun. *Industrie und Inflation*. (Hamburg: Hoffmann und Campe, 1977).

Bibliography

Fischer, Alfons. *Geschichte des deutschen Gesundheitswesens.* (Hildesheim: Georg Olms, 1965).

Fischer, Fritz. "Der Stellenwert des ersten Weltkriegs in der Kontinuitätsproblematik der deutschen Geschichte," *Historische Zeitschrift,* 229/1 (1979), 25–53.

Fishman, Sterling. *The Struggle for German Youth: The Search for Educational Reform in Imperial Germany.* (New York: Revisionist Press, 1976).

Fleming, Jens, et al. *Die Republik von Weimar.* (Düsseldorf: Athenäum, 1979).

Fritzsche, Klaus. *Politische Romantik und Gegenrevolution. Fluchtwege in der Krise der bürgerlichen Gesellschaft: Das Beispiel des "Tat-" Kreises.* (Frankfurt/Main: Suhrkamp, 1976).

Fuld, Werner. *Walter Benjamin: Zwischen den Stühlen.* (Frankfurt/Main: Suhrkamp, 1981).

Funcken, Liliane, et al. *L'uniforme et les armes des soldats de la guerre 1914–1918.* (Paris: Casterman, 1970).

Fussell, Paul. *The Great War and Modern Memory.* (New York: Oxford University Press, 1975).

Gadamer, Hans-Georg, and Gottfried Boehm, eds. *Seminar: Philosophische Hermeneutik.* (Frankfurt/Main: Suhrkamp, 1979).

Garraty, John. *Unemployment in History.* (New York: Harper & Row, 1979).

Gay, Peter. *Weimar Culture.* (New York: Harper & Row, 1968).

Geiss, Imanuel. *Das deutsche Reich und der erste Weltkrieg.* (Munich: Carl Hanser, 1978).

Genno, Charles, and Heinz Wetzel, eds. *The First World War in German Narrative Prose.* (Toronto: University of Toronto Press, 1980).

von Gersdorff, Ursula. *Frauen im Kriegsdienst, 1914–1945.* (Stuttgart: Deutsche, 1969).

Gibbons, Floyd. *The Red Knight of Germany.* (New York: Bantam, 1964).

Girouard, Mark. *The Return to Camelot.* (New Haven: Yale University Press, 1981).

Gladen, Albin. *Geschichte der Sozialpolitik in Deutschland.* (Wiesbaden: Franz Steiner, 1974).

Glaser, Hermann. *Sigmund Freuds Zwanzigstes Jahrhundert.* (Frankfurt/Main: Fischer Taschenbuch, 1979).

Glatzer, Nahum. *Franz Rosenzweig.* (New York: Schocken Books, 1961).

Gollbach, Michael. *Wiederkehr des Krieges.* (Kronberg/Ts.: Scriptor, 1978).

Grebing, Helga. *Geschichte der deutschen Arbeiterbewegung.* (Munich: Deutscher Taschenbuch, 1970).

Grebler, L. *The Cost of the World War to Germany and Austria-Hungary.* (New Haven: Yale University Press, 1940).

Grossmann, Kurt. *Ossietzky. Ein deutscher Patriot.* (Munich: Suhrkamp, 1973).

Hafkesbrink, Hanna. *Unknown Germany.* (New Haven: Yale University Press, 1948).

Halperin, S. William. *Germany Tried Democracy.* (New York: Norton, 1965).

Hamilton, Nigel. *The Brothers Mann.* (New Haven: Yale University Press, 1978).

Hardach, Gerd. *The First World War.* (Berkeley: University of California Press, 1977).

Hardach, Karl. *Wirtschaftsgeschichte Deutschlands im 20. Jahrhundert.* (Göttingen: Vandenhoeck & Ruprecht, 1976).

Hartenstein, Wolfgang. *Die Anfänge der deutschen Volkspartei, 1918–1920.* (Düsseldorf: Droste, 1962).

Heiber, Helmut. *Die Republik von Weimar.* (Munich: Deutscher Taschenbuch, 1979).

Henning, F. W. *Das industrialisierte Deutschland, 1914–1976.* (Paderborn: Ferdinand Schöningh, 1978).

Hervier, Julien. *Deux individus contre l'histoire: Drieu la Rochelle, Ernst Jünger.* (Paris: Klincksieck, 1978).

Herzfeld, Hans. *Der erste Weltkrieg.* (Munich: Deutscher Taschenbuch, 1979).

Hofstätter, Peter. *Gruppendynamik.* (Hamburg: Rowohlt, 1976).

Höhn, Reinhard. *Die Armee als Erziehungsschule der Nation.* (Bad Harzburg: Verlag für Wissenschaft, Wirtschaft und Technik, 1963).

———. *Sozialismus und Heer.* (Bad Harzburg: Verlag für Wissenschaft, Wirtschaft und Technik, 1969).

Hohorst, G., J. Kocka, and G. A. Ritter, eds. *Sozialgeschichtliches Arbeitsbuch.* (Munich: Beck, 1975).

Horn, Daniel. *The German Naval Mutinies of World War One.* (New Brunswick, N.J.: Rutgers University Press, 1969).

Hunt, Richard. *German Social Democracy.* (Chicago: Quadrangle, 1964).

Jones, Larry. "Inflation, Revaluation and the Crisis of Middle-Class Politics: A Study in the Dissolution of the German Party System, 1923–1928," *Central European History,* 12 (1979), 143–168.

Kaiser, Helmut. *Mythos, Rausch und Reaktion. Der Weg Gottfried Benns und Ernst Jüngers.* (Berlin: Aufbau, 1962).

Kaupen-Haas, Heidrun. *Stabilität und Wandel ärztlicher Autorität.* (Stuttgart: Ferdinand Enke, 1969).

Kayser, Wolfgang. *The Grotesque.* (Bloomington: Indiana University Press, 1963).

Keegan, John. *The Face of Battle.* (New York: Vintage, 1977).

Kitchen, Martin. *The German Officer Corps, 1890–1914.* (London: Oxford University Press, 1968).

———. *The Political Economy of Germany, 1815–1914.* (Montreal: McGill-Queens University Press, 1978).

Klein, Fritz. *Deutschland 1897/'98–1917.* (Berlin: VEB Deutscher Verlag der Wissenschaft, 1977).

Kliche, Christian. "Die Stellung der deutschen Militärärzte im ersten Weltkrieg." (Berlin: Diss., 1968).

Kocka, Jürgen. "The First World War and the Mittelstand," *Journal of Contemporary History,* 8 (1973), 101–124.

———. *Klassengesellschaft im Krieg.* (Göttingen: Vandenhoeck & Ruprecht, 1978).

———. *Sozialgeschichte.* (Göttingen: Vandenhoeck & Ruprecht, 1977).

Kolb, Eberhard. *Die Arbeiterräte in der deutschen Innenpolitik, 1918–1919.* (Düsseldorf: Droste, 1962).

Koszyk, Kurt. *Zwischen Kaiserreich und Diktatur. Die sozialdemokratische Presse von 1914 bis 1933.* (Heidelberg: Quelle & Meyer, 1958).

Krause, Werner. *Werner Sombarts Weg vom Kathedersozialismus zum Faschismus.* (Berlin: Rütten & Loening, 1962).

Krohn, Claus-Dieter. *Stabilisierung und ökonomische Interessen: Die Finanzpolitik des deutschen Reichs, 1923–1927.* (Düsseldorf: Bertelsmann, 1974).

Kuczynski, Jürgen. *Die Geschichte der Lage der Arbeiter unter dem Kapitalismus.* (Berlin: Akademie, 1966).

Laqueur, Walter. *Weimar: A Cultural History.* (New York: Putnam, 1974).

Laursen, Karsten, et al. *The German Inflation, 1918–1933.* (Amsterdam: North-Holland, 1964).

Leed, Eric. "Class and Dissillusionment in World War I," *Journal of Modern History,* 50 (1978), 680–699.

——. *No Man's Land. Combat and Identity in World War I.* (New York: Cambridge University Press, 1979).

Lepenies, Wolf. *Melancholie und Gesellschaft.* (Frankfurt/Main: Suhrkamp, 1972).

Levine, Frederick. *The Apocalyptic Vision. The Art of Franz Marc as German Expressionism.* (New York: Harper & Row, 1979).

Lifton, Robert Jay. *The Broken Connection.* (New York: Simon and Schuster, 1979).

——. *Death in Life.* (New York: Simon and Schuster, 1967).

——. *History and Human Survival.* New York: Random House, 1970).

——. *Thought Reform and the Psychology of Totalism.* (New York: Norton, 1969).

Lindenlaub, Dieter. *Richtungskämpfe im Verein für Sozialpolitik.* (Wiesbaden: Steiner, 1967).

Loewenberg, Peter. "The Psychohistorical Origins of the Nazi Cohort." *American Historical Review,* 56 (1971), 1457–1502.

Löffler, Fritz. *Otto Dix. Leben und Werk.* (Munich: Anton Schroll, 1967).

Mann, Gunter, ed. *Biologismus im 19. Jahrhundert.* (Stuttgart: Ferdinand Enke, 1973).

Mann, Gunter, et al., eds. *Medizin, Naturwissenschaft, Technik und das zweite Kaiserreich.* (Göttingen: Vandenhoeck & Ruprecht, 1977).

Mannheim, Karl. *Ideology and Utopia.* (New York: Harcourt, Brace, and World, 1936).

——. *Man and Society in an Age of Reconstruction.* (New York: Harcourt, Brace, and World, 1940).

Marwick, Arthur. *War and Social Change in the Twentieth Century.* (New York: St. Martin, 1975).

Mason, Tim. "Women in Germany, 1925–1940," *History Workshop,* no. 1 (1976), pp. 74–113.

Mayer, Hans. *Steppenwolf and Everyman.* (New York: Crowell, 1971).

Meier-Welcker, Hans, and Wolfgang von Groote, eds. *Handbuch zur deutschen Militärgeschichte.* (Frankfurt/Main: Bernard & Graefe, 1968).

Mendelssohn Bartholdy, Albrecht. *The War and German Society.* (New Haven: Yale University Press, 1937).

Merkl, Peter. *The Making of a Stormtrooper* (Princeton: Princeton University Press, 1980).

Meyer, Jacques. *La vie quotidienne des soldats pendant la grande guerre.* (Paris: Hachette, 1966).

Michalka, Wolfgang, and Gottfried Niedhart, eds. *Die ungeliebte Republik.* Munich: Deutscher Taschenbuch, 1980).

Mills, C. Wright. "Situated Actions and Vocabularies of Motive," *American Sociological Review,* 5 (1940), 904–913.

Mitscherlich, Alexander. *Massenpsychologie ohne Ressentiment.* (Frankfurt/Main: Suhrkamp, 1972).

———. *Society without the Father.* (New York: Harcourt, Brace and World, 1969).

Mitscherlich, Alexander, and Margarete Mitscherlich *Die Unfähigkeit zu Trauern.* (Munich: Piper, 1979).

Mitzman, Arthur. *The Iron Cage.* (New York: Grosset & Dunlap, 1969).

Mockenhaupt, Hubert. *Weg und Wirken des geistlichen Sozialpolitikers Heinrich Brauns.* (Munich: Ferdinand Schöningh, 1977).

Mommsen, Hans, et al., eds. *Industrielles System und politische Entwicklung in der Weimarer Republik.* (Düsseldorf: Droste, 1977).

Mommsen, Wolfgang. *Max Weber. Gesellschaft, Politik und Geschichte.* (Frankfurt/Main: Suhrkamp, 1974).

Moore, Barrington. *Injustice: The Social Bases of Obedience and Revolt.* (New York: M. E. Sharpe, 1978).

Motteck, Hans, et al. *Wirtschaftsgeschichte Deutschlands.* (Berlin: VEB Deutscher Verlag der Wissenschaften, 1977).

Netzband, Karl-Bernhard, et al. *Währungs- und Finanzpolitik der Ära Luther, 1923–1925.* (Tübingen: Mohr, 1964).

Nussbaum, Manfred. *Wirtschaft und Staat in Deutschland während der Weimarer Republik.* (Berlin: Akademie, 1978).

Omodeo, Adolfo. *Momenti della vita di guerra.* (Turin: Einaude, 1968).

Ottmüller, Uta. *Die Dienstbotenfrage: Zur Sozialgeschichte der doppelten Ausnutzung von Dienstmädchen im deutschen Kaiserreich.* (Munster: Frauenpolitik, 1978).

Pentzlin, Heinz. *Hjalmar Schacht.* (Frankfurt/Main: Ullstein, 1980).

Peschke, Paul. *Geschichte der deutschen Sozialversicherung.* (Berlin: Tribüne, 1962).

Petzina, Dietmar. *Die deutsche Wirtschaft in der Zwischenkriegszeit.* (Wiesbaden: Franz Steiner, 1977).

Picht, Werner. *Vom Wesen des Krieges und vom Kriegswesen der Deutschen.* (Stuttgart: Friedrich Vorwerk, 1952).

Pittcock, Malcolm. *Ernst Toller.* (Boston: Twayne, 1979).

Piven, Frances Fox, and Cloward, Richard. *Poor People's Movements.* (New York: Vintage, 1979).

———. *Regulating the Poor: The Functions of Public Welfare.* (New York: Vintage, 1971).

Plessen, Marie-Louise. *Die Wirksamkeit des Vereins für Sozialpolitik von 1872–1890.* (Berlin: Duncker & Humblot, 1975).

Plessner, Helmuth. *Die verspätete Nation.* (Stuttgart: Suhrkamp, 1974).

Pogge von Strandmand, H., ed. *Die Erforderlichkeit des Unmöglichen.* (Frankfurt/Main: Europäische, 1965).

Preller, Ludwig. *Sozialpolitik in der Weimarer Republik.* (Stuttgart: Franz Mittelback, 1949).

Pressel, Wilhelm. *Die Kriegspredigt 1914–1918 in der evangelischen Kirche Deutschlands.* (Göttingen: Vandenhoeck & Ruprecht, 1967).

Prost, Antoine. *Les anciens combattants et la société française, 1914–1939.* (Paris: Presses de la Fondation Nationale des Sciences Politiques, 1977).

Prümm, Karl. *Die Literatur des soldatischen Nationalismus der 20er Jahre (1918–1933).* (Kronberg Taunus: Scriptor, 1974).

Quataert, Jean. *Reluctant Feminists in German Social Democracy, 1885–1917.* (Princeton: Princeton University Press, 1979).

Reich-Ranicki, Marcel, ed. *Gesichtete Zeit: Deutsche Geschichten 1918–1933.* (Munich: Deutscher Taschenbuch, 1981).

Reichsarchiv. *Der Weltkrieg.* (Berlin: E. S. Mittler, 1925–1944).

Ringer, Fritz, ed. *The German Inflation of 1923.* (New York: Oxford University Press, 1969).

Ritter, Gerhard. *Staatskunst und Kriegshandwerk.* (Munich: R. Oldenbourg, 1960).

Ritter, G. A., und J. Kocka, eds. *Deutsche Sozialgeschichte.* (Munich: Beck, 1974).

Rohe, Karl. *Das Reichsbanner Schwarz–Rot–Gold.* (Düsseldorf: Droste, 1966).

Rohr, Donald. *The Origins of Social Liberalism in Germany.* (Chicago: University of Chicago Press, 1963).

Rosenberg, Arthur. *Entstehung der Weimarer Republik.* (Frankfurt/Main: Europäische, 1979).

———. *Geschichte der Weimarer Republik.* (Frankfurt/Main: Europäische, 1978).

Rowe, Barbara. *Testimony to War: Literature by French Soldiers in the Great War.* (Ph.D. diss., University of Massachusetts, 1979).

Ronge, Wolfgang. *Politik und Beamtentem im Parteistaat: Die Demokratisierung der politischen Beamten in Preussen zwischen 1918–1933.* (Stuttgart: Ernst Klett, 1965).

Ruge, Wolfgang. *Deutschland, 1917–1933.* (Berlin: VEB Deutscher Verlag der Wissenschaften, 1978).

Rutherford, Andrew. *The Literature of War.* (London: Macmillan, 1979).

von Saalfeld, Lerke. "Die ideologische Funktion des Niebelungenliedes in der preussisch-deutschen Geschichte." (Berlin: Diss., 1977).

Saul, Klaus. "Der 'Deutsche Kriegerbund:' Zur innenpolitischen Funktion eines 'nationalen' Verbandes im kaiserlichen Deutschland." *Militärgeschichtliche Mitteilungen,* Feb. 1969.

Schadewaldt, Hans, ed. *Studien zur Krankenhausgeschichte im 19. Jahrhundert im Hinblick auf die Entwicklung in Deutschland.* (Göttingen: Vandenhoeck & Ruprecht, 1976).

Schieder, Theodor. *Das deutsche Kaiserreich von 1871 als Nationalstaat.* (Cologne: Westdeutscher, 1961).

Schlaffer, Heinz. *Der Bürger als Held.* (Frankfurt/Main: Suhrkamp, 1976).

Schramm, Gottfried. "Klassengegensätze im ersten Weltkrieg." *Geschichte und Gesellschaft,* 2, no. 2 (1976), 244–260.

Schramm, Gottfried. "Militarisierung und Demokratisierung: Typen der Massenintegration im ersten Weltkrieg." *Francia*, 3/1975, p. 376–397.

Schuster, Kurt. *Der rote Frontkämpferbund, 1924–1929.* (Düsseldorf: Droste, 1975).

Sheehan, James. *The Career of Lujo Brentano.* (Chicago: University of Chicago Press, 1966).

Sokel, Walter. *The Writer in Extremis.* (Stanford: Stanford University Press, 1959).

Sontag, Susan. *Illness as Metaphor.* (New York: Vintage, 1978).

Sontheimer, Kurt. *Antidemokratisches Denken in der Weimar Republik.* (Munich: Deutscher Taschenbuch, 1978).

Steffen, Hans, ed. *Der deutsche Expressionismus.* (Göttingen: Vandenhoeck & Ruprecht, 1970).

Stolper, Gustav. *Deutsche Wirtschaft seit 1870.* (Tübingen: J. C. B. Mohr, 1964).

Stribrny, Wolfgang. *Bismarck und die deutsche Politik nach seiner Entlassung, 1890–1898.* (Paderborn: Ferdinand Schöningh, 1977).

Syrup, Friedrich. *Hundert Jahre staatliche Sozialpolitik, 1839–1939.* (Stuttgart: W. Kohlhammer, 1957).

Theweleit, Klaus. *Männer Phantasien.* (Reinbeck bei Hamburg: Rowohlt, 1980).

Thönnessen, Werner. *The Emancipation of Women.* (New York: Urizen, 1976).

Treue, Wilhelm, ed. *Deutschland in der Weltwirtschaftskirse.* (Düsseldorf: Karl Rauch, 1967).

Tucholsky, Kurt. *Politische Texte.* (Reinbeck bei Hamburg: Rowohlt, 1971).

Turner, Victor. *Dramas, Fields and Metaphors.* (Ithaca: Cornell University Press, 1974).

——. *The Ritual Process.* (Ithaca: Cornell University Press, 1969).

Ullmann, Hans-Peter. "Industrielle Interessen und die Entstehung der deutschen Sozialversicherung, 1880–1889." *Historische Zeitschrift.* 229/3 (1979), 574–610.

Urlanis, Boris. *Bilanz der Kriege.* (Berlin: VEB Deutscher Verlag der Wissenschaften, 1965).

Vondung, Klaus, ed. *Kriegserlebnis.* (Göttingen: Vandenhoeck & Ruprecht, 1980).

Wandrey, Uwe. *Das Motiv des Krieges in der expressionistischen Lyrik.* (Hamburg: Hartmut Lüdke, 1972).

Ward, Stephen, ed. *The War Generation.* (Port Washington: Kennikat, 1975).

Weber, Hermann. *Die Wandlung des deutschen Kommunismus.* (Frankfurt/Main: Europäische, 1969).

Wehler, Hans-Ulrich, ed. *Geschichte und Psychoanalyse.* (Cologne: Kiepenheuer & Witsch, 1971).

Weisbrod, Bernd. *Schwerindustrie in der Weimarer Republik.* (Wuppertal: Peter Hammer, 1978).

Wells, Donald. *The War Myth.* (New York: Pegasus, 1967).

Werth, German. *Verdun.* (Gladbach: Lübbe, 1979).

Widmaier, Hans Peter. *Sozialpolitik im Wohlfahrtsstaat.* (Reinbeck bei Hamburg: Rowohlt, 1976).

Willett, John. *Art and Politics in the Weimar Period.* (New York: Pantheon, 1978).

Williams, John. *The Other Battleground.* (Chicago: Henry Regnery, 1972).

Wohl, Robert. *The Generation of 1914*. (Cambridge: Harvard University Press, 1979).

Wolf, Heinrich. *Die Entstehung des jungdeutschen Ordens und seine frühen Jahre, 1918–1922*. (Munich: Wolfgang Lohmüller, 1970).

Wurm, Franz. *Wirtschaft und Gesellschaft in Deutschland, 1848–1948*. (Opladen: Leske, 1969).

Zucker, Stanley. *Ludwig Bamberger: German Liberal Politican and Social Critic, 1823–1899*. (Pittsburgh: University of Pittsburgh Press, 1981).

Zunkel, Friedrich. *Industrie und Staatssozialismus. Der Kampf um die Wirtschaftsordnung in Deutschland, 1914–1918*. (Düsseldorf: Droste, 1974).

Index

Adenauer, Konrad, 184
Adorf, Hans, 119–121
Alverdes, Paul, 26, 56, 117
Atherton, Gertrude, 108
Auxiliary Service Law (1916), 114

Bauer, Gustav, 100
Berliner Frauenbund, 90–91
betrayal (as cultural theme), 31–32
Beumelburg, Werner, 44
Biese, Alfred, 26
Bismarck, Otto von, 83–85, 91–93
blockade, 71–72
Blücher, Evelyn, 37, 72, 98, 109, 113
Braun, Otto, 28
Brüning, Heinrich, 168
Bund erblindeter Krieger, 117, 120–121,
   175
Bund der Kreigsbeschädigten. See
   Reichsbund der
   Kriegsbeschädigten
Bund der Landwirte, 98–99

casualties:
   age, 41
   German, 39–40, 63, 67, 95
   by occupation, 41
   by rank, 42
   by weapon, 42–43

total, World War I, 38–39
   See also disease; wounds
children, 77–81. See also orphans
Cordemann, Margarette, 125
cost of living, 75. See also inflation;
   pensions
crime, 80–81

death, metaphors for, 22, 24, 29–30,
   32–33, 37, 43, 45, 47, 182–186
dementia praecox, 63
demonstrations, 116–117, 123–125, 149
depression (economic), 168–170
Dernberg, Bernhard, 131
Deutscher Offiziersbund, 34, 126, 173
disease, 42, 52–53
   as metaphor, 84
Döblin, Alfred, 186
doctors, 59–61, 64, 67, 112, 136–137, 188
Donner, Louis, 98

Ebert, Friedrich, 33, 184
Einheitsverband, 128
Essen Verband, 120–122

Fatherland Party, 123–124
Faulhaber, Michael von, 187
Flex, Walter, 26–27, 43, 45, 183

Library of Congress Cataloging in Publication Data

Whalen, Robert Weldon, 1950–
  Bitter wounds.

  Bibliography: p.
  Includes index.
  1. Veterans—Germany—History—20th century.   2. Military dependents—
Germany—History—20th century.   3. World War, 1914–1918—Social aspects—
Germany.   4. Germany—Social conditions—1918–1933.   5. Germany—Social
conditions—1933–1945.   6. Germany—Politics and government—1918–1933.
7. Germany—Politics and government—1933–1945.   I. Title.
UB359.G3W43   1984   355.1′15′0943   83-45938
ISBN 0-8014-1653-1 (alk. paper)